Sugarlandia Revisited

International Studies in Social History
General Editor: Marcel van der Linden
International Institute of Social History, Amsterdam

SUGARLANDIA REVISITED

Sugar and Colonialism in Asia and the Americas, 1800 to 1940

Edited by
**Ulbe Bosma, Juan Giusti-Cordero
and G. Roger Knight**

Berghahn Books
NEW YORK • OXFORD

First published in 2007 by

Berghahn Books

www.berghahnbooks.com

Library of Congress Cataloging-in-Publication Data

Library of Congress Cataloging-in-Publication Data

Sugarlandia revisited : sugar and colonialism in Asia and the Americas, 1800-1940 / edited by Ulbe
Bosma, Juan Giusti-Cordero, and G. Roger Knight.
    p. cm. -- (International Institute of Social History ; v. 9)
    Includes bibliographical references and index.
    ISBN 978-1-84545-316-9 (hardcover : alk. paper)
    1. Sugar trade--Indonesia--Java--History. 2. Sugar trade--Southeast Asia--History. 3. Sugar trade--
West Indies--History. I. Bosma, Ulbe, 1962- II. Giusti-Cordero, Juan A. III. Knight, G. R.

HD9116.I53J356 2007
382'.4136--dc22

                                                                              2007012582

British Library Cataloguing in Publication Data
A catalogue record for this book is available from the British Library
Printed in the United States on acid-free paper

ISBN 978-1-84545-316-9 (hardback)

CONTENTS

1

INTRODUCTION

Sidney W. Mintz

A book that breaks new ground in dealing with an old subject merits a simple introduction – one that, minimally, does not obstruct the serious reader's search for enlightenment. I shall try here to be simple, and brief.

A powerful and apparently innate human liking for the sweet taste, tied particularly though not exclusively to honey in the ancient world (as well as globally, among all peoples known to live among bees), was wholly transformed by the spread of crystalline sugar, processed from the juice of domesticated sugar cane, which began its diffusion from Southwest Asia, after about 300 BC. It was only several centuries later that sugar began to reach Europe in sizable quantities, both overland and via the Mediterranean. Following the Islamic conquest of Spain and Portugal, near the middle of the eighth century, sugar cane was also planted for the first time, and sugar made from it, on European soil, along Spain's southern littoral. Although now only of minor economic importance, its cultivation has continued there for the last 1250 years.

By the fourteenth century, sucrose (crystalline or liquid $C_{12}H_{22}O_{11}$), won from sugar cane by heat and clarification, had become a coveted good in the West. Its consumption trajectory thereafter was ascendant, especially in Europe. It has begun to falter only in the last half-century or so; but it has continued to rise meanwhile in much of the so-called developing world, including Algeria, Egypt and Indonesia.

The chronology accompanying that trajectory can be broken down into different sorts of stages or epochs. But from nearly every perspective, the history of sugar up to now has been viewed as a triumph of New World production, resting from the outset on an abundance of fertile land and the labour of coerced peoples, especially African slaves. That American history began with Columbus's second voyage in 1493, which brought the plant to the island of Santo Domingo, and it has continued until present times. The epoch of slavery and the implantation of sugar factories in the New World colonies before 1500, and its sequels with free labour since, has dominated most historical inquiries about sugar, tending to set both the boundaries and the goals of research. But in truth, and in spite of the primacy of New World production, the growing of cane and the making of sugar in the world outside the Americas has long been enormously important and complexly differentiated. In spite of some important work (e.g., Sucheta Mazumdar's for China, Donald Attwood's for India, Chih-Ming Ka's for Taiwan, and that of many students of the Australian, Indian Ocean and Philippine industries),[1] the number of historians of sugar that have shown as much interest in the Old World centres as in the New has been modest. Hence our vision of the global compass of sugar and of its later stages as a world industry has inclined towards being incomplete and simplistic. This book is an important initial step towards addressing that deficiency.

The New-World-centred history of sugar seems to have suffered from an additional shortcoming, linked to sugar's New World beginnings as a large-estate, slave-based, field-and-factory industry in what were the West's first overseas possessions. Inevitably, sugar, rum and molasses first became commodities for the Western world. The history of their production lent itself to convenient polarities of description – large-scale production versus small; unified field-and-factory versus separated cultivation and processing; coerced labour versus free labour, and the like – in the construction of historical portraits of the American centres of production. Each such contrast proved useful for building in broad terms a description of what happened with sugar in particular New World settings, such as Brazil, or in one or another of the various Caribbean 'sugar islands'.

There have been added polarities of this sort, too. Since about 1830, a new one was imposed on sugar production history, which called for a transatlantic perspective: that between sucrose won from cane and sucrose extracted from the sugar beet. Since sugar is made from a temperate-zone crop and cane from a tropical one, quite different implications for political economy lay in this new development. Economically successful beet sugar signalled for the first time in history that a tropical product could be perfectly copied by a temperate one. And since 1960, there has been room for other such descriptive polarities, including that between sucrose and high-fructose corn syrup (HFCS), in which the industrial uses made of the product inflect the comparison; and between sugars and non-caloric sweeteners – a rivalry now intensified by the global epidemic of obesity.

Such polarities of description and analysis can sometimes serve to highlight contrasts in the nature of markets in the sphere of consumption, or differing features of local systems in the production sphere – as in Cuba, say, or Brazil. But what happens in each such system of production on the ground, in terms of land use, labour arrangements, milling, distribution, the identity of the planters, and much else, is specific; so are the consequences of these distinctive features. Case A – Cuba, say – resembles case B, Jamaica; but it is not the same; Case C – Trinidad, say – resembles them both, but it is also different in detail from them both. The student seeks abstractable regularities among the cases; but while using the polarities and finding the regularities, he discovers to his surprise that he can easily 'lose' the cases themselves. Indeed, some interpretations were wrong, simply because the contrasts were not so marked as the analyst had argued, or the implications of one or another local difference had not been grasped. So the polarities are helpful, yes; but they can also mislead, because they leave out so much, especially in the form of relevant historical detail. There seems to be little virtue (as Karl Marx famously wrote) in being super-historical.

Many of the previous students of sugar, including this writer, who have tried to make sense of its New World history, have played interesting games by polarising concepts, and have had to face up to the peculiar way in which historical detail can lay low the most imaginative typologies, whether of isolated features of the sugar industry (such as the relationship of milling the product to the form of landownership), the nature of peasantries and plantations (such as the definition of labour that oscillates between them), or the character of whole social systems. At the same time, as the editors also realise, if the contrasts posed by polarities and tentative periodizations are fruitful, they can sometimes help to unlock relationships that might otherwise remain concealed behind the specific details of the individual cases. If typologies compel us to think harder about the variables that they handle as clusters of traits – if on reading a comparison of plantations defined by their size and the basis of their labour force, we are made to look more closely and critically at exactly those two factors – then they serve a useful purpose, even if as a result they have to be replaced by a more exact and informed typology. Successive approximations of sugar's historical development and spread ought to result in some cumulative improvement of our understanding of the relevant variables, such as the status of labour, its relationship to non-sugar cultivation, the role of an indigenous planter class, the expansion of the market, and so on. Otherwise, why bother?

The contributors to this collection have tried to walk the golden mean between excessive particularism on the one hand, and too much abstraction on the other. What has made their task complicated – as the editors make clear in their lengthy introductory essay – is the size of the main conceptual undertaking: to bring Asia into the world sugar system, and to unite its fate with that of the Americas. They have tackled this difficulty head on, and have acquitted themselves handsomely. They begin by taking the term 'Sugarlandia', long associated with 'a mono-crop, sugar-based regional economy' in the Philippines, and freeing it from its local, original meaning. 'Sugarlandia' for them becomes the world of sugar, or the sugar world, 'the social classes, cultures and political economies' implicated in the production of sugar, and shaping that production. Within this new Sugarlandia, they invited their colleagues to look at both Old World and New World sugar economies, and to ponder previously neglected linkages between these economies, mediated through the world sugar market and the evolving politics of a not-too-remote colonialism. The results are impressive and important.

The editors undertake to disequilibrate – to knock off balance and then to re-balance anew – a picture of the world of sugar, centred on the Americas. At the same time, they see a need to re-periodise world sugar history. They aim to tie what I would dub the first world of sugar to the mercantilist era, and the second to the industrial era; and they move the dividing line between these eras a century backward in history. The various interpretations of colonialism and imperialism that follow are readjusted accordingly. Very importantly, it seems to me, the editors call for a serious re-examination of what might be called the mechanics of colonial-imperial rule. Today's governing view of colonial rule may underestimate the role of indigenous power holders, ignoring the weight of kinship and family for the way power is held and transmitted. In effect, the editors call for a serious re-examination of the genealogies of power in the colony. That makes good sense. In the Caribbean region, for example, differences in planter rule in the late eighteenth century among British Jamaica, French Saint-Domingue and Spanish Cuba make alarmingly clear how inadequate have been the pan-Caribbean generalities floated about the origins of the sugar plantocracies. A re-examination of the sort the editors call for, perhaps particularly when applied to major erstwhile Old World colonies such as India and Java, could throw considerable additional light on the varying character of European colonialism, and on the question of who might be most entitled to speak for the oppressed.

The individual contributions are concentrated upon three cases: Java, the Philippines, and parts of the hispanic Caribbean (Cuba and Puerto Rico). The Antillean cases provide a useful link between New World and Old, through the character of the Hispanic overseas colonial system and its sequelae. Although they bring into plain view some parts of the Old World industry that are not dealt with – Fiji, for example, or China, or South Africa and now New Guinea[2] – they carry us forward to a new vision of world sugar.

But by now this prefatory note has become neither simple nor brief. I only hope that readers' appetites will have been whetted.

Notes

1.   Mazumdar, *Sugar and Society in China*; Attwood, *Raising Cane*; Chih-Ming Ka, *Japanese Colonialism in Taiwan*.
2.   Errington and Gewertz, *Yali's Question*.

2

Sugarlandia Revisited: Sugar and Colonialism in Asia and the Americas, 1800 to 1940, An Introduction

Ulbe Bosma, Juan Giusti-Cordero and G. Roger Knight

Sugar was the single most valuable bulk commodity traded internationally before oil became the world's prime commodity. In the first colonial era, from the sixteenth to the eighteenth century, cane sugar production was pre-eminent in the Atlantic Islands, the Caribbean, and Brazil. Subsequently, cane sugar industries in the Americas were transformed by a fusion of new and old forces of production, as the international sugar economy incorporated production areas in Asia, the Pacific, and Africa. A spectacular growth of beet sugar production in the 'metropolitan' countries added a critical new dynamic to the sugar industry world-wide and to that of 'colonial', cane-based industries in particular. At the height of the second colonial era, circa 1914, cane and beet sugar was a truly global commodity, embracing both the New World of the Americas and the Old Worlds of Europe and Asia. Cuba, the Indonesian island of Java and the beet sugar industry of Imperial Germany stood at the apex of this development.

Sugar is also the single most 'colonial' commodity, as it is the product most closely associated with the history of colonialism; indeed also like oil, sugar was similarly associated with metropolitan domination. In the first colonial era sugar was integral to mercantilism, the slave trade, inter-metropolitan rivalries, and other processes that marked the very formation of Western colonialism. Even in the second (post-1800) era of world sugar production, the continuing nexus between (cane) sugar and colonialism was reaffirmed. Although seriously threatened by beet in terms of its market share and profitability in the decades before the First World War, during the inter-war period it was again colonial cane producers (in both the Caribbean and Asia) that accounted for the bulk of the world's international trade in the commodity.

Sugar's global economic importance and its intimate relationship with colonialism offer an important context for probing the nature of colonial societies. This book questions some major assumptions about the nexus between sugar production and colonial societies in the Caribbean and Southeast Asia, especially in the second (post-1800) colonial era. Major themes include the sugar plantation's complex articulation of agriculture and manufacturing the specific role of 'creolized' groups in sugar manufacturing and financing and their interaction with indigenous landholders; the local ethno-cultural spaces associated with sugar production generally; and the intertwined transformations in sugar production and colonial power, with 1800 posited as a more significant turning point than 1900. The perspectives offered in this book imply rethinking the relationship between the two major eras and the two major zones of colonial sugar production from the sixteenth to the twentieth centuries: the Americas and (Southeast) Asia. The New World – especially several Caribbean islands – is generally viewed as a paradigm of the first era of Western colonialism and sugar power, while the Old World of Asia – and Java in particular – is associated with the later era. This neat conception is premised on 1900 as the general chronological marker between the two major colonial and sugar eras; yet 1800 may be the more significant interface. The peculiar relationship between New World and Old World sugar regions after 1800 – in which, as far as the commodity production of sugar was concerned, both 'worlds' were juxtaposed as well as transposed – tells us a great deal about the nature of Western colonialism and its role in an evolving global economy.

Two Eras, Two World Regions

The book's overriding assumptions are that we need to establish comparisons and contrasts between the sugar-producing colonies of the New World and the Old; that we need to do this across the two eras of sugar and colonialism; and that the temporal boundaries of these two eras need to be redrawn (with 1800, not 1900, as the major 'divide').

Therefore, this book 'crosses' two world regions (Southeast Asia and the Caribbean) and two eras (of colonialism). We contend that several major misconceptions in the study of sugar and colonialism in both the Caribbean and Southeast Asia result from the absence of such perspectives; and that the study of sugar and colonialism in the Caribbean and Southeast Asia, and hence globally, will not much advance further until such a comparative perspective gains a foothold.

We do not propose merely a cluster of geographical locations (or a mere counterpoint between two world regions) but also connected circuits of commodity production that include refineries, shipping and credit systems. As such, our perspective provides a basis for comparisons and linkages that we hope will enrich, challenge and transform our understandings of sugar history. While possessed of an often outstandingly rich regional historiography, the history of sugar's production and circulation has suffered from a dearth of global perspective. These interactions sometimes occurred,[1] as we shall see, in circumstances in which sugar did not enjoy the status of a mono-crop but where its presence was nonetheless pervasive.[2]

This book also assumes a third 'crossing': between economy and culture. Particularly in this context, the choice of the term 'Sugarlandia' is not an arbitrary one. Although in its original usage (in the Philippines), Sugarlandia signified a mono-crop, sugar-based regional economy,[3] it is employed here as an evocative, global synonym for the social classes, cultures and political economies with which the large-scale production of the commodity was enmeshed and which equally shaped sugar production. In contrast with much postcolonial scholarship, the book locates culture and ethnicity in close interaction with a material domain whose boundaries are fluid and contested.

A fourth crossing essayed here is between metropolis and colony. On the whole, the authors of this book also do not subscribe to postcolonial notions that treat of colonies as 'zones of hybridity' yet nonetheless depict them primarily as the product of metropolitan initiatives. Instead, colonies are viewed here as historical crucibles for developments that were far from being simply a copy of metropolitan exemplars. In the second colonial era in particular, colonial power and local social classes were characterised by intense hybridity and by fluid boundaries between coloniser and colonised. Precisely because colonialism was already several centuries old, societies imprinted by old colonial rule (under one or more metropoles) featured planter groups of metropolitan origin who had become 'creolized' in close interaction with native social groups. This close if complex interaction engendered a large, hybrid ethnic-cultural milieu. Under these circumstances, any notion of a necessary common identity between sugar capital and colonial state needs to be treated as highly problematic; to an extent, indeed, that may distinguish sugar from other colonial commodities. Such patterns were unheard of in the first colonial era, at least in the sphere of production.[4] It is an apparent paradox that this second era led in most cases to decolonisation.

Despite differences in approach and focus, all the contributors share a common, strongly revisionist aim: the need to see Sugarlandia in a fresh light rather than one refracted through the prism of late imperialism, of the anti-colonial nationalism which shared many of the former's key premises, and of the dichotomous conceptual perspectives nourished by these intellectual and political currents. Hence the issues addressed by the contributors to the present volume are world-wide in their implications, even though the context within which they are addressed is (for the most part) geographically specific. They range from concerns with the emergence and growth over time of a 'sugar bourgeoisie' in locations as geographically separate as Cuba and Java through to analyses of the political culture of Sugarlandia in southeast Asian and Caribbean contexts.

The Colonial Sugar Complex

In working out the connection between global processes and local histories, our point of departure is hybrid: the sugar complex as an entity which combined a world-wide convergence towards industrial manufacture with a very marked – and continuing – disparity in sugar cane agriculture and labour patterns. Indeed, the book highlights the composite and highly convoluted agro-industrial nature of cane sugar production world-wide, its ambiguously rural-urban location, and its complex production processes at both ends. Perhaps no other major commodity has been as intensely dual, and 'paradoxical': at once profoundly 'agricultural' and elaborately 'industrial'.

Most immediately, this duality stems from a combination of two factors. One was the uniquely unstable nature of sugar cane as raw material, which required immediate, on-site processing. In cane sugar production, capital and labour were brought together in one spatial unit, as the processing of cane had to be done on the spot. In this context, the need for an optimal level of field-factory co-ordination brought steam and steel into tropical colonial dependencies where they would otherwise have been absent. Thus the entire global complex of capital, technology and labour was nominally played out in the micro-social realities of Sugarlandia. The second reason for the 'duality' of cane sugar production, increasingly in evidence around 1830, was the cane sugar producers' need to compete in the manufacturing sector with a virtually identical commodity, beet sugar. This was obtained from an entirely different raw material that was cultivated and processed in industrialised conditions in 'metropolitan' Europe and North America.

While Caribbean sugar production in the seventeenth and eighteenth centuries was a crucial element in the emerging European capitalist economy,[5] its nineteenth-century successor emerged as a key vehicle for the global dissemination of the industrial production modes associated with steam and steel, although its successful operation was conditioned by the availability of local knowledge and skill.[6]

The dissemination of the new industrial production modes extended, moreover, well beyond the gates of the sugar factory itself. Cuba – the rising sugar giant of the mid-nineteenth century – was also only the seventh country in the world to embark on the construction of railways. Major shipping and dock facilities were established in many sugar-producing territories, as well as state-of-the-art telegraph, and later telephone, communications;[7] and research into cane varieties and fertilizers in the sugar-producing territories was at the forefront of innovation in, respectively, plant biology and chemistry.

In this context, global-industrial became a central element of sugar's late colonial trajectory. It did so, however, with respect to a commodity that retained deeply local agrarian and social dimensions, characterised by ample variation both between regions and intra-regionally. The degree of global convergence in the manufacture of sugar cane into marketable forms of sucrose was not closely matched by similar developments in the production of sugar cane and its forms of labour subordination. Methods of cultivation and associated forms of labour process diverged – and continued to diverge – profoundly throughout the nineteenth and early twentieth centuries.

Indeed, even the industrialisation of sugar production is more complex than it might seem. There is, of course, no single pace-setting model of what constitutes industrialisation. One widely accepted focus – but one that is not so unambiguous as it first appears – is technological innovation, which in this instance invokes the transformation of manufacture by a combination of steam, steel and applied chemistry. Far from constituting a clean and decisive break with the past, however, this transformation took place (at least until the late nineteenth century) on a largely incremental basis, which mixed the new with the old in a myriad of possible permutations.

The 'revolution' in the technology of sugar manufacture was paradoxically a slow and patchy affair.[8] Steam-driven iron and steel mills, vacuum pans, multiple effect condensers and centrifuges – all the panoply, in short, of industrialised manufacture – did not come swiftly. By the end of the nineteenth century, nonetheless, it had become possible to envisage the 'advanced' manufacture of sugar in terms of a more-or-less common, complete, defining and global technology.

The 'Concept' of Plantation

This phenomenon of a dual industrial-agricultural identity – with its parallel metropolitan-colonial resonance, and what it portended for the labour process demands a more rigorous attempt to historicise the 'plantation' as a unit of commodity production than has generally been attempted. The concept of the 'plantation' issues from a historical trajectory of sugar production, often in relatively large units with generally resident, coerced or semi-coerced labour – often enslaved – that began in the eleventh century; and whose antecedents lie in ninth-century Mesopotamia. Despite (or because of) their antiquity, plantations have been characterised by a broad spectrum of unit sizes, products (and types of products, e.g. for direct consumption, for processing and consumption, or for industry) as well as a range of coerced and free forms of labour.[9] Yet despite these variations, 'plantation' has retained the sense of a large, centralised agricultural unit of forced labour engaged in monocrop production.[10] This definition is much too constraining. Also notable in the concept of plantation is a deliberate archaism that tends to deny plantations the possibility of modernity and change.[11]

But perhaps the most problematic dimension of the concept of plantation is the pervasive sense of a single unit of production. That is, the estate with hard and fast boundaries, in the case of the slave plantation and of the 'land-and-factory combine' that eventually superseded it. Such a plantation construction tacitly replicates on a micro scale the colonial economy and society, viewed in similar terms as strongly bounded and resistant to change; and plantation and colony reinforce each other as concepts. When the colony is an island, as was the case of the 'sugar islands', that insularity attained seemingly self-evident expression.

The critical flaw in the 'insular' plantation perspective, of course, is that both plantation and colony are singularly extroverted spaces; and that such extroversion cannot be compartmentalised away merely as unilateral metropolitan control. Like other agrarian formations, and surely more so than most, in plantation production labour form, crops, scale, and productive space are informed by and inform a larger space of social production relations. Yet the confines of the 'plantation' as a pre-industrial, unitary space of production worked with slaves and lorded by expatriate, or rather, absentee planters, still looms over the discussion. It is a paradigm in the literature of both the New and Old Worlds where plantation, planter and plantation labour are denied the complexity of capitalist modernity (as if 'insularity' for some odd reason was synonymous with simplicity).

'Plantation', like slave, has been much the dichotomous opposite of 'industrial', 'capitalist', and 'merchant', rather as 'slave' has been the opposite of 'free'. In fact, the global focus of the present volume points up comparisons between the Old World and the New that demonstrate, in particular, the fallacy of supposing that the spread of industrial technology was contingent on the suppression of servile forms and their replacement by 'free' wage labour. The historical and conceptual links between the sub-regions of the Caribbean that became leading sugar producers in the nineteenth and early twentieth centuries (that is, Cuba, Puerto Rico, and the Dominican Republic) and their counterparts in Southeast Asia during the same period have been eclipsed by a 'plantation' perspective that continues to generalise unduly from the experience of the slave plantations of the English Caribbean in the first era of Western colonialism.

On the whole, the concept of plantation is in dire need of full-scale reappraisal; to a large extent, such a reappraisal would need to rethink the intellectual history of plantation scholarship. This was probably at its most fecund in the 1940s to 1960s.[12] Among the numerous studies of plantations at the time, the papers by Sidney Mintz and Eric Wolf remain the most supple and challenging. Mintz's and Wolf's celebrated joint paper was long a touchstone for defining plantations along a series of material indicators, although the plantations it discussed were modern, wage-labour plantations (while coerced labour relations were found in the hacienda).[13] Mintz later noted that the paper had serious weaknesses; among them, that 'the plantation worker who is also a peasant appears to be straddling two kinds of socio-cultural adaptation', and not just the plantation's.[14] Caribbean rural proletarianisation has historically been partial and exceptional, Mintz argued, and the 'plantation-peasant relation' (and not just 'the plantation') is central to Caribbean history. Moreover, peasantries tended to coexist with plantations over a considerable period of time, in a 'state of flux equilibrium'. Mintz stressed the relative complementarity between plantation and peasant production.[15] Mintz's perspective – which he extended into a reconception of 'proto-peasantries' under slavery – implies that plantations could be neither bounded nor defined easily, at the very point where plantations were deemed to be transparent: the control of labour.

Similarly, Wolf shifted the focus from the estate to the labourer and contended that plantation labourers in contemporary plantations led 'double lives, with one foot in the plantation way of life, while keeping the other foot in the peasant holding'.[16] In Asia generally, the 'plantation' form as a spatially unified land-and-factory combine was clearly not dominant, nor was sugar cane inevitably and invariably a monocrop cultivation. Indeed, in the case of Java, it was anything but that: the world's second largest producer-exporter of cane sugar was located agriculturally in the midst of the 'peasant' cultivation of a multitude of potentially competing crops. Mintz's and Wolf's unorthodoxy concerning plantations travelled well to Java and Southeast Asia.

Echoing Mintz and Wolf, Clifford Geertz characterised Javanese plantations labourers as having 'one foot in the rice terrace and the other in the mill'.[17] He described Java's modern sugar plantations as 'odd centauric social units' where 'the Javanese cane worker remained a peasant at the same time that he became a coolie', that is, 'a part-time proletariat'. Almost three decades later, in her major work on Sumatran plantation labourer politics, Ann Laura Stoler cited Wolf's 'one-foot-and-the-other' dictum as key to her conceptual framework.[18] On the whole, these approaches dispense with superficial distinctions between plantations and their immediate social contexts, help to connect the rural social history of the Caribbean with that of southeast Asia (as their sugars were connected in the world sugar market), and suggests major linkages and points of comparison between the two regions. None of this negates the importance of also examining, as in Java, how capitalist social relations significantly shaped village sugar production and labour recruitment; and how these social relations can even recreate nominally 'peasant' social relations, in an effort to subdue 'proletarian' class conflict through deproletarianisation.[19] These continue to be major historical issues.

In a sense, the liberal critique of plantation societies, long in a 'united front' of sorts with specifically anti-colonial and anti-racist optics, may have outrun its considerable conceptual power and has become a major obstacle to a broader and more historical understanding of plantation production, plantation societies, and plantation labour. The search for a definition of plantation may not be fruitless, but besides the point. At some level, of course, plantations (and agrarian units of any size, including households) need to be viewed as relatively self-contained social space; the point is not to stop there, but to intertwine broader as well as more specific levels. We urgently need the capacity to envisage and connect multiple levels of analysis; from world-scale to households to individual labourers' multiple social relations. These various levels raise rather different issues, involve different concepts and invoke distinct intellectual traditions. None is more distinctly important. This book happens to focus on more local and regional levels, but does so in a comparative, world-scale perspective that actively underscores the importance of all levels and connections.

The industrialisation of sugar manufacture took place in the context of a global market and global spread of manufacturing technology: but also in a context characterised by a variety of labour relations and by a variety of political configurations.[20] The notion of 'plantation society', defined as a place of insular character, where the political form was a 'plantocracy' and where sugar enjoyed untrammelled hegemony over agrarian resources, has obscured the real variety of forms taken by both sugar production itself and the polities, societies and economies with which it was associated.

A Colonial Bourgeoisie?

Our second major argument flows directly from this general critique of the 'plantation' paradigm. It focuses on the plantation construct's inability to take cognisance, not only of the precocious character of sugar production globally, and of the rooted-ness of sugar production in local agrarian relations, but also of the associated presence at the heart of Sugarlandia of a capitalist bourgeoisie of planters, manufacturers and traders. It draws attention to the absence of any substantial or 'real' bourgeois presence in the orthodoxy concerning 'plantation society' and the 'planters' who formed its backbone.

Denial of the reality of a colonial bourgeoisie was reinforced by key tenets of anti-colonial nationalism. On this reading, the entrepreneurs and owners of capital in colonial Sugarlandia were not a 'proper' bourgeoisie because they did not belong ethnically to the majority, 'indigenous' population. Typically, the local sugar bourgeoisie, while not necessarily absentee, was *mestizo*, Creole – or even expatriate. Whatever the precise designation, they did not 'belong', their loyalties lay elsewhere and their history as a bourgeoisie (if, indeed, they had one) was a bastard offshoot of the history of the metropolitan, colonising power that could not also be an intrinsic dimension of the history of the colonised, 'native' people. The colonial bourgeoisie, a class without history, was no match for the oppressed classes of the colony, who were the bearers of history itself.

Within a quasi-feudal terminology of 'sugar barons', 'sugar lords' and the like, the colonial planter bourgeoisies in the late nineteenth and early twentieth centuries are cast (overtly or tacitly) as essentially *compradors* – as the 'mere' clients and intermediaries of dominant metropolitan capital in its dealings with 'native' colonials. The diffusionist implications inherent in this interpretation were reinforced by theories of Underdevelopment and the currency of Mao's political thought, which brought the term *comprador* into wide circulation during the second half of the twentieth century, but also by the late (and neo-) imperialist world-view which underdevelopment sought to challenge. Both perspectives assumed unilateral domination by metropolitan capital and the diffusion of capitalist production from its 'core' in the West.

From (ostensibly) opposite angles, both underdevelopment and late/neo imperialist perspectives denied the existence, complexity and historical significance of a 'peripheral' bourgeoisie – especially in the domain of the 'classic' colonial terrain of cane sugar production.

In contrast, our contributors are at one in advocating a historically informed understanding of the social and cultural evolution of the bourgeoisie, and (as we shall see) of the political developments contingent on that evolution. No one characterisation of Sugarlandia's bourgeoisies fitted every case or every period. As is illustrated in the individual contributions to this book, specific historical situations differed, even profoundly, both within the same region and inter-regionally. The characterisation of these local, planter bourgeoisies is complex and problematic, and we do not aim to substitute one conceptual cliché for another. We consider these bourgeoisies in the context of a globalising capital whose own origins in Europe and its original overseas colonies were shaped out of 'non-capitalist' relations, with plantation production and the slave trade playing major roles. In this reading, the historical and conceptual presuppositions of capital are, and remain, contradictory.[21] Capital, to put it succinctly, has been hybrid all the time.

Labour and Non-Wage Industrialisation

Our third, closely related, argument for the reconfiguring of Sugarlandia concerns labour and what might be termed 'non-wage industrialisation'. As we have already seen, sugar's manufacturing sector experienced a globally precocious degree of industrialisation that began around 1830 and reached its apogee in the 1920s. Although it may once have appeared axiomatic that technological advance of this kind was contingent on (and perhaps the spur to) the emergence of proletarian and hence 'industrial' labour, reality was rather different. In Cuba, the country that was the world's largest and most technologically advanced manufacturer of cane sugar for much of the nineteenth century, the numbers of slaves rose exponentially until a decade or so before abolition in the 1880s. Likewise in Java, Cuba's coeval in the Old World of Asia, the industrialised manufacture of sugar took place for much of the nineteenth century in a context characterised by the 'servility' of a significant proportion of the workforce.

Multiple and contemporaneous forms of labour, both in the factory itself and – very obviously – in the field, characterised the large-scale commodity production of sugar throughout the late colonial era. 'Pre-industrial' forms either continued or were called into existence alongside stereotypically industrial ones. There was a singular absence of a linear progression, as was once widely supposed, from slavery or other forms of servility towards 'free labour'. Here again, the global focus of the present volume points up the comparisons between the Old World and the New that demonstrate conclusively the fallacy of supposing that the spread of industrial technology was contingent on the suppression of servile forms and their replacement by 'free' wage labour.

The nineteenth-century evolutionist model assumed a fixed nexus between capitalism, technology and (free) labour – and similarly assumed that plantations, which embodied the very acme of servile labour, were a key obstacle to technological advance. In fact this linear reading was belied by historical instances scattered over the globe.[22]

Crossing the 'Great Divide'

Our critique also addresses the oft-repeated but inadequately researched notion of a late nineteenth-century rupture or 'great divide' throughout virtually the whole of Sugarlandia. In our interpretation, that divide from 1880 to 1900 was less significant than generally construed, and merely separated early and late periods of the second era of colonialism (and colonial sugar production) Two major events ostensibly occasioned this divide.

First, the severe commercial crisis of the mid-1880s, brought about by a fall of almost 50 percent in the world price of sugar, and its ramifications for the financing and ownership of the sugar industry.

Second, the 'insular wars' of the Spanish empire in the Caribbean and Asia in the final decade of the nineteenth century; the subsequent re-colonisation (de facto or de jure) of the former Spanish territories by the United States; Japan's new, comparable colonial career in east Asia; and changes world-wide in the international sugar economy in the age of 'New Imperialism' inaugurated at the end of the nineteenth century.

In relation to the first of these arguments, there is this to be said. Although it appeared an epoch-marking calamity to those affected by it, in retrospect, the 'sugar crisis' of the mid-1880s was grossly inflated in terms of its impact. In fact, it was preceded by a fall in the world price of sugar for the previous two decades and simply worsened in the 1880s. The 1880s 'crisis' simply served to accelerate developments in the financing and ownership of sugar industries world-wide that were already underway. The 'sugar crisis' was far less dramatic in its impact than has often been imagined.

The second reason for positing an 1880 to 1900 'Great Divide' concerns the 'New Imperialism' and the entry of the U.S.A. (and Japan) on to the world colonial stage. Yet the 'new' aspects of fin-de-siècle imperialism may also have been overstated. If anything, the greater differences are to be located in the pre- and post-1800 eras rather than in the period before and after 1880 to 1900. The post-1900 decades of Sugarlandia did not bear the stamp of unbridled metropolitan authority – financial or otherwise – any more than earlier decades had been characterised by unbridled autonomy. The contributors to this volume are virtually at one in rejecting binary readings of this kind and in asserting the nineteenth-century roots of late colonial Sugarlandia and the continuity between earlier developments and those of the first half of the twentieth century. Social and political configurations, which first got underway in the mid-nineteenth century, were still crystallizing in the 1920s. This was as true for those parts of Sugarlandia affected by civil commotion and conquest in the late nineteenth century as it was for territories that knew of neither war nor revolution. For the former – for Puerto Rico, Cuba and the Philippines[23] – the concept of 'a sugar revolution' in the late nineteenth century has been replaced by the concept of 'sugar evolution', beginning in the early 1800s and continuing into the opening decades of the twentieth century. In the case of the latter – Java is the prime example and Barbados probably another – an evolving trend in the historiography is to underline the incremental nature of change rather than sudden shifts in society and politics.[24]

Reconsidering Sugar Centrals

In this context, how are we to understand the prevalence towards 1900 of a new way of organising the manufacture of sugar – the *central* or centralised factory-in-the-field? Do not *centrals* underpin the strongest case for a real divide marking off the late colonial era? A conceptualised definition of the *central* is that of a single, large, sometimes even massive and capital-intensive unit of sugar manufacture that drew its supplies of cane from a diversity of sources that were not owned by the factory itself, and which emerged in response to the economies of scale required by the high cost of fully industrialised factory production.

As we shall go on to argue, this definition is highly problematic. Were it to be accepted, it might appear that the onset of the *centrals* was the watershed that indeed underpinned the 'Great Divide' in the history of Sugarlandia. In fact, however, the ambiguities surrounding the issue of the *centrals* are so considerable as to undermine any such assumption.

Changes in sugar manufacturing technology associated with the appearance of the *centrals* were nothing like so 'revolutionary' as has sometimes been implied. The *centrals* are often viewed as a 'state-of-the-art', continuous-production manufacturing unit. Yet the *centrals* inherited many technological advances that had been incorporated incrementally into advanced sugar manufacture world-wide since at least the 1830s. Technologically speaking, the *central* represented a culmination rather than a revolution. In some cases, this culmination was associated with an extensive reconstruction of the organisation of manufacture and the manner in which raw material was accessed, and resulted in the total physical replacement of the existing units of manufacture. This happened, notably, in parts (at least) of the Caribbean and elsewhere in the international (cane) sugar economy. There, the appearance of the *centrals* did indeed correspond to (although did not necessarily cause) a significant break with the past. But this deep shift very explicitly did not occur in Java, the world's second largest exporter of cane sugar for virtually the whole of the late colonial era. In early twentieth-century Java, many of the island's fully industrialised factories rose on foundations that had been laid in the 1830s and 1840s.

Moreover, the arrangements under which the *centrals* were provided with their raw material, cut sugar cane, need closer scrutiny. Far from being associated with any single or novel mode of accessing cane, the *centrals* in fact relied on a great diversity of such modes. Indeed, the advent of the *centrals* often multiplied the modes of procurement of the cane. The absolute lack of uniformity in such modes makes it difficult if not impossible to see the *centrals* as global agents for epoch-making change in the agricultural sphere of Sugarlandia.

In fact, both procurement and the agricultural conditions under which cane was grown varied considerably, not only in sub-regional industries generally but often, also, in the case of individual *centrals*. At one end of the spectrum was direct farming carried out by and under the supervision of the factory itself, on land owned or rented by the factory owners; at the opposite pole was the production of cane carried out by a myriad of smallholders with the framework of 'peasant' agriculture. These differences existed between sugar colonies, and even between regions of the same colony. For instance, in northern and eastern Java direct farming of cane by the factory predominated, with substantial state intervention, close supervision by factory personnel and heavy dependence on industrial work routines performed by wage labourers. On the other hand, in Java's mountainous centre (Yogyakarta) an indigenous Javanese 'precolonial' state and supra-peasant elites survived into the late colonial era. In Yogyakarta, sugar was embedded within a broader agriculture of smallholder production that included rice and 'second crops'.

Significant contrasts in the agrarian configurations of *centrals* also existed between eastern and western Cuba, or between northern and southern Puerto Rico.

Elsewhere on the Pacific Rim, direct farming of cane by the sugar factories did indeed take place. In Taiwan, there was a considerable amount of direct cane farming carried out by the big Japanese-owned factories established there early in the twentieth century, and in Hawaii and Peru it was virtually the sole manner in which the production of raw material was organised. However, in the Philippines, relations between the *centrals* and the production of cane was much more characteristic of the diversity found in the New World, where direct farming of cane existed alongside many other forms. In the key New World production areas of Cuba, Dominican Republic and Puerto Rico, the 'production of cane was carried out by rural producers ranging from large corporations employing workers in the thousands to small farmers who produced cane with family labour'.[25]

On the whole, the appearance of the *centrals* did not necessarily usher in a new era in the agricultural sector of cane production in Sugarlandia. Rather, in accessing cane, many sugar regions built on extant and often fluid local arrangements complex enough to suggest a future research agenda of their own. Prominent in this research agenda will surely be spatial relations, regional differences, ecological profiles and labour patterns – as these are all of major consequence for the trajectories of the *centrals* and for understanding their differential impacts.

In sum, our contributors underscore the fundamental ambiguities inherent in the terminology of difference inherited from the archive of imperialism with respect to ethnic identity; they challenge crudely diffusionist notions of global economic development fostered by imperialist discourse from the late nineteenth century onward; and they seek to problematise a variety of simple binaries: inter alia, those that juxtapose metropolitan and colonial, industry and agriculture, merchant and industrial capital, urban and rural, peasant and proletarian, and capitalist and pre-capitalist. In so doing, moreover, they probe the very meaning of 'modernity' and of the process of 'industrialisation' with which it is frequently, even ubiquitously associated.

Java and the 'Old' World of Asia

The *Cultuurstelsel* or System of State Cultivations, provided the framework for the revival and expansion of colonial sugar production in nineteenth-century Java. From the 1830s until the 1880s in Java's 'government lands' (the directly ruled areas of the colony), in particular, the *Stelsel* provided contracting manufacturers with raw material, labour, capital (until circa 1850) and a secure market for much of their output. The standard version of the *Stelsel* posits a situation in which commodity production in mid-nineteenth-century

Java was dominated by the Dutch colonial state and its hierarchy of European and 'native' officials. G. Roger Knight, in Chapter Three, challenges this view by arguing for the significant presence of an Indies bourgeoisie at the very heart of the *Cultuurstelsel*. The role played by the Dutch colonial state did not exclude – and, indeed, promoted – the rise of an *Indisch* or Indies bourgeoisie of factory owners and merchants, and of a state officialdom linked to the *Indisch* bourgeoisie through family ties and direct financial interests.

During the middle of the nineteenth century, changes within this bourgeoisie saw it take on an increasingly Indies-Dutch or creole character, in tandem with the partial relegation of its long-standing Indies-Chinese component to a position as the 'pariah entrepreneurs' of colonial capitalism. Yet this latter was never a complete development, and what later came to be termed Indonesian-Chinese capital continued to play a significant, if often understated, role in the sugar industry (with important affinities to mestizo capital in the Philippines). There are also large questions concerning changes in the status of other groups. This is particularly so with respect to the 'Eurasians', who comprised the majority of the 'Indies-Dutch'. In Dutch Java's 'colonial society ', the Eurasians were persons of mixed ethnicity who were nonetheless accorded a legal and social status as 'Europeans'. In contrast, strict racial/cultural bars were upheld between 'native' and 'colonial' in the Anglo-Saxon colonies in Asia. As already suggested, it has been generally assumed that a sequence of events, beginning with the opening of Suez Canal in 1870, and including the crisis of 1884 and the modernisation and drastic re-financing of the sugar industry that purportedly followed in its wake, was attended by a demise of the colony's 'mestizo society' and a consequent marginalisation of Dutch Java's Eurasian population.[26]

Drawing on a remarkable mid-nineteenth-century census of the colonial population of the small coastal Residency of Pekalongan – the same area in which the sugar factory manager Thomas Edwards spent most of his Java years – Van Schaik and Knight present a two-fold argument. Their Chapter Four discusses the provincial colonial status system in the context of the big expansion of the sugar industry during the 1830s and 1840s. It suggests that the impact of the development on the fortunes of the Dutch Eurasians who constituted the bulk of the provincial Dutch community in Pekalongan was highly complex. On the one hand, the industry offered new opportunities for employment and advancement. On the other, it drew expatriate Europeans into the Residency whose social prestige may have belied their small numbers – and whose arrival may have signified an important milestone in the long-term evolution of Dutch colonial society.

But, as Van Schaik and Knight argue, this was only part of the story revealed by the census and related data. The second, and indeed overriding, theme of their chapter stresses the extent to which expatriate newcomers were absorbed into and became part of provincial Dutch colonial communities that continued to be dominated, culturally, socially and economically, by the Indies bourgeoisie. In fact, the arrival of the sugar industry may have tended, taken as a whole, to reinforce rather than undermine the existing hierarchy of Dutch Indies society. In this important sense, the mid-nineteenth-century expansion of the colonial sugar industry reflected long-term and on-going power relationships at least as much as it saw the creation of new ones.

In nineteenth-century Yogyakarta, an ancient fiscal system was gradually transformed into a way of requisitioning labour by market producers of both sugar and indigo.[27] Using recently recovered sources from the courts of Yogyakarta, Sri Margana documents remarkably hybrid fiscal arrangements, legal administration and patterns of coercion.

The unit of production in late-nineteenth-century Yogyakarta was hardly a plantation, at least as defined as a physical, unitary space of production. In Yogyakarta the sugar factory was physically and legally quite distinct from the surrounding village lands: a 'field-and-factory-combine' without the 'field'. Peasants could move away, take legal action and otherwise confront the 'planters', notwithstanding the fact that the sugar factories consistently strove for complete control over land and labour. Yet there is no mistaking the situation in the Yogyakarta area for an instance of 'peasant smallholders' integrated into large-scale commodity production.

At the other extreme of the social relations of sugar production in Yogyakarta, Ulbe Bosma dissects the colonial 'planter class' of that Principality-Residency in the nineteenth century. As a 'class', the planters became famously 'profligate' figures in the quasi-legendary *Tempo Doeloe* of mid-nineteenth-century Java. *Tempo Doeloe* (literally 'time past') eventually came to have a similar status and mythical potency to the 'Old South', the antebellum southern states of the United States of America. It was significant that the Indies Dutch of the mid-nineteenth century were 'far from home' both as regards their seigneurial nonchalance and their social and cultural mores, which had little in common with those of 'Calvinist' Holland. However, the cultural and social nexus between Europe and the Indies in the mid-nineteenth century was a good deal more intimate, and colonial identity significantly more ambivalent, than enduring stereotypes might allow. Concubinage, for example, did not necessarily equate with loose sexual mores (the Spanish Antilles offer arresting parallels in this respect) whereas marriage did not preclude polygamy. As the case of the planters of Yogyakarta demonstrates, marriage might coexist quite harmoniously with having children by concubines. The fact that the Creole planters' matrimonial behaviour did not entirely fit with some nineteenth-century mores should not lead to the conclusion that they were a leisured class of oriental nabobs. This is a false impression created by nineteenth-century novels on 'Company Java' that set out quite explicitly to evoke a sense of exoticism among their readers. It is indeed ironic that novels on 'Company Java' have been so popular among students of colonial cultures eager to take a short cut into the complexities of the era.

Hence the persistence of the myth of 'Company Java', as dominated in the last decades prior to 1800 by local Creole elites, who continued to hold seigneurial sway into the final decades of the nineteenth century, when they were finally swept away by a relentless, metropolitan modernity.

Bosma concludes, however, that the period after 1884 certainly represented a far greater influx of metropolitan capital than had been available to the sugar industry in earlier decades: it did not represent, however, the eradication of the Yogyakarta planter class nor of the Indies bourgeoisie in general. Rather, they continued to own a minority of factories, continued to serve on boards of sugar companies and continued to play a significant role in the upper echelons of industry management. Bosma's findings for the micro-world of Yogyakarta highlight a pattern that was not uncommon for Java or elsewhere in Asia, or indeed for the Caribbean (where, as in Java, this pattern was often profiled by a spatial division between metropolitan and local capital).

New and Old Worlds Juxtaposed:
The Philippines and the Caribbean

The picture around the turn of the century is definitely one of capital concentration, but incremental rather than revolutionary. The very idea of continuity speaks against any assumption of erstwhile colonial sugar industries becoming the exclusive preserve of metropolitan – American and European – capital by the late nineteenth century.

In the case of the Philippines and Puerto Rico (which came under American direct colonial rule after 1898) and in Cuba (where informal empire held sway), a revisionist historiography is pointing towards the problematic nature of metropolitan financial domination as well as the relatively short duration of whatever hegemony United States sugar capital actually enjoyed. Indeed, in the Philippines, American capital was never dominant in situ, and by the 1930s American disinvestment was the key theme. Even in the Spanish Antilles, despite its proximity to the centres of United States capital, the majority of the *centrals* (and the canefields) remained in local hands.

As Juan Giusti-Cordero points out in his chapter, the sugar bourgeoisies of the Philippines and Puerto Rico exhibited common patterns of complex subordination to American capital that belie stereotypes of formal colonial rule. In both territories, regional differences were important. In Puerto Rico's north coast, the *centrals* were less important as landholders than the long-established hacendados and the area remained under the sway of Spanish and Spanish-Creole *centralistas*.[28] In the Philippines, the Creole (particularly *mestizo* of Chinese-Filipino descent) and Spanish-Creole presence was important throughout, but especially in the archipelago's 'sugarlandia', Negros. In that island, somewhat larger than Puerto Rico, all the cane milled by the *centrals* was grown by independent growers under long-term contracts.

In Puerto Rico, local capital was concentrated through interlocking stock ownership and directorates, while in the Philippines the Philippines National Bank (directly subsidised by the colonial government) was instrumental. The sugar planters in both colonies were involved in multiple economic activities and social identities. This resiliency was associated with political roles that went far beyond being middlemen. Thus 1898 did not merely represent a shift from 'Spanish' to 'United States' rule over passive colonial formations. Sugar planters, like other local social groups in the Philippines and Puerto Rico, actively shaped the relationship between the pre- and post-1898 colonial eras. While the Filipino and Puerto Rican planter elites may not have had the strength and self-assurance of other peripheral bourgeoisies, they had much of their complexity; hence these planter bourgeoisies should be analysed in terms of negotiation as well as subjugation.

Yoshiko Nagano captured this complexity in asserting the Filipino sugar oligarchy's 'Janus-faced role as both subjects and beneficiaries of imperial rule'.[29] Discussions of 'compadre colonialism'[30] and 'cacique democracy'[31] in the Philippines, and 'colonial democracy' in both the Philippines[32] and Puerto Rico resonate with this 'Janus-faced role'. Indeed, even Spanish elites rooted in the pre-1898 era had a notable economic and political trajectory in the American colonial regime, quite visibly so among *centralistas* and associated bankers.

Comparison between Puerto Rico and the Philippines 'sugar island', Negros – the main sugar-producing area of the Philippines – is especially useful in making connections between landownership, *central* development, ethnocultural profiles, and modes of control over land and labour. Giusti-Cordero concludes that in Puerto Rico as in Negros, the indigenous and Creole-Spanish sugar corporations accounted for most sugar production into the late 1920s; and several of the most important corporations continued to be under the control of Spanish citizens.

Significantly, in Negros as elsewhere in the Philippines, American capital was entirely absent from sugar landholding, and had a limited, refracted presence through Hawaiian-American control of a handful of *centrals*. In both Puerto Rico and Negros, these ownership patterns signalled profound characteristics of *central* structure that involved an agrarian sector firmly under the control of locally-rooted social groups and labour patterns whose global import cannot be separated from highly specific local histories. As in Java, an expatriate Chinese merchant class was displaced as well as transformed; in the Philippines, by Chinese-Filipino *mestizo* and in Java by Eurasians. As in Puerto Rico and Cuba, in the Philippines a Spanish elite intermarried with local groups. Historical analysis of the role of sugar planter elites in the Philippines and Puerto Rico allows a closer appraisal of cultural and political developments such as post-1898 'Hispanophilia' in Puerto Rico[33] and a post-1898 'Spanish presence' in Filipino culture.[34]

Ibarra's Chapter Nine takes up the issue of the post-1898 role of Spanish elites in Cuba and Puerto Rico and sets forth striking contrasts between the two islands. In Puerto Rico, the pre-1898 Spanish presence was somewhat less conflictive than in Cuba; the Spanish in Puerto Rico were also less numerous, both in absolute and relative terms, and were less concentrated in the cities than was the case in Cuba. In Cuba, a bitter independence war created significant divisions between Spanish and Cuban with lasting consequences for relations among sectors of the Spanish and Cuban populations. Moreover, the resilient Spanish elites in sugar, banking, and commerce sometimes struck common chords of protest with Cuban nationalists (in a sense, even despite themselves) in the face of American neo-colonial rule, in patterns that have parallels in Puerto Rico.

In Cuba as in Puerto Rico and the Philippines, growing concentration of capital and the decline of some elite sectors coexisted with more densely interwoven stock-owning local family networks linked to banking interests. This was also a phenomenon experienced in Java, where the *Indische* bourgeoisie even had a presence in metropolitan banking. In the former Spanish colonies, these familial financial networks remained under the American aegis. Here again the Caribbean-Java comparison is important and deserves further research. Any attempt to answer the question of who are the colonisers and who the colonised, in the context of sugar production, would probably lead to a re-categorisation of many locals as foreigners. Yet, as Ibarra points out, on the ground the Spanish sugar colonies presented a variety of intra-elite struggles that were all the more intense because they turned on the possibility, or impossibility, of future nationhood.

Beyond Taxonomies of Sugarlandia

Our authors' perspectives on Sugarlandia call into question an entire taxonomy – one rendered problematic by its reliance on such key terms as 'metropolitan', 'indigenous', 'comprador', 'Creole' as a way of articulating discussion of the establishment of 'nationhood', paradoxically enough in the context of a phenomenon which was essentially global, namely the growth of the international sugar economy. In the nineteenth-century Cuban or Puerto Rican or Java sugar colonies, the role of local capital was early and substantial. This is reflected, for example in Manuel Barcia's Chapter Eight on the Havana bourgeoisie and importation of slaves into early nineteenth-century Cuba.[35]

Barcia clearly establishes the key role of the Havana bourgeoisie in promoting both the trade in slaves and the sugar industry. From the late eighteenth century onwards the merchants and planters of the Cuban capital and its environs largely took over the importation of slaves into the Spanish colony, with the backing of the colonial authorities and largely regardless of policy in Madrid. This locally-based slave trade prospered until well into the mid-nineteenth century. The merchants tended to be of metropolitan Spanish origin (*peninsulares*) while the planters tended to be locally-born Creoles; yet they made common cause in the slave trade. Barcia's particular contribution, based on access to important new data in Cuba itself, is to reveal that the extent of the imports of slaves into early nineteenth-century Cuba was considerably greater than has been previously supposed, and hence a more significant basis for the accumulation of capital by the colonial bourgeoisie than has been appreciated hitherto.

As Margana and Bosma argue, it is problematic to analyse the development of the sugar industry in Yogyakarta through the prism of a coloniser-colonised dichotomy. It would be far too easy to claim that these Creole or comprador classes were mere instruments of overseas capitalism. In some cases metropolitan and local actors were adversaries, in other circumstances they were working together, more like the *compadres* of Hispanic co-parenthood.[36]

The age of high imperialism, and particularly its periods of low sugar prices, did generate sharp tensions among the 'bourgeoisies' of Sugarlandia, which were often spelled out in terms of 'metropolitan' versus 'colonized' or 'Creole' elites. Yet, the picture was far more complicated. For one, the Creole population groups did not have such a strong sense of national identity. In Java, for example, as Joost Coté points out in Chapter Seven, German, British, or American flags were not per se viewed as foreign. Moreover, Creole sugar property, including its associated trading houses, loyalties and identities, was predicated upon free access to the world market and free access to (not necessarily free) labour.[37]

Should we suggest that the moment of rupture and the onset of a colonial versus Creole relationship was quintessentially a perception of a reconfiguration of capital, ignited by a shake-up of the political configuration among world powers in the era of high imperialism? That would mean that the concept of 'colonial capital' was predicated upon this process of re-categorisation of who was local and who metropolitan. Clearly, in Java, a change of discourse became visible, and the shift in Dutch colonial policy may have been in some ways more significant than the change in metropolis in the Spanish colonies.

In Chapter Seven, Joost Coté analyses how sugar became part of a colonial discourse, throwing up new questions about civilisation and inclusion in modernity. The discourse in the port town of Semarang shifted in the 1880s from the old style 'laissez faire' liberalism to an appeal for an interventionist colonial policy. The late nineteenth-century leaders of public opinion in this town were part of a metropolitan group of progressive liberals, who arrived at a subtle re-appraisal of the State Cultivation System, which was heavily associated with colonial government and Dutch colonial interests. In their view, the Cultivation System was at least orderly, in contrast to the prior vices of uncontrolled private enterprise in Java and the chaos and misery in other European colonies in Asia, particularly British India.

In the age of high imperialism, 'colonial' could mean many different things. To arrive at a comparative understanding of the position of the local sugar bourgeoisies in this matrix of colonial, coloniser and colonised, we need to take stock, for example, of the very different situations with regard to labour patterns and cultural-racial divisions in the various Sugarlandias. The way in which progressive colonialists in Java tried to define the sugar production as a colonial problem was therefore unthinkable in the Spanish realm, where societies were much more of the 'settler' type. In colonial Indonesia, newcomers and trading houses favoured an interventionist policy to curtail the disintegrating effects wrought by 'Creole' sugar producers on the Javanese peasantry, whereas in Cuba and Puerto Rico it was the Creole landholders who advocated (especially after 1930) various restrictions on the expansion of the sugar industry.

The progressive colonial interventionist discourse about the chaos and misery caused by unbridled capitalism, which took shape in Java and in the Netherlands in the late 1880s, denied the citizen status of the Creole planters. There was no room for a 'hybrid' sugar complex in this discourse, for it would blur the distinction between coloniser and colonised, and endanger the concept of the 'white man's burden' vis-à-vis the weaker races. Yet locally, lines between 'coloniser' and 'colonised' were often drawn among the Creole population.

To Conclude ... and To Continue

This introduction has built on the perspectives of the book's authors, and has addressed the connections between studies dealing with widely separated geographical areas, in different time periods, and along different social dimensions. At the same time, and in important ways, the introduction has also condensed the editors' own changing conceptions of Sugarlandia, as these evolved in the process of editing the studies and connecting their arguments. Hence this introduction is in a sense also an epilogue, and a call for further research along lines that these studies are among the first to demarcate.

The studies presented here analyse various aspects of 'Sugarlandia' in Southeast Asia and the Caribbean, from peasant production and taxation to technological change; to the economic activity, culture and politics of the Creole sugar bourgeoisies; to state policy and ideology. The studies span two world regions and two eras, and they raise significant questions about the relationship between these (and other) binary constructs. Persisting demarcations between Southeast Asia and the Caribbean even in the study of a single commodity such as sugar seems to be related to persisting constructions of colonial history premised on a 1900 fault-line. Sugar invites us to look otherwise at these binary couplings, and to highlight hereto neglected dimensions in the respective colonies' histories.

Other binary constructs have drawn the critical attention of the book's contributors: economy and culture, tradition and modernity, field and factory ... These polarities, too, have hamstrung the historiography of sugar and have limited its conceptual depth. For one thing, the distinction between field and factory in sugar plantations, and their close interrelation, is both a key to this 'anomaly' and a privileged space in which to study it. Thus we need to study the social relations in field and factory in their own right, but not only so. For instance, even if early twentieth-century cane field labour in Java was not mechanised, the scale and sophistication of its technological and scientific development bears some relationship with advances in its *centrals*. The 'factory in the fields' could not obliterate the 'fields' as historical spaces of social relations, and indeed we might well search for the 'fields in the factory', e.g. in the factories' seasonal rhythms, fluid labourer populations, and ethno-racial stratifications. Yet the massive 'modern' presence that the sugar mills presented – and their often adjacent settlements – cannot be underestimated. What we need is a full conceptual perspective on the *centrals* of the nineteenth and early twentieth centuries. The comparison and connection between Southeast Asia and the Caribbean, such as is essayed here, will surely be a major component of that analysis.

The relationship between economy and culture in the sugar colonies is a major theme that leads us away from the crude economicism that often characterises plantation societies. Culture can indeed periodise and condition economic patterns, and reinterpret them; culture is also a major 'bridge' between historical periods, and one of the most telling continuities between the pre- and post-1900 eras is in the ethnocultural profiles of the colonial planter groups. The evidence for cultural patterns is more easily available for the literate sectors of sugar society, but matters do not end there: and vigorous research needs to be done on the plantation labourers (often also peasants) and their own complex and changing world views.

Under colonialism and neo-colonialism, societies in Asia and the Caribbean that were shaped to a significant extent by sugar production exhibited widely diverging characteristics, in the context of societies that were already profoundly different. This book takes on that historical complexity and difference as the vehicle for novel, encompassing ways of thinking about sugar plantation societies and their eras. The most colonial and global of commodities dramatises, like perhaps no other, the tensions and complexity of globalisation as a secular process.

Table 2.1. Ten largest producers of Cane Sugar in 1923 (World production 13,697 thousand tons)

Country	Size in square kilometers	Hectares planted with Cane	Number of Factories	Production in 1000 tons	Average production per Factory per 1000 tons
Cuba	113,960	747,460	179	4,000	22,34
India	–	1,186,812	Unknown	3,266	
Java	125,957	171,130	194	1,771	9,12
Brazil	–	–	More than 2000 small factories	647	
Hawaii	15,635	90,000	53	479	9,03
Puerto Rico	8,040	80,000	40	398	9,95
Formosa	34,974	110,000	46 (and hundreds of small factories)	348	
Philippines	330,500	98,000	32 large (and hundreds of small factories)	335	
Australia	–	56,879	54	280	5,18
Peru	1,382,832	49,800	33 (and a number of small factories)	275	

Source: Prinsen Geerligs, *De rietsuikerindustrie in de verschillende landen van productie* (1924).

Notes

1. In the Asia-Pacific region, the most appreciable single study to address the mind as well as the matter of Sugarlandia has been Larkin, *Sugar and the Origins of Modern Philippine Society*, a study which brought the term 'Sugarlandia' into wide scholarly circulation. In Southeast Asia, it is probably in the field of Philippines studies that discussion of the culture and society of Sugarlandia, rather than simply its political economy, has been at most advanced (e.g. McCoy, 'A Queen Dies Slowly'; McCoy, 'Sugar Barons'; Lopez-Varga, *The Socio-Economic Politics of Sugar;* Billig, *Barons, Brokers and Buyers;* Aguilar, *Clash of Spirits*).
2. Recent studies of sugar production in the nineteenth and twentieth centuries (e.g. Tomich, 'Small Islands and Huge Comparisons'; Tomich, *Through the Prism of Slavery;* Dessens,

Myths of the Plantation Society, De Cauna, *Au Temps des Isles à Sucre*; Shepherd, *Slavery Without Sugar*; Piqueras, *Azúcar y esclavitud*; Thompson, *In the Shadow of the Plantation*; Ayala, *American Sugar Kingdom*; Higman, *Montpelier, Jamaica*; Boomgaard and Oost-indie, *Changing Sugar Technology*), while richly documented and conceptually far-reaching, have focused on to the Caribbean region and the Americas (but see Moitt, *Sugar, Slavery and Society*). Conversely, on Southeast Asia, see Elmhirst and Saptari, *Labour in Southeast Asia* and Jain, *Plantation Labour in South and Southeast Asia*. In other studies, emphasis has shifted to issues of race and culture (Isfahani-Hammond, *The Masters and the Slaves*). At the same time, 'international' histories of sugar have concentrated almost exclusively on pro-duction per se (the major exception is Mintz, *Sweetness and Power*, on consumption) and have been heavily weighted towards developments in the Americas (e.g. Galloway, *The Sugar Cane Industry*). In the 1980s, two composite volumes addressed broader issues of the political economy of sugar in a genuinely global setting (Albert and Graves, *Crisis and Change*, and Albert and Graves, *The World Sugar Economy*), but, in the absence of all but the most abbreviated editorial discussion, the enterprise remained essentially fragmentary.

3. In the Philippines, 'Sugarlandia' has long been used to refer to the 'sugar island' of Negros. See for instance López-Gonzaga, *Crisis in Sugarlandia*, and Nagano, 'The Oligopolistic Structure'. On Negros island, see Giusti-Cordero in this volume.

4. The slave trade, however, exhibited various important intermediary forms among coastal West African sovereigns; while in Java and Southeast Asia until the nineteenth century, locally-controlled production spheres were linked only indirectly to European trade.

5. James, 'French Capitalism and Caribbean Slavery', and Mintz, 'The Caribbean as a Socio-cultural Area'. Major elements in the evolution of industrial (factory) work routines found their origin in the slave-operated 'factory-in-the-field' of Caribbean sugar production in the seventeenth and eighteenth centuries .

6. Bosma and Knight, 'Global Factory and Local Field'.

7. In the early twentieth century, the proto-multinational corporation, International Tele-graph and Telephone (ITT) was founded by Creole sugar traders of Puerto Rico (with a complex Caribbean background) doing business with the American Virgin Islands and Cuba, with family backgrounds in St. Thomas and Curaçao. In *The Sovereign State of ITT*, Anthony Sampson seems rather baffled by this peculiar 'offshore capitalism', as he calls it. See Sampson, *The Sovereign State of ITT*.

8. A similar argument, indeed stressing the importance of trial and error, has been made for the archetypal Caribbean 'sugar revolution', that of Barbados in the seventeenth century. McCusker and Menard, 'The Sugar Industry in the Seventeenth Century', 290.

9. Dockès, 'Le paradigme sucrier', 115. Under the Abassid caliphate, Basra became a centre for large scale sugar production, refining and commerce that drew heavily, if indirectly, on the labour of large numbers of east African slaves. The slaves' labour on the drainage of the wetlands of southern Mesopotamia was the vital foundation for the industry's growth.

10. Bosma and Knight, 'Global Factory and Local Field'.

11. Best, 'The Mechanism of Plantation Type Societies'.

12. Mintz and Wolf, 'Haciendas and Plantations'; Mintz, 'The Plantation as a Socio-cultural Type'; Wolf, 'On Peasant Rebellions'; Steward et al., *The People of Puerto Rico*.

13. Mintz and Wolf, 'Haciendas and Plantations'.

14. Mintz, 'The Plantation as a Socio-Cultural Type', 43.

15. Mintz, 'Petits cultivateurs et prolétaires ruraux', 225.

16. Mintz, 'The Plantation as a Socio-cultural Type', 143. An early, perhaps unexpected con-tributor to this discussion was Julian Steward, who directed the *People of Puerto Rico* research team where Mintz and Wolf did their important early research in the 1940s (Steward et al., *The People of Puerto Rico*). Steward was skeptical of overly broad 'plantation' conceptions and called for closer attention to (a) history, especially of land dispossession by the planta-tion or its forebears and (b) the peasant and small farmers who survived land dispossession and continued to live in proximity to the plantations: 'the varied subcultural groups who

did not lose their land' (Steward, 'Perspectives on Plantation'). Interestingly, Steward also recommended examining situations of plantation inexistence, i.e. where plantations did not arise (for instance, Java?).

Steward rejected the possibility of '[a] single definition that covers plantations of all periods and areas' (Steward, 'Perspectives on Plantation', 5). With regard to the 'field and factory combines' – which Mintz and Wolf had equated with modern plantations (see Mintz and Wolf, 'Haciendas and Plantations') Steward perceptively noted that the 'combines' were rather exceptional anyway: modern plantations tend to be afar more like the Hawaiian pineapple 'plantations', the modernised coastal Peruvian cotton haciendas, or the California Del Monte fruit orchards and canneries (Steward, 'Perspectives on Plantation', 8). In those operations, field and factory operations are not combined, and processing plants purchase the crop from independent growers (Steward's point was also valid for half of the Puerto Rican sugar industry as well). Moreover, even granting the existence of the 'field-and-factory combines', there were 'many variations within this general type' (Steward, 'Perspectives on Plantation', 11). While hardly a specialist on plantations, Steward set forth lines of investigation that went beyond the plantation 'as is' to its history and its immediate periphery as essential to understanding the plantation itself. At the same time, Steward raised hard questions about the 'internal' organisation of modern plantations.

17. Geertz, *Agricultural Involution*, 89.
18. Stoler, *Capitalism and Confrontation in Sumatra's Plantation Belt*. Edward Kamau Brathwaite's study of Creole society in Jamaica eventually turned the plantation model on its head (see Brathwaite, *The Development of Creole society*), although Brathwaite's far-reaching reconceptualisation has not received all the attention it deserves, and indeed has been all but ignored where it should have resonated the most: in the hispanophone Caribbean. Walter Rodney's parting opus, *A History of the Guyanese Working People 1881–1905*, is even more germane, for Rodney articulated the political economy of Guyanese *centrals* with that of the associated smallholders, including dimensions of race and culture. In Rodney's perspective, late nineteenth-century British Guyana is unique in the anglophone West Indies for the 'overwhelming presence of plantation capitalism' and a labour force that was mostly 'a permanent hybrid of plantation and proletarian' (See Rodney, *A History of the Guyanese Working People*, 218), existing in close interaction with self-employed farmers.
19. Knight, 'The Java Sugar Industry as a Capitalist Plantation'.
20. Bosma and Knight, 'Global Factory and Local Field'.
21. Tomich, *Through the Prism of Slavery*.
22. Moreno Fraginals, *El Ingenio*; Scott, *Slave Emancipation in Cuba*, and Scott, 'Labour Control in Cuba'; Bergad, *Cuban Rural Society in the Nineteenth Century*; Tomich, *Through the Prism of Slavery*.
23. Larkin, *Sugar and the Origins of Modern Philippine Society*; Ramos Mattei, *Azúcar y esclavitud*; Ayala, *American Sugar Kingdom*; Allahar, *Class, Politics, and Sugar in Colonial Cuba*.
24. Bosma and Raben, *De oude Indische wereld*; Knight, 'The Visible Hand', and Knight, 'The Sugar Industry of Colonial Java'; Sleeman, 'The Agri-Business Bourgeoisie of Barbados and Martinique'.
25. Ayala, *American Sugar Kingdom*, 121.
26. Taylor, *The Social World of Batavia*.
27. The production by 'peasant' labour of this organic dyestuff was a major counterpart of the sugar industry throughout Java in the middle decades of the nineteenth century. Its manufacture provides an outstanding instance of attempts under colonial aegis to adapt and expand a long-existing 'peasant' industry to the requirements of world market production. By the final decades of the nineteenth-century, production of this latter type was concentrated largely in the Yogyakarta region and in the adjacent 'Principality' of Surakarta.
28. The north/south distinction in Puerto Rico had its west/east counterpart in Cuba, with Puerto Rico's north coast being closer to Cuba's Occidente, and the south coast to Oriente.
29. Nagano, 'The Oligopolistic Structure', 109.

30. Owen, *Compadre Colonialism.*
31. Anderson, 'Cacique Democracy in the Philippines'.
32. Paredes, *Philippine Colonial Democracy.*
33. Vivoni Farage and Alvarez Curbelo, *Hispanofilia.*
34. Ileto, *Pasyón*; Rodao, ' Spanish Falange in the Philippines', and Rodao, 'Spanish Language in the Philippines'.
35. Recent scholarship on Caribbean sugar history notes the role of local settler initiatives vis à vis metropolitan and international forces even in Barbados's 'sugar revolution' in the seventeenth century, the classic plantation-building process: McCusker and Menard, 'The Sugar Industry in the Seventeenth Century'.
36. See Owen's reading of '*Compadre Colonialism*'
37. Tomich, *Through the Prism of Slavery.*

3

Technology, Technicians and Bourgeoisie: Thomas Jeoffries Edwards and the Industrial Project in Sugar in Mid-Nineteenth-Century Java

G. Roger Knight

In November 1865, the English-born Thomas Jeoffries Edwards died near the north Java town of Madjalengka, situated in the Residency of Cirebon and itself in the vicinity of the colonial sugar factory at Gempol where Edwards had taken over in the previous year as *administrateur* or general manager. Death appears to have overtaken him fairly suddenly, although perhaps not unexpectedly, within a few weeks of the end of the Campaign, as the sugar industry's manufacturing season was termed. Aged 50, he had been born in Shropshire, in the English borders of Wales, the eldest son of a skilled leather worker (currier) and leading member of the local community of Unitarian Dissenters. His mother, Marian Edwards, came from a well-to-do artisan family in the county town of Shrewsbury and an uncle subsequently became a wealthy merchant in Liverpool. Thomas Edwards had first arrived in Java in 1842, and had lived there for over twenty years with a locally born and almost certainly Eurasian woman, Anne Baird, with whom he had three surviving children, all girls. Some ten years his junior, Baird outlived her erstwhile partner by more than four decades, and died in the West Java town of Bogor in 1910.

Edwards' life story belongs, obviously enough, to an increasingly rich narrative of the colonial communities of Dutch Java. Its conjoint themes of bourgeois domesticity – the *administrateur* of a mid-century sugar factory and his partner were people of some social consequence and financial substance – and long-term cohabitation provide a nice counterweight to more exaggerated notions of the 'good old days' of a colonial *Tempo Doeloe* (literally 'time past') characterised by bucolic excess and sexual license. Altogether less obvious, on the other hand, is the extent to which Edwards' story also underpins a largely unfamiliar narrative of the engagement of a mid-nineteenth-century Indies bourgeoisie, composed of sugar manufacturers, merchants and state officials. They sustained an industrial project in Java, sugar manufacture, which saw the colony emerge as Asia's first successfully industrialised producer of the commodity, half a century or more ahead of any of its erstwhile counterparts in the eastern hemisphere.

Technology and the Industrialisation of Sugar Manufacture in Nineteenth-Century Java

Between the late 1830s and the crisis, precipitated in 1884 by a dramatic fall of the world price of sugar, which threatened to engulf its factories in financial ruin, the output of exported cane sugar from Java increased sevenfold, from less than 50,000 tons annually to a figure in excess of 350,000 tons. It did so, moreover, on the basis of a degree of industrialisation in manufacture that singled out Java as unique in nineteenth-century Asia and as the 'Oriental' antipode of Cuba, which from the mid-nineteenth century onwards came to represent the very acme of the industrialised manufacture of cane sugar in the West. At the heart of Java's achievement lay the capacity of the island's colonial sugar producers to incrementally absorb all the major appurtenances of a nineteenth-century revolution in sugar-manufacturing technology, founded on steel, steam and their attendant chemistries. Access to the agricultural resources of the 'Garden of the East', guaranteed in terms of land and labour commandeered under the impress of the Indies Government's *Cultuurstelsel*, was crucial in making this possible. From 1830 onwards, under the impress of what can best be translated as the System of State Cultivations, the Indies Government, through the agency of its provincial state officials, made available to the industry both cane itself and a field Campaign and factory workforce levied from among the peasantry of the surrounding villages.[1]

Taken by itself, raw material and labour alone were no guarantee of industrialisation. The transition from a modified version of pre-industrial production, on however enlarged a scale – which was what the *Cultuurstelsel* initially seemed to promise – was dependent on other factors. Foremost among them was a reconstruction of sugar capital in Java in the mid-century decades that both ensured the emergence of a bourgeoisie and facilitated its role in sustaining moves towards an industrialisation of manufacture. This was initiated but only partly carried through in the 1830s and 1840s by the Indies state. Industrialisation of this kind was founded technologically on the mechanised grinding of cane in increasingly sophisticated iron and steel mills and – crucially in terms of global best practice – in the (reciprocal) exploitation of steam energy in the processes through which cane juice was transformed into sugar. In consequence, the boiling house (or sugar house) of the advanced mid-nineteenth-century sugar factory came to be dominated, first and foremost, by the vacuum pan. There were also attendant but essentially subsidiary apparatus,[2] based to varying degrees on the re-circulation of steam heat, for the prior defecation and condensing of the expressed cane juice before it went into the pan for the final stage of conversion into quasi-crystalline sugar.

These advances in the application of steam heat under reduced air pressure, most of them initially developed for the big sugar refineries and beet sugar industries of Western Europe, formed the very core of a revolution in sugar manufacturing. By the end of the nineteenth century, these developments had transformed the industry from one heavily dependent on manual labour and 'rule of thumb' in the manufacturing sector into one dominated by the most technically sophisticated form of continuous, scientifically based mass production that the world had yet seen. The earlier stages of this development, during the mid-nineteenth-century decades, were characterised world-wide, nevertheless, by technologically mixed systems of manufacture in which the most advanced equipment was apt to be found in the factory cheek-by-jowl with apparatus of a much earlier vintage. Such was certainly the case in Java, where, by the late 1850s, some 50 or so factories, representing around half the island's colonial industry, were equipped with vacuum pans which operated in conjunction with a great variety of arrangements further back down the production line, some of them as up-to-date in design as the pan itself, others a good deal more primitive. In this respect, mid-century Java was roughly comparable with other 'modern' cane sugar industries world-wide. Cuba, at the cutting edge of technological advance in the New World, and shortly to become Java's coeval as one the world's two largest producer-exporters of cane sugar, provides a particularly potent comparison. Around 1860, rather more factories in the Spanish colony (around 60) were equipped with the vacuum pan than was the case in Java, but, as in Java, the majority of such pans operated in the context of 'mixed' systems of manufacture.[3]

In Java as elsewhere in the colonial world, the technology associated with the industrial revolution in sugar manufacture was almost entirely imported, literally in packing cases, from manufacturers in Great Britain and continental Europe. It required a considerable investment of capital, not only in equipment but also in freight and insurance. Between 1830 and 1850, the necessary finance was provided to selected manufacturers, in part at least, in the form of low-interest capital loans from the Indies Government's treasury. These were made in conjunction with formal contracts that committed the manufacturer to supply the Government with sugar made from cane compulsorily grown on village land by peasant landholders and their dependents. After 1850, this direct state subvention ceased, and the role of capital supplier to the industry was taken over by the Batavia Branch – universally known as the Factorij – of the Netherlands Trading Corporation or NHM, the largest Dutch firm operating in the colony. Thanks to royal support for its establishment in 1824 and its position as commercial agent to the Indies Government (prior to 1850 it was also its banker), it also enjoyed exceptionally close links with the colonial state.

It was the Factorij, in close conjunction with the emergent Indies bourgeoisie – and hence with a variety of sugar manufacturers, local and metropolitan trading houses and (though covertly) ranking officials of the Indies state – that sustained this industrial project in Java from about 1850 onwards. As a result, the incremental re-equipment of the industry was almost continuous during the mid-century decades, culminating in the late 1870s in the commencement of the installation throughout the Java industry of the multiple effect condenser, usually in the form known as 'Double' or 'Triple Effet'. It was this apparatus that took to its logical conclusion in the sugar factory (it had already been widely used in European and North American refineries) the principle, prefigured in equipment devised some decades earlier, of the re-circulation of steam heat in a totally enclosed system of defecation and condensing of cane juice prior to its arrival at the vacuum pan.[4]

The Indies Bourgeoisie and the Sustaining of the Industrial 'Project'

It is the role of the mid-century Indies bourgeoisie, acting with and through the NHM's Batavia Factorij, in sustaining the industrial project in Java sugar that is highlighted by Thomas Edwards' career in Java. This spanned almost two and a half decades from the 1840s through to the 1860s. Edwards' story does more than reflect what was going on in a wider context: it nuances and sometimes contradicts that larger, less personal narrative. First and foremost, however, it makes it abundantly clear that an integral part of the industrial project was not simply the cases of equipment that arrived by shiploads from the West, but also the personnel who accompanied them, often in a quite literal sense. These were people who went on, under the patronage of the Indies bourgeoisie, to form a core of experienced operatives, engineers (*ingenieur*) or mechanics (*mechanist*) – the distinction seems to have been a fairly fluid one – and skilled artisans, who were as vital to the industrial project as the equipment itself. Edwards, although pre-eminent among such people on account of his abilities, education and (very probably) social status, was by no means alone in pushing forward the industrial frontier during the mid-century decades. In the same locality on the north Java coast where Edwards spent most of his Java years, for example, there also were individuals like the Scot Alexander Lawson (1819–1877), a *machinist* originally 'brought out' to Java to supervise the assembly of a pair of paddle steamers for the Indies Government and subsequently employed for the remainder of his life in one of the north coast's best-equipped factories.[5] Likewise, his Dutch counterpart, Franciscus Adrianus Bergmans, 'in life, *ingenieur* at the sugar factories in Tegal' whose death notice, inserted by his grieving mother, appeared in a Rotterdam newspaper in May 1859.[6]

Potentially Euro-centric assumptions of the diffusion of skill from the metropolitan core have to be tempered, nonetheless, by a realisation that the mid-nineteenth-century sugar factory in colonial Java was also critically dependent for its successful technical operation on the abilities of 'local' Chinese and Javanese artisans and workman.[7] At the apogee of his Indies career (see below), Edwards himself was employed as the *administrateur* (general manager) of what was, in effect, a 'model factory', developed as an exemplar to other manufacturers in matters technological. He had scarcely been in the position a year, however, before he brought in skilled local or *peranakan* 'Chinese' (Java-born individuals of mixed ethnicity and of part-Chinese descent) to oversee, in tandem with an expatriate European 'sugar maker', the day-to-day operation of the boiling house. Edwards evidently had grave doubts as to whether or not Javanese workman in this 'remote' rural area were capable of managing the processes involved in boiling sugar with steam, but he equally had no doubt whatsoever that experienced local Chinese were on hand in the colony to do precisely that. Similar individuals, distinguished inter alia by their 'curious' adoption of the bowler hat, are to be seen in some of the few contemporary photographs of the mid-nineteenth century Java factory.[8]

Edwards 1815 to 1842: From Shropshire to Java

Precisely what led Thomas Edwards to Java in 1842 is not entirely clear. His father, John Edwards, died at the age of 35, leaving a widow and a young family of five children, of whom Thomas, aged ten, was the eldest boy. As a youth of seventeen, he was at work (probably as an apprentice and thanks to his connections among the area's Unitarian communities) at a large colliery in the south of Lancashire in the north-west of England,[9] in a district that lay near the heart of the most rapidly industrialising part of the United Kingdom (and hence, at that date, of the world).[10] The colliery itself would have familiarised him with the steam engines and steam pumps on which its operation was dependent, while nearby was the newly-established Vulcan Foundry, already on its way in the mid-1830s to becoming one of the leading steam engine manufacturing enterprises in the entire country, specialising in the production of railway locomotives and their export world-wide.[11] His whereabouts thereafter are uncertain, but is clear that when he arrived in Java he did

so as what the Dutch termed at the time a *werktuigkundige* – literally, someone 'knowledgeable' with machines.

Edwards was twenty-seven years old when he landed in Batavia in August
1842 on a ship, *The Warlock*, that had cleared the English port of Liverpool
at the end of April of that year.[12] It looks as if it were no chance journey, and
that Edwards had been 'brought out' to Java for a specific purpose by a
wealthy Indies landowner and sugar manufacturer. The point is worth
emphasising. On the face of it neither his new employer, Thomas Benjamin
Hofland – the man who supported Edwards' application to the colonial
authorities for permission to remain in the colony a few weeks after his land-
ing[13] – nor his brother Pieter were very likely exemplars of a 'progressive'
Indies bourgeoisie. Indeed, both men were subsequently immortalised as the
very epitome of the old-fashioned *suikerlord* (a later but useful coinage), the
seigneurial figure, whose improvident and 'oriental' lifestyle was represented
as the very antithesis of bourgeois identity. Yet the Hoflands' patronage of
Edwards is a revealing instance of just how multifaceted that identity actually
was. Together with their business partner, the Schleswig-born Johann Erich
Banck, this pair of *Indisch* Dutchmen, born of a Dutch father and an Asian
woman on the Coromandel coast of India, had made their money as sugar-
manufacturing contractors to the Indies Government in Java's eastern salient
or *Oosthoek*, and enjoyed the financial backing of both the NHM's Batavia
Factorij and local Chinese business interests in East Java.[14] Recently, they had
bought from its bankrupt British owners the Pamanoekan & Tjiassem estate
in the Krawang Residency of West Java. This vast property, running from the
Java Sea up into the Preanger mountains to the south, and equipped at Subang, some forty kilometres back from the coast, with what had been planned
in the 1820s as the most elaborate 'sugar works' in the entire colony, was
often referred to as a virtual principality.[15]

It was almost certainly at Subang that Java's first vacuum pan had been
installed at a precociously early date at the beginning of the 1830s, when the
pan had only just begun its global career.[16] By the time that the Hoflands and
Banck took it over, the Subang factory was run down and its vacuum pan
(most probably) sold off to another sugar maker elsewhere in the colony.
What evidence there is, however, points to the brothers' intention to follow-
up the success in East Java by restoring and adding to Pamanoekan & Tjiassem's sugar manufacturing capacity. Indeed, within a few years they had
built a second factory elsewhere on the estate.[17] Thomas Benjamin Hofland's
application to the Indies Government for permission to prolong Edwards'
stay on the estate made explicit reference to the fact that the sugar works were
of 'such a character that a capable *machinist* needed to be continually
employed there.'[18] Indeed, to Edwards' expert eye the problems were evidently more far reaching than that. Within a very few months, he was to be
found accompanying some of the equipment from Subang for repair at the
East Java workshops of the expatriate Englishmen W.J.F. Dudman and T.R.

Stavers in Pasuruan.[19] The workshops' very existence, like that of Edwards himself, was an indication of the advancing frontier of the industrialised manufacture of sugar in mid-nineteenth-century Java. The establishment was described by the Dutch Resident there as being of *groot nut* to the area's sugar factories. In 1842, the Indies Government had agreed to lend Stavers and Dudman 12,000 guilders to buy and ship from Europe 'a large iron smelting furnace and the equipment belonging to it' ('groote ijzer smeltoven en de daarbij behoorende gereedschappen.').[20] Both men's careers in Java were a reminder that Edwards' own trajectory, in some respects a singular one, was by no means unique. Thomas Reid Stavers (1798–1867) had been born in Deptford on the Thames estuary and was described as a 'master shipwright and seaman' (scheepsbouwmeester en zeevarende') at the time of being given permission to settle in Pasuruan in 1840.[21] He had a nephew, Francis Dawson Stavers (1823–1864) who was a partner in the 1850s in the Koning Willem II sugar factory – one of the best equipped of its day – in Surabaya Residency. The London-born William J.F. Dudman (1816–1868) later became partner in an Indies Government sugar contract in the Rembang Residency on the north Java coast, while his brother Robert's career had striking parallels with that of Thomas Edwards. In the early 1840s, Robert Dudman was in Java attempting to repair machinery on plantations belonging to the great and recently deceased *Vorstenlanden* landholder J.A. Dezentjé, in Central Java.[22] He, again like Edwards, subsequently became *administrateur* at a sugar factory in Pasuruan, married an Indies born and almost certainly Eurasian woman and died in Surabaya at the age of forty-one in 1855.

On this trip to the sugar belt of the *Oosthoek*, then by far the most flourishing sector of the Java industry, Edwards may well have seen enough to convince him that his future lay there rather than in West Java, where there were few factories and where it appears that the Hoflands had drawn back from any plans to install up-to-date steam equipment.[23] His younger brother John temporarily joined him at Pamanoekan & Tjiassem in 1845, apparently to recover his health after a voyage from Europe.[24] By the end of the following year, however, Thomas Edwards, accompanied, it would appear, by Anne Baird, the young Eurasian woman (who was born in 1826) whom he had met there,[25] left Subang for the East Java city of Surabaya. He took up work at F.J.H. Baijer's recently established iron works and repair shop, the 'Phoenix' *Fabriek voor Stoomwerktuigen* (Factory for Steam-Machinery).[26]

Celebrated in the decades that followed as the 'Iron King' of Surabaya, Baijer was the proprietor of a series of iron foundries and machine workshops in and around the town, from the early 1840s until his death there in 1879. At the height of his operations, Baijer employed 700 or more people, the great majority of them Indonesian.[27] Baijer was not a solitary figure, however, and even by the date of Edwards' arrival there, around 1846, Surabaya was already on the way to becoming the key centre for servicing the emergent industrial project in Java sugar, with its iron masters, foundries and engineering workshops.[28] As sugar factories and warships shared in the same steam technology, Surabaya was also the site of the Netherlands Indies' main naval base. In this way, the two different dimensions of the colonial frontier complemented each other both figuratively and literally.

Technological Advance and Edwards' Rise to Prominence in the Java Industry

The presence of people like Baijer, and of the enterprises in which they were involved, was one important index of the industrialised nature of mid-nineteenth-century sugar manufacture in colonial Java. It also betokened the support of an Indies bourgeoisie far more committed to the industrial project than has often been assumed. The point underlines the historical deficiency of the notion (already briefly alluded to) that the Dutch colonial communities of mid-century Java were so immersed in a 'pre-modern' *Tempo Doeloe* as to vitiate any truly 'bourgeois' tendencies among their members. On this reading, the prevailing seigneurial ethos – sometimes compared to that of the antebellum American South – was profoundly at odds with the growth of an economically vigorous middle class. Of course, not all of this was caricature. There were indeed 'backwoodsmen' in Java's *Tempo Doeloe* and Edwards was engaging in more than hyperbole when he wrote of the 'ease and nonchalance' then still 'so much in vogue' in the mid-century sugar industry.[29] The secular trend, however, was in the opposite direction, and the notion of nineteenth-century Indies colonial elites who were 'far from home' and in enervating proximity to decadent 'oriental' models, needs to be substantially revised, entailing important implications for the history of their involvement in the sugar industry. Such a revision insists on the intimacy of connection – rather than the putative distance – between the colony and Holland, and on the fact that the Indies bourgeoisie were recognisable cousins – often quite literally – of the contemporary Dutch middle and upper classes. These were people of multiple rather than single identity. What was reputed to be an 'Eastern' 'seigneurial' style of living did not preclude a taste for industrialising their factories *à la mode*. Edwards' career at the end of the 1840s, when he moved on after two years of working with Baijer, illustrates the point well enough.

By the middle of 1848, Edwards was at the Padjarakan sugar factory further east along the coast from Surabaya, in the *Oosthoek* district of Probolingo. The owner of Padjarakan, the Dutch-born Abraham Gerrit de Roock was an Indies veteran, having already been a sugar-maker in East Java in the late 1820s and resident in the colony since 1811. Indeed, by the 1840s he was an absentee owner, having repatriated to the Netherlands in 1835.[30] His ostensibly unambiguous status as an absentee *rentier* – another of the classic stereotypes of the mid-nineteenth-century sugar owner – was belied, however, by developments at Padjarakan. In 1848, when Edwards arrived there as an employee, the factory was in the process of being extensively re-equipped with Dutch- or Belgian-made steam operated apparatus, said to be comparable with the best available from the French firm of De Rosne & Cail.[31] In Probolingo, moreover, Edwards would have found himself located, at the end of the 1840s, among a group of some half-dozen or more factories, all equipped with reasonably up-to-date steam equipment, some of it Derosne, while further west in the Surabaya Residency there were two or three more such factories

In 1848, there was no other such concentration of comparable size anywhere else in Java. Its nearest equivalent was to be found in the island's north coast sugar belt extending eastward from Cirebon towards the major port city of Semarang, where its heavily and precociously industrialised core consisted initially of some five Derosne & Cail equipped factories in the Tegal Residency. It was in this sugar belt, struggling until the 1860s to match the productivity and profitability of the *Oosthoek*, that Edwards was to spend the rest of his life, first at the Tjipiring factory in Semarang Residency and subsequently at factories further west along the narrow coastal plain which, from the 1830s onwards, was increasingly filled with sugar cane and the factories that processed it for export. Edwards reached the top of the ladder in the incipient hierarchy of *Europees Personeel* (European personnel) that was later to be characteristic of the colonial sugar industry by becoming *administrateur* of Tjipiring in 1850.[32] Tjipiring was part-owned a by a scion of the Netherlands patrician merchant family of Van den Broek. Four of the Van den Broek brothers were active in Java during the 1840s. Like many of their counterparts in the mid-century Indies bourgeoisie, they maintained close social and economic links with Europe, something entirely compatible with their 'Indies' personae.

Ulbe Bosma has recently argued that such ties with the metropolis were a vital element in the perpetuation of bourgeois status in the colony.[33] This gave rise, in turn, to quite distinct but related family trajectories. Of the four Van den Broek brothers, for example, Frangois Guillaume (born in Antwerp in 1812) repatriated to Europe, where his immediate family was, broadly speaking, 'metropolitan', in so far as his wife came from a Dutch family (though they married in Naples, and he remarried late in life to woman born on the Ile de France/La Réunion), his business interests were primarily in Europe and he himself died in Paris.[34] His elder brother, Prosper Hypolite André van den Broek, on the other hand, was a partner in several sugar factories including Tjipiring, married a locally born, and probably Eurasian woman, Sophie Le Leu (1829–1893), and ,among other things, established a colonial dynasty of sugar manufacturers. He himself died in Semarang Residency in 1893, most probably at Tjipiring itself, as indeed did his eldest son some fourteen years later.[35] Typically, his financial backers, in succession to the NHM's *Factorij*, were both colonial, the great Batavia trading house of Maclaine Watson, and metropolitan, the Amsterdam-based Nederlandsch-Indische Handels-bank.[36] Typical also were his 'bourgeois' pre-occupations with improvement: it was no accident, for example, that Prosper van den Broek pioneered the experimental use of the steam plough on the sugar fields at one of his Semarang factories in the early 1860s.[37]

Tjipiring and its contract with the Indies Government for the manufacture of sugar was a recent purchase for Van den Broek, who also had sugar inter-ests in the *Oosthoek*.[38] Edwards was the lynch pin in the re-equipping of what had been an old-fashioned factory in which sugar was manufactured without any of the advantages of steam apparatus.[39] Within eighteen months of his arrival at Tjipiring, however, Edwards had moved on yet again, this time to a position at a factory owned by the NHM, in which he was to remain for the next ten years. Located in Pekalongan Residency, mid-way along Java's north coast, Wonopringo had been taken over, somewhat reluctantly, nearly a decade earlier, in 1844, by the NHM's Batavia Factorij as part of a settlement with a bankrupt client. Unable to find a buyer, they eventually settled for an expensive and extensive reconstruction. In so doing, they set out to turn Wonopringo into a model colonial factory – an exemplar to other industrial-ists – parallel to the similar models which, under the urging of the Dutch King Willem I, the company had created in the metropolitan Netherlands a decade or more earlier.[40] In Thomas Edwards, moreover, the company found a model manager.

Around the mid-century, as a result of NHM investment, the *fabriek* at Wonopringo had no less than four newly assembled vacuum pans, two water-driven mills (there was nothing retrograde about a preference for water power in the local circumstances of production) and was about to gain a centrifuge in which sugar was spun dry at the end of the production line. With good rea-son, Edwards was subsequently to observe to his employers:

> … nothing has ever been refused by you which I have thought might conduce to an improved manufacture, and although other administrators may have shown more ability, not one, I dare to affirm, has been more animated by a more constant and earnest desire for improvement than myself.[41]

At the same time he justifiably lauded Wonopringo as 'one of the most com-plete' factories in the whole of Java. At the outset, however, the Factorij's ren-ovation there had gone anything but smoothly, and something of the everyday reality of the industrial transformation of the mid-nineteenth-cen-tury sugar industry in colonial Java is conveyed both by the considerable delay attendant on dragging heavy apparatus 'up-country' (this was several decades before the first railway) and by the fact that those parts of the equip-ment supplied by Dutch (as opposed to Belgian or French) manufacturers were found on arrival to be so badly made that they had to be sent to work-shops in the East Java city of Surabaya (see above) for modification. Nor did it expedite matters that no packing list was enclosed with the many crates of remarkably anonymous-looking pipes and valves that were an integral part of the steam-operated system.[42] Begun in 1848, the NHM's renovation of Wonopringo dragged on into the following decade. By the time of Edwards' arrival there in August 1852, however, the 'new' factory was largely complete.

The position of *administrateur* at Wonopringo had been advertised locally in the *Javasche Courant*, the official gazette-cum-newspaper of the Netherlands Indies, and there had been scores of applicants. His new employers justified appointing Edwards 'even though an Englishman', on the strength of his repute as a manager and because of his technical skills, 'a quality rarely found here.'[43] The circumstances of his appointment, and its clear implications for the rise of the professional manager, demonstrate the seriousness with which the Batavia Factorij, in this context the flagship of the Indies bourgeoisie, set about furthering the industrial project. Edwards' position was a salaried one – the NHM rejected subsequent attempts on his part to lease the factory from them[44] – and he received 500 guilders a month which was the same base salary as an Assistant-Resident in the Government service, together with an annual bonus linked to the factory's output, free accommodation at Wonopringo and 'all that which is normally provided free of charge to the *administrateur* of a sugar factory.'[45] It was not spelled out, but judging from other contemporary evidence it would have included accommodation, rice and oil as well as stabling and feed for his horses. By the time of his departure from Wonopringo some ten years later, his employers were prepared to offer him a guaranteed minimum of 20,000 guilders per year, a sum well in excess of the base salary of a Resident, the highest ranking provincial official.[46] Commensurate with all that was the fact that, as *administrateur*, Edwards now occupied distinctive accommodation in the proximity of the factory. The first (Chinese) individual to run a sugar factory on the Wonopringo site, early in the 1830s, had lived in a bamboo shed which doubled as boiling house and living quarters.[47] Edwards' immediate predecessors had been forced to live either at the derelict Karang Anjer sugar factory, three or more kilometres away, a location which meant, among other things, that the *administrateur* was not always on hand to supervise operations, and that at night the factory had to be left in charge of a subordinate. In case of necessity, he had to make do with accommodation in some outhouses (*twee rijen bijgebouwen*) that formed part of the factory compound at Wonopringo itself. By the time of Edwards' arrival, however, a dedicated *administrateur's* house had been built adjacent to the factory, complete with stabling.[48] For some years, however, he found himself providing lodging under the same roof for the factory's bachelor *mechanist-suikerkoker*, a situation which only changed in 1860 when the latter's forthcoming marriage became the occasion to press the NHM for the building of separate accommodation. An additional incentive was that such quarters for the factory's second-in-command were apparently commonplace elsewhere in the industry, and that without them the man might be tempted to move to a rival employer.[49]

Salaried, professional status – and a new attention to outward appearances – was an index, moreover, to the growing importance that the Indies bourgeoisie as a whole began to ascribe to capitalist management. As Dipesh Chakrabarty has argued in the context of the advance of the industrial project elsewhere in colonial Asia,[50] prior to the mid-nineteenth century, management was conceived pre-eminently in terms of the successful manipulation of costs of raw materials and labour in relation to a carefully observed market. In Java, until the 1830s, sugar (with few exceptions) was made at the *fabriek* using techniques that dated back to the seventeenth century. The key concern of the industry's owners and managers – beyond the securing of adequate supplies of cane and labour – was in scaling production to meet the requirements of a notoriously fluctuating export trade to Asian, and, sometimes, European and North American markets. By the mid-century, however, the hallmarks of management were being transformed, as a concern with the production process overtook the predominantly mercantile pre-occupations of a previous era. Indeed, one of the things that stands out very clearly from Edwards' management at Wonopringo was the extent to which the exploitation of the factory corresponded to what Moreno, for example, in his discussion of the contemporary, nineteenth-century Cuba industry, described as the essentially capitalist pre-occupation with 'the constant renovation of the means of production ... to fight for lower costs, better quality and the steady growth of the enterprise's productive capacity.'[51] Indeed, these are key themes in the steady stream of letters exchanged between Edwards and the NHM's Batavia Factorij, a great many of which (thankfully for the historian) were forward by the branch to head office in Amsterdam and hence preserved.

It was this same 'capitalist pre-occupation', in tandem, no doubt, with a certain acerbity of Edwards' part (there is some suggestion that he was not the easiest of colleagues), that underpinned his relationship with the visiting 'expert' Armand Montclar. Edwards styled himself as *ingenieur-civil* when the French savant spent some time at Wonopringo during an extended stay in Java at the beginning of the 1860s. Collaboration between the two, based on Montclar's attempts to increase the total output of sugar from condensed juice by a far more extensive (and expensive) use of bone charcoal than had hitherto been the case, was initially enthusiastic, but deteriorated so sharply that the latter resorted to the print warfare so characteristic of (at least) the Dutch colonial enterprise in the mid-century decades. Montclar's 'Exposé de Mon Operation à Wonopringo' appeared in Surabaya in 1862 from the publisher Le Roy as part of his larger treatise *De La Situation Industrielle et Manufacturiere du Sucre à L'île Java*. A few years later, this time in Amsterdam, he was to be found reiterating a theme dear to the hearts of metropolitan refiners but less warmly received in the colonies (whose manufacturers it

would have condemned to perpetual clientage), namely that colonial producers should manufacture no more than the crudest sugar which should
then be shipped to Holland for refinement.[52] In short, Montclar's work
became part of an evolving discourse about the 'failings' of Java's manufacturers, which had been the underlying text of a vituperative exchange in
which Edwards had been engaged a few years earlier, when the distinguished
University of Utrecht chemist G.J. Mulder had been called in for consulta-
tions by the Dutch Colonial Office, to propose 'improvements' to the way in
which cane was crushed in the Java factories.

Sent a copy of Mulder's proposal, Edwards responded in the most scathing
terms. 'I beg to say', he wrote to employers at the Batavia Factorij (who were
clearly only too happy to pass on his comments), 'with all deference to the
great name and world-wide reputation of that gentleman' that Mulder's proposal was quite 'the worst that has ever come under my notice' and that
although its author 'may be the first chemist in the world ... I take leave to say
that he knows nothing whatever about Sugar mills'. The point, nonetheless,
was not that Edwards was evidently a man who did not suffer fools gladly, but
rather that underlying such contestation was an on-going commitment to
improve the quality and quantity of the output of the manufacturing process
that Edwards shared with many of his colonial contemporaries. Indeed, it was
the apparent ignorance of this among 'experts in Europe' which accounted for
his ire with Mulder. The problem, from the colonial manufacturers' point of
view, was that 'improvements' in the mill advocated by Mulder would undermine an economy of production predicated on the extensive use of cane trash
in the boiler house. More intensive crushing left it virtually useless as fuel and
double crushing as advocated by Mulder notoriously fouled the mills with
broken cane. If there was an economically feasible alternative to the use of
cane trash, Edwards had no doubt whatsoever that 'no recommendation will
be needed to induce [the manufacturers] to obtain the best presses that can be
had for money. They have already given evidence by the general adoption of
steam machinery that they are ready to spend their money freely when a fair
chance of a profit can be shown.'[53]

Over and above the immediate issue, however, the fascination of this whole
episode,[54] one that involved the Dutch Colonial Office and the Indies Government's Director of Cultivations S.D. Schiff (who sided with Edwards) as
well as Edwards and Mulder himself, is what it reveals about the manufacture,
not of sugar, but of a potent metropolitan myth about the 'backwardness' of
Java's colonial manufacturers and their illusory 'resistance' to change, fostered in this case by officials in the Hague and by a professor as absurdly
pedantic as any of his kind.

Underscoring this quest for improvement, as these exchanges themselves
strongly imply, were values hard to reconcile with notions of a *Tempo Doeloe*
'remote' from Europe and the concerns of a 'modern' business class and culture. In fact, even in the most literal sense, for the well-to-do bourgeois the

distance between the colonial Indies and metropolitan Holland was significantly less in the mid-century decades preceding the opening of the Suez Canal (and direct steamer connections between Europe and Asia) than has often been supposed. Indeed, the single most important development (before the arrival of the aeroplane) in closing the physical gap between Europe and 'the East' had taken place some decades earlier, with the establishment during 1840s of a regular 'Overland Mail' passenger steamer route from Singapore to Marseilles or Southampton via the Red Sea and the Egyptian land bridge. A journey that had previously taken three and a half or four months via sail and the Cape was reduced to a little over five weeks.[55] One immediate consequence for Edwards personally was that it was possible for his employers to pay for him to make a swift return journey to Western Europe to order new equipment for the *fabriek* and specify his requirements in person at the Millwall Iron Works & Engine Factory of the well-known manufacturing firm of H.O. & A Robinson,[56] on the eastern outskirts of London. This ensured that the new machinery would be ready in time for installation at Wonopringo in the 'dead' period at the end of the 1858 Campaign. Departing for Europe in October 1857, thanks to the 'Overland Mail', Edwards could be securely back at Wonopringo by early May 1858, in good time for the beginning of the manufacturing season for which his presence was indispensable.[57] Baijer, the 'Iron King' of Surabaya and Edwards' erstwhile employer (see above) was to make a similar journey with a similar purpose from 1864 to 1865,[58] and one of the Hofland brothers, the estate-owners and sugar manufacturers who had brought Edwards to Java in the first place, was to die in Malta en route to Europe via the 'Overland Mail'.

Such developments were indicative more generally of the close ties which the Indies bourgeoisie and their agents maintained with the advancing frontier of technology. Edwards, situated in 'remote' Wonopringo in the 1850s could yet allude to his veritable library of recent scientific work on the manufacture of sugar: 'Of late years many scientific and practical men have written on the manufacture of sugar from cane juice' he was able to inform his employers in 1861, ' [and] ... I have a long list of extracts from different writers ... now before me.'[59] It was the pursuit of interests of this kind that no doubt led him, in the mid-1850s, to join the newly established *Nederlandsch-Indische Maatschappij van Nijverheid* (Netherlands Indies Society for Industry) which had been founded in Batavia in 1854, and whose journal the *Tijdschrift voor Nijverheid* (Journal for Industry) began to appear annually from a publisher in the colonial capital in that same year. In 1856, the third issue of the Journal, characteristically enough, carried a lengthy paper reporting on a 'Physisch en chemisch onderzoek van der gronden der suikerfabriek Wonopringo in Pekalongan', by the chemist D.W. Rost van Tonningen.[60] Within a few years of its inception the Society itself had a membership list that read like a roll-call of the colony's more 'progressive' bourgeoisie. In Pekalongan-Tegal, where Wonopringo was located, the members included, along with Thomas Edwards, Resident G.P.J. van der Poel, the sugar manufacturer Theodore R.N. Lucassen and his brother-in-law G.J. Netscher, a qualified 'steam engineer' and sometime de facto sugar factory manager.[61] The very existence of the Society, in short, was another reminder that the ostensible factor of 'distance' and the patriarchal and spendthrift *suikerlord* was only one dimension of the mid-century Indies bourgeoisie. Significantly enough, its setting up had been preceded in 1851 by the establishment in the 'industrial capital' of Surabaya (see above) of the East Java branch of the *Koninklijk Instituut voor Ingenieurs* (Royal Institute of Engineers), whose headquarters were in The Hague, where the *Instituut* had been founded, only three years earlier, in 1848.[62]

Edwards: The Final Years

By 1862, Edwards' tenure as *administrateur* at Wonopringo was nearing its end. Under his management, productivity at the factory had more than tripled over a ten-year period, and Wonopringo was accurately rated by its proud owners as 'one of the finest in the whole of Java'.[63] The NHM was therefore dismayed at the prospect of their *administrateur*'s departure, and did their best to retain him. As early as 1860 he had indicated his desire to leave, and in the following year, in response to their entreaties to stay on until at least the end of the 1864 Campaign, he had replied that, 'I have been nineteen years in India [i.e 'the Indies'], and am now forty-seven years old. I am still healthy and strong, but I think it is at least doubtful whether I can stand four years more of this climate and retain for that period the activity and energy necessary to do full justice to this fabriek.'[64] He persisted in this resolve, now alluding primarily to 'the poor state of his health' and late in 1862, terminated his employment with the NHM and handed over Wonopringo to his Dutch successor, J.C. Heijning.[65]

What happened to Edwards in the final three years of his life is something about which (on present evidence) we can do little more than speculate. In 1860, the *Factorij* was apparently under the impression that if he left their employ, he would return 'home' to Scotland – an error of location (if such it was) easily explained by the North British origins of many of Java's mid-nineteenth-century 'Englishmen'.[66] In fact, nothing of the sort happened. Thomas Edwards remained on Java, and in 1864 took up employment with the Batavia firm of Maclaine Watson (together with its close affiliates in Semarang and Surabaya, they were second only to the NHM's *Factorij* in terms of the extent of their sugar interests) as *administrateur* at their Gempol sugar factory, some 150 kilometres to the west of Wonopringo, in Cirebon Residency. What had happened to make him abandon his apparent plan to repatriate? Had he lost his money? The year 1862, in which he took his long-projected departure from Wonopringo, was a bad one for agricultural speculations in Java, and many firms and individuals had their fingers badly burnt.[67] One can only wonder whether Thomas Edwards was among them. An alternative explanation based on altogether more personal, domestic reasons may have been the impossibility of returning to provincial England with his 'Java' family and, equally, the impossibility of deserting them. In the event, death intervened. His own father had died in Whitchurch, Shropshire, at the age of 35, his grandfather at 57. Thomas, aged 50, died near the Gempol factory, at the hillside village of Agalinga, where the family had perhaps gone to escape the heat of the plains, on 13 November 1865.

Conclusion

Colonial sugar capital was reconstructed in Java in the middle decades of the nineteenth century in ways that placed it predominantly in the hands of an *Indisch* or Indies bourgeoisie of manufacturers, commercial interests and (through both family ties and direct financial interests) members of the 'half-formed' bureaucracy of the Indies colonial state. Such people played an important role in supporting the importation of both the technology and the trained personnel who were crucial to an incremental 'revolution' in the manufacture of sugar that was already well under way in Java by the 1850s. Lacking both kin and capital in the colony, the 'Shropshire Lad' Thomas Edwards was yet able to prosper in Java the under the patronage of an Indies bourgeoisie that valued his technical skills and managerial abilities in furthering a sustained industrial project in the manufacture of sugar which had no counterpart elsewhere in Asia prior to the twentieth century. His personal history, in short, serves both to illuminate and fill out a broader narrative of the global dissemination of industrial technology during the course of the nineteenth century and of the role of the colonial bourgeoisie in making this possible.

Notes

1. For major recent discussions of the *Cultuurstelsel*, see Elson, *Javanese Peasants and the Colonial Sugar Industry*; Elson, *Village Java under the Cultuurstelsel*; Fasseur, *The Politics of Colonial Exploitation*; Fernando, 'Peasants and Plantation'; Knight, *Colonial Production in Provincial Java*; Suryo, 'Social and Economic Life in Rural Semarang under Colonial Rule in the Later Nineteenth Century'.

2. For a succinct description, see Martineau, *Sugar*, 66: 'It is (…) a slightly flattened sphere of copper, provided inside at the lower part with a coil of steam pipe, and also a vacuum jacket. An air-pump creates a partial vacuum, and a condenser, through which the steam from the boiling juice passes on its way to the air pump, by rapidly condensing the vapour, greatly helps to increase the vacuum.'

3. According to Leidelmeijer, *Van Suikermolen tot Grootbedrijf*, 138. Nearly 60 percent of Java's colonial sugar factories (58 in all) were equipped with vacuum pans by 1857. By international standards, this was a substantial number. The comparison here between Java and Cuba is a particularly potent one, given the fact that the Caribbean island overtook Brazil in the mid-nineteenth century as the world's single largest producer-exporter of cane sugar – and had a reputation for innovation in the field of manufacturing technology. At the beginning of the 1860s, Cuba had 64 factories equipped with vacuum pans and associated steam equipment in the boiling house. Moreno Fraginals, *The Sugar Mill: The Socioeconomic Complex of Sugar in Cuba*, 85–86. This was only a very few more than were installed in Java (although this does not take into account productive capacity and provenance), and reflected the fact that Java's colonial bourgeoisie of sugar contractors and their backers was no more averse to technological improvement than its mid-nineteenth-century Cuban counterpart.

4. As Martineau remarks (*Sugar*, 67): 'The French call it the 'triple-*effet*' and that is now its name (…) The apparatus may roughly be described as consisting of three vertical cylindrical vessels, with dome-shaped heads, ending in a wide neck which turns over and downwards to carry the vapour to its next destination.'

5. Indisch Besluit 8.1.1849/3, NA Archief Ministerie van Koloniën (hereafter MK) 2714. In 1874, Th.R.N. Lucassen (son of the factory's original owner) appointed Lawson as *administrateur*, an arrangement which included the latter taking a 25 percent stake in the factory itself. See NHM Factorij 'Register Overeenkomsten', NA NHM 4978.

6. Bergmans was recorded as living in Tegal from 1853 onwards. See *Regeerings-Olmanak voor Nederlandsch Indië* 1853. For the report of his death, see newspaper clipping ('Heden ontving ik het treurige berigt van het overlijden van mijnen geliefden oudsten Zoon den Heer Franciscus Adrianus Bergmans, in leven Ingenieur aan de Suikerfabrieken te Tagal, overleden te Pelatoegang, op den 20sten Maart 1859, in den ouderdom van bijna 37 jaren. Rotterdam, 28 Mei 1859, [signed] De Wed. A. Bergmans, geb. Van Den Broeke') in the files of the IGV, The Hague.

7. The placing of skilled Javanese workers in both the sugar industry and in other technologically advanced sectors of the mid-nineteenth-century industrial economy of colonial Indonesia could stand further investigation. The visiting Dutch parliamentarian Gevers Deynoot, for example, in his brief contemporary mention (around 1860) of the Baijer's Stoomfabriek en IJzergietery (Steam Works and Iron Foundry) at Surabaya in East Java (see text below) remarked that 'for the most part, it was Javanese whom I found doing the work, and was given excellent reports of them. They are skilful and clever (handig en gevat)'. See Jhr. Mr. Gevers Deynoot, *Herinneringen eener Reis naar Nederlandsch Indie in 1862*, 95.

8. In 1854, it was found advisable to engage 'for the forthcoming grinding-season four Chinese conversant with the manufacture of sugar (…) it is proposed that two of them, under the supervision of the European sugar boiler, are to be responsible for the vacuum boiling of sugar, and the two others will keep on eye on the operation of the defecators.' Factorij

to Amsterdam 26.4.1854/284, 2de Afd., NA NHM. For visual evidence of the 'Chinese' presence, see e.g. the photograph (taken around 1870) of the staff of the Tjipiring sugar factory (Semarang Residency) in Breton de Nijs, *Tempo Doeloe*, 61.

9. See copy of the letter from Thomas Edwards (Tom) to Robert Hill Edwards (Robert), his younger brother, dated Haydock Colliery (some four miles from the village of Winwick, where Edwards was lodging), 26 June 1833, in 'Diary and Copybook' kept by Robert Hill Edwards in the mid-1830s, in private possession.

10. On the development of mechanical engineering and steam technology in nineteenth-century Lancashire, see Timmins, *Made in Lancashire*, 85–124 and 178–215; Howe, *The Cotton Masters, 1830–1860*, 61–62, stresses the strong representation, by 1850, of Unitarians among (south) Lancashire cotton masters (meaning cotton entrepreneurs/employers of labour). Dissenters accounted for around 50 percent of the cotton masters (49 percent were Anglicans) and of these 36 percent were Unitarians.

11. For information on the Vulcan Foundry in the 1830s and 1840s, see *The Story of Vulcan Works from 1830 to 2002*, prepared by Malcolm Siberry for MAN B & W Diesel Ltd, Ruston, U.K., posted at http://www.enginemuseum.org/bbv.html.

12. *Javasche Courant*, 13 Augustus 1842.

13. Indisch Besluit 13.9.1842/1, NA MK 2637.

14. The NHM's Batavia Factorij advanced the Hoflands more than 1 million guilders to buy Pamanoekan & Tjiassem, on the security of its output of sugar and coffee. See Factorij to Amsterdam, 5.9.1840/1527 & 29.11.1841/1819, NA NHM 7334–5. As to the brother's financial relation to the East Java Chinese, it was reported by the Factorij in the early 1850s 'that the Chinaman Kwee yang Ho, died on July 7 (1851?) and that the Hoflands had considerable sums [groote sommen] on loan from him'. See 'Aantekeningen uit de Correspondentie Factorij', in file 588, NA NHM 3122.

15. On Subang in the 1820s, see Knight, 'From Plantation to Padi Field'.

16. John Pitcairn (*administrateur* of Pamanoekan & Tjiassem) to J. van den Bosch 14.8.1830 (NA Collectie Johannes van den Bosch, 426): 'I am anxious to inform your Excellency that a machine lately invented in England for boiling sugar by steam has been sent out to me, which will likely arrive in the course of this year. It possesses many advantages over the present mode of boiling sugar'. And see also J.E. de Sturler (Secretaris Residentie Pekalongan) to Van den Bosch 2.9.1830 (NA, Van den Bosch, 216), describing what he supposes to be a draft-furnace ('Trek Fournius') erected at Subang (more probably a steam boiler or some such) which he says ought to be copied by the Indies Government's own sugar contractors, and that 'de Heer Loudon [formerly *administrateur* of P&T, now in Pekalongan] told me that it was of the most recent design and that an engineer had been sent out from England to set it up'.

17. In 1842, the NHM Factorij remarked on the 'substantial improvements recently effected' at Pamanoekan & Tjiassem, without, however, going into any detail. See Factorij to Amsterdam 8.1.1842/1858, NA NHM. On further developments on the estate during the 1840s, see below.

18. Indisch Besluit 11.2.1843/4 NA MK 2642.

19. Indisch Besluit 1.7.1843/23 NA MK 2647.

20. Indisch Besluit 15.4.1842/14 & 1.7.1843/23, NA MK 2632 & 2647.

21. Indisch Besluit 15.8.1840/20 NA MK 2609. Other information relating to Thomas Reid Stavers and Francis Dawson Stavers in this paragraph from the files of the IGV in The Hague.

22. Indisch Besluit 29.6.1841/5 NA MK 2619. Other information relating to the Dudman brothers in this paragraph from the files of the IGV in The Hague.

23. For a description of the sugar-making equipment at Pand T in the 1840s, see Assistant-Resident Krawang, 'Verslag omtrent den Toestand der Verkoopte en den Verhuurde Landen in der Afd. Krawang' 16.3.1850, Arsip Nasional Republik Indonesia, Jakarta, Arsip Daerah, Krawang no. 9.

24. For John Edwards' arrival in Java in 1845, see *Javasche Courant*, 31 May 1845 and for subsequent permissions for him to reside temporarily on Pamanoekan & Tjiassem, see Indisch Besluit 18.6.1845/1 and 10.1.1846/3 NA MK 2670 and 2677.
25. Anne Baird's connection with Pamanoekan & Tjiassem is presumably explained by the fact that her presumptive father, the Scots-born Robert Webster Baird, was, until his death there in January 1826, Superintendent of the Subang sugar works on that estate, where he had arrived some five years earlier. See the notice of his death in *Bataviasche Courant*, 23.2.1826.
26. Indisch Besluit 2.11.1846/22 NA MK 2688.
27. On Baijer (aka Bayer) and his contemporaries, see Von Faber, *Oud Soerabaia*, 170–77.
28. Dick, *Surabaya, City of Work*, 257–61.
29. Edwards to Factorij 24.12.1860, enclosure in Factorij to Amsterdam 2.1.1861/ 915. NA NHM.
30. De Roock was born at [Zalt] Bommel, in Gelderland, The Netherlands, around 1786. For this and other brief data on his Java years, see NA MK 3117 & 3142.
31. See the information about this factory in: 'Opgave wegens de op Java werkende suikerfabrieken, Juni 1848'. NA NHM 9207: it was fitted up 'with steam apparatus from [the firm] of [Van Vlissingen and Dudok van Heel], closely resembling the system of De Rosne & Cail, the principle of which is boiling [sugar] in a vacuum and the purification of the cane juice by means of bone-charcoal'. This was one of a small group of factories in Besuki Residency that incorporated steam heat/vacuum pan/charcoal defecation systems in the late 1840s. Its only parallel was in Tegal Residency, where the four sugar factories belonging to Theodore Lucassen and O.C. Holmberg de Beckfelt operated in a similar fashion. This equipment had been newly installed at Padjarakan in the late 1840s. In 1844/5, for example, Padjarakan was described as still working 'in the [then] common fashion', i.e. without steam boiling and associated refinements. See NA NHM 9207, 'Aanwijzing der op Java bestaande en in werking zijnde suikerfabrieken' (c.1844).
32. This and other brief details of Edwards' career in the Indies prior to this appointment at Wonopringo come from his application (in 1857) for naturalisation as a Dutch citizen in NA, Archief Ministerie van Justitie, 4862.
33. See elsewhere in this volume.
34. In the 1840s, the other 'Java' members of this francophone family (Prosper, for example, communicated with the Factorij in French – see Van den Broek to Factorij, 30.8.1863 in Factorij to Amsterdam 14.9.1863/1189) were Jean Gillaume Pierre and Bartholemus Petrus van den Broek. See *Regeeringslmanak Nederlandsch Indië* 1843, 1849.
35. For an extensive genealogy of his and his brothers' families, see *Nederland's Patriciaat*, 1924 (14), 46–57.
36. Mansvelt, *Geschiedenis der Nederlandsche Handel-Maatschappij*, II, 366.
37. Factorij to Amsterdam 18.9.1860/1189, 2de Afd. NA NHM. By this date, Prosper van den Broek was also the owner of the nearly factories of Gemoe and Pegoe. The upshot of the experiments, however, was disappointing: according to the Factorij, it was found 'impossible to use profitably such a heavy, difficult to handle and expensive piece of equipment'.
38. The owners of Tjipiring in 1849 were P.H.A. van den Broek, J.H. Horst and M.G. van Heel. Horst and Van Heel also owned Sf. Gayam in Pasuruan (Horst also owned Sf. Geneng in Pasaruan). See 'Kultuurinrigtingen Java' 1844, 1848, NA MK, Exh 1.2.1847/2 & 9.5.1851/4.
39. After they took over Tjipiring, Van den Broek and his partners installed equipment that included three Van Vlissingen vacuum pans, of either Dutch or Belgian manufacture. See Jaarverslag NHM Factorij Batavia 1859–60 (35), 132–33, NA NHM.
40. I am grateful to Professor Richard Griffiths of Leiden University for drawing my attention to this point.

41. T.J. Edwards to the Batavia *Factorij* of the Nederlandsche Handel-Maatschappij (hereafter Factorij) 24.12.1860, enclosure in Factorij to *Hoofdkantoor* of the Nederlandsche Handel-Maatschappij in Amsterdam (hereafter Amsterdam), 2.1.1861/915, Nationaal Archief, The Hague (hereafter NA) Archief Hoofdkantoor Nederlandsche Handel-Maatschappij (hereafter NHM).
42. For some of the difficulty attendant on the renovation, see e.g., Factorij to Amsterdam 26.8.1848/325 & 28.11.1848/338 2de Afd., NA NHM.
43. Notulen Factorij Batavia (hereafter NFB) 10.7.52/67 NA NHM.
44. NFB 7.4.1855/153 NA NHM.
45. NFB 10.7.1852/67 NA NHM.
46. NFB 687/20.4.1861 NA NHM. At that time, the Resident of Pekalongan would have been in receipt of a salary of 15,000 guilders and *cultuurprocenten* (cultivation bonuses) of around 3000 guilders annually.
47. 'Rapport Omtrent de Suikermolen te Wonopringo', in Louis Vitalis to Director Cultivations, 10.3.1834/25, Arsip Nasional Republik Indonesia, Jakarta (hereafter ANRI), Archief Cultures 333, Exh. 761/13.3.1834. I am grateful to Dr Radin Fernando who, a quarter of a century ago, was so kind as to point me towards the location of this important documentation.
48. 'Taxatie Staat der Fabriek Wonopringo en bij dezelve behoorende Bijgebouwen 30.6.1845', in Factorij to Amsterdam 30.9. 1845/237, 2de Afd. NA NHM; 'Nota betreffende de Fabriek Wonopringo door den Heer C.A. Granpré Molière' 23.12.1844, in NFB 31.12.1844/669, NA NHM.
49. NFB 17.1.1860/549 NA NHM.
50. Chakrabarty, *Rethinking Working Class History: Bengal 1890–1840*, 14.
51. Moreno, *Sugar Mill*, 133.
52. Montclar, *La 'Sucrerie' Indo-Néerlandaise et la 'Raffinerie' Néerlandaise*. Oddly enough, Montclar's greatest contribution to developments at mid-century Wonopringo was his advocacy of the extensive use of bone charcoal in the manufacturing process, an innovation designed to produce high rather than low-grade output. On Montclar and his activities in Java, see Leidelmeijer, *Van suikermolen tot grootbedrijf*, 141 and Van Dolder and Morbotter, *Verslag Omtrent hunne Bevindingen in de fabriek Poerwoedadie van A. baron Sloet van Oldruitenburgh*. For Edwards' account of his dispute with Montclar, see Factorij to Amsterdam 14.11.1860/900 & 905, 2de Afd. NA NHM.
53. Edwards to Factorij, 2.8.1856/1036, enclosed in Factorij to Amsterdam 9.8.1856/480 2de Afd., NA NHM. I would like to thank Dr. Margaret Leidelmeijer for drawing my attention to Edwards' dispute with Mulder.
54. It is documented, together with its broader context, in Leidelmeijer, *Van suikermolen tot grootbedrijf*, 195–224.
55. See e.g., Junghuhn, *Terugreis van Java naar Europa met de zoogenaamde Engelsche Overlandpost*, 4–14; Gevers Deynoot, *Herinneringen*, 1–25.
56. A *Description of Robinson's Steam Cane Mill* appeared in London in 1845. An eight page pamphlet, it carries the notice: 'Further particulars (...) on application to Messers H. O. and A. Robinson, Engineers, Mill Wall Iron Works and Engine Factory, Poplar, near London (where specimens may be seen), or at 12 Old Jewry-chambers, Cheapside, London.'
57. 'Edwards leaves for Europe with this Mail' the Batavia Factorij informed Head Office early in October 1857, and asked them to put 5000 florins at his disposal in Europe (Factory to Amsterdam 10.10.1857/2105, Ie Afd. NA HHM). He began his return voyage 'end February 1858' in company with some of the machinery from Robinsons, and resumed management at Wonopringo on fourteenth May (Factorij to Amsterdam 25.3.1858/633 2de Afd.; Factorij to Amsterdam 7.6.1858/650, 2de Afd. NA NHM).
58. Von Faber, *Oud Soerabaia*, 173.
59. Edwards to Factorij 24.12.1860, enclosure in Factorij to Amsterdam 2.1.1861/ 915, NA NHM.

60. Rost van Tonningen, 'Physisch en chemisch onderzoek van der gronden der suikerfabriek Wonopringo in Pekalongan'.
61. Gerhardus Johannes Netscher (born in The Hague 1822, died in Stuttgart 1877). In 1845 he was in Java, as an assistant to the Indies' Government's 'Chief Engineer for Steampower' and in 1858 was himself acting in that position, and based in Surabaya. In between times, in 1847, he had married Mathilde Theodora Charlotta Lucassen (born in Semarang 1828, died in The Hague 1906). See *Nederland's Patriciaat*, 1967 (53), 169–70; 'Stamboek NI Ambtenaren', Lett H, NA MK.
62. The *Regeeringsalmanak* 1857, 303, carries information that the East Java branch ('afd. Oost Java') was set up in Surabaya in 1851. The brief entry in *Encylopaedie van Nederlandsch-Indië*, Tweede Druk, vol. II, 158 gives the date for the metropolitan foundation of the Instituut, but is appears confused as to precise chronology of the Java branch.
63. Jaarverslag NHM Factorij Batavia 1859–60 (35), 253–55; 1861–62 (37), 142–48, NA NHM.
64. NFB 20.4.1861/687 NA NHM.
65. NFB 21.8.1860/623 NA NHM; NFB 2.6.1862/788 NA NHM.
66. Jaarverslag Factorij Batavia 35 (1859–1860), 252.
67. On the crisis of 1862, see De Bree, *Gedenkboek van de Javasche Bank*, vol 2, 47–62.

4

An Anatomy of Sugarlandia: Local Dutch Communities and the Colonial Sugar Industry in Mid-Nineteenth-Century Java

Arthur van Schaik and G. Roger Knight

During the course of the mid-nineteenth century, the presence of the sugar industry had an increasing impact in colonial Java. Through the scale of its buildings, the extent of its fields, and the number of people involved in it, the sugar industry deeply affected rural conditions. Its influence on the social organisation in the villages, on peasant agriculture and ecology has been discussed amply elsewhere.[1] Here we address the question of the evolving relationship between the sugar industry and local European communities in provincial Java. The potential impact of the advance of (quasi-) industrialised sugar manufacture was obviously considerable. Among other things, it notionally brought into mid-nineteenth-century provincial Java a minor flux of newcomers from Europe whose arrival had the potential to challenge the existing social order of the colonial communities in which they found themselves and to upset existing hierarchies. Along with the state-sponsored owners of sugar factories, usually referred to as Contractors, the influx included people with claims to expertise in the industrial manufacture of sugar and the management of factory production.

The argument of this chapter, however, based on the microcosmic colonial community of the Residency of Pekalongan in central Java, is that such communities largely absorbed the newcomers without major changes to status and rank with the proviso that arrival of Dutch government contractors (see below) in both sugar and indigo potentially challenged a social order in which ranking officials of the Indies State had hitherto stood at the apex. In particular, the present argument contends that the complex interweaving of class and ethnicity that characterised Indies Dutch colonial society in Pekalongan, as elsewhere on the island, proved singularly resilient in the changed economic circumstances associated with the arrival of large-scale sugar production. Indeed, it goes on to argue that the real dynamic of the colonial communities like those of mid-nineteenth-century Pekalongan was largely to be found in factors other than the advance of the sugar industry.

The European communities in mid-nineteenth-century Java consisted of several groups. There were newcomers of European birth, mostly but not exclusively from metropolitan Holland, whom it is convenient to call Caucasians, but whom contemporaries were increasingly apt to describe as *totoks*, (born elsewhere) in imitation of the parallel usage among Java's Chinese communities, where the majority were also of mixed descent and locally born or *peranakan*; there were Creoles, Indies born white Europeans, or Europeans purporting to be white; and finally there were European residents of mixed blood, *mestizos* whose parents were almost invariably born in the Indonesian archipelago, and who formed the majority of the colonial population: indeed, the great majority of the Dutch colonial communities, more then 80 percent, were born in the Indies. Among this latter group, in turn, there was an evident and long-standing class divide between those who were to be found among the colonial elites and the 'best' Dutch families and those of a lower class who were increasingly likely to be termed 'Indo' (i.e. Indo-Europeans): these were the people who, late in the nineteenth century, began to be seen as a 'problem' by writers concerned with 'eugenics' and the 'danger' of miscegenation.

Literature on European societies in the Netherlands Indies is biased towards the elite. As has been implied, if it discusses miscegenation it is either in the pejorative meaning of pauperism and barrack concubinage or – alternatively – in mythical terms of a *Mestizo Patriciaat* which flourished at the end of the eighteenth century and was in decline thereafter.[2] These so-called mestizo elites, however, usually considered themselves to be Creoles, often had parents who were born in Europe and might well be referred to as white because of their familiarity with Europe where, in the case of boys, at least, they had often been educated. In fact, as we have implied, the distinction between Creole and *mestizo* was often highly confusing as it was a class distinction framed in terms of race.[3] Generally speaking, the information necessary to flesh out the structure and dynamics of the Dutch colonial communities of mid-nineteenth-century Java is either non-existent or segmented in discrete family genealogies. In the case of Pekalongan, however, thanks in part to a remarkable provincial census of 1855, which was recently found in the National Archives of Indonesia, we can present some new insights into patterns of occupation and marriage related to class and ethnicity.[4]

Sugar in Rural Pekalongan

The Residency of Pekalongan, in the form in which it existed in the nine-teenth century, was the smallest such colonial administrative unit in the colony. Situated in the island's northern littoral, the town of Pekalongan itself, the Residency's centre of government and only major urban centre, was some 60 kilometres to the west of the major port-city of Semarang, and four hours or more away by coach along the great post road built in the 1810s. It was home in the 1840s to a Dutch colonial community of more than 400 souls, around 1,900 mostly locally-born Chinese[5] and 600 or so Arab settlers and an Indonesian, mostly Javanese, population reckoned to number 15,000. The location of the town in a narrow coastal plain between the Java Sea and the foothills and mountains of the island's central massif was said to give it a salubrious climate, while the price of necessities was generally reckoned to be low.[6] For whatever reason, since the Dutch East India Company (VOC) had first built a fort and trading post there in the mid-eighteenth century, the town had attracted a larger Indies Dutch (and Chinese) population than any of its counterparts along the coast, apart from the 'metropolis' of Semarang itself. As we shall see, the resultant community was characterised by the pres-ence of a small, largely Caucasian-Creole elite and several hundred *mestizos,* some at least of whom by the mid-nineteenth century already multi-genera-tional settlers either in Pekalongan itself or elsewhere in Java and the Indies in general.

The colonial sugar industry that was to establish such a massive presence in Java in the nineteenth and early twentieth centuries only arrived in Peka-longan in the 1830s and took nearly three decades to fully establish itself. Before that, commercial agriculture in the Pekalongan lowlands had been dominated by rice production, largely in the hands of the Residency's Chinese merchant community and their associates and clients among the Javanese *priyayi* elite, and by the cultivation of indigo leaf and its manufacture into a transportable form of the dyestuff. Indigo in one form or another had been produced in Pekalongan since the late eighteenth century and probably ear-lier. During the 1820s, however, it had been taken up by a handful of colo-nial European entrepreneurs, who had sought to expand the industry on the basis of the centralisation of manufacture in a small number of large but tech-nologically quite rudimentary 'factories' located both in the lowlands and in the foothills to the south. It was the presence of this industry and its heavy demands on local labour that was one of the factors in the initial slow expan-sion of sugar in Pekalongan in the 1830s and 1840s. During the following decade, however, the production of indigo in the Residency was scaled back and then largely abandoned on a commercial scale: in the lowlands, sugar became king, a position which it continued to hold until the 1930s, when it too was drastically scaled down in the face of falling international demand.

By the middle of the nineteenth century there were a total of five colonial sugar factories operating in the Pekalongan lowlands, covering approximately 1,000 hectares of rice fields with their cane plantations (on an annually rotational basis) and producing around 3,000 tons of sugar for export. This constituted less than 4 percent of Java's total exports of sugar in 1850, and serves to alert us to the fact that Pekalongan, with its handful of factories and relatively small share in the industry's overall output, may not have been 'typical' of the colonial sugar industry as a whole. Nonetheless, its factories themselves appear to have followed a similar pattern to those in more heavily 'sugared' parts of the colony, in so far as they exhibited a typical mid-century mix of older and new technologies of manufacture. All of them had mills driven not by steam engines but by water wheels (as was, indeed, the predominant mode throughout the colony in the 1850s) and boiling houses in which steam technology came into own in the shape of vacuum pans in which cane juice, once clarified and thickened, was 'boiled' under reduced air pressure until the point was reached at which it was ready to turn into sugar. At one mid-century Pekalongan factory, at least, this was done by way of a set of centrifuges, while at others the older style method of 'claying' the sugar in large conical pots still held sway. As elsewhere in Java, vacuum pans, centrifuges and the steam engines and steam boilers which operated them were very largely imported in packing cases from Europe, although this did not preclude – indeed it positively demanded if the new machines were to be kept in working order – the establishment of small repair shops at the factories themselves and the creation (principally at the city of Surabaya in East Java) of quite extensive workshops to handle repairs and renovations.

All told, though somewhat remote from the main centres of production, the colonial sugar factories of mid-nineteenth-century Pekalongan were as technologically advanced as most of their kind elsewhere in the colony. Indeed, one of them, the Wonopringo factory, owned and managed by the Batavia Office (the *Factorij*) of the NHM or Netherlands Trading Society, was one of the most technologically progressive and well-equipped factories in the whole of Java. The implications of this expansion of the sugar industry and its concomitant (relative) technological advance meant for the Dutch colonial community in Pekalongan are something to which we shall shortly return.

A Colonial Community

The great bulk of the Residency's Dutch colonial community, Caucasian newcomers, Creoles and *mestizos* lived in the town of Pekalongan itself.[7] Colonial descriptions of the town, from the late eighteenth century through to the mid-nineteenth, point to its considerable size ('very large' was how Nagel described it in the 1820s), suggest an urban centre where the community's public life was focused on Main Street B. In typical Dutch fashion it was the *Heerenstraat* B, lined with canary and tamarind trees and on a large and shady square – the reference here was distinctly eastern – where, inter alia, the Resident's house and offices were located, together with the post office and the remains of the mid-eighteenth century VOC fort, called appropriately enough, *De Beschermer* (Protector). By the 1830s this had undergone a dual conversion into indigo warehouse and prison. The houses of what one contemporary writer termed the 'Europeesche Kamp' were said to be airy and built in brick, and together with their gardens presented a 'most inviting' appearance. There was also an inn (*herberg*), presumably located on the main road, as were two 'European' shops, run by a German and a Frenchman, providing European food and beverages, cloth and fashion articles. Still apparently in the 'European' sector of the town, there were other shops owned by Chinese.

The great bulk (and perhaps all) of the town's Chinese community, however, was located across the 'fine river' that divided Pekalongan into western and eastern sectors. According to a late eighteenth-century description, the Chinese quarter 'faces the hills and borders on the sea; it consists of a row of dwelling houses, amounting to perhaps 50 of 60. To the north and south it is defended by wooden palisades ... The houses are joined one to another, with high stories; towards the west is the Kappittans residence, to the right of which is a garden, which may be about one acre in extent, beautifully shaded with trees ...'. Likewise in the eastern sector, the main part of the 'native' town was where the Javanese *Bupati* or Regent held court in his *dalem*, and where the markets and the town's main mosque were located. Surrounding this urban core were the *kampongs* of the mass of the town's Indonesian population. Until the early 1830's the majority of the Europeans who were not self employed (small traders and artisans) or retirees had jobs in the embryonic colonial bureaucracy, the small local military establishment or had occupations connected with the manufacture of indigo. Out of a total of 66 male heads of households living either in the town itself or the surrounding lowlands in the period 1819 to 1823 (the earliest period for which such figures are available), the majority – twenty-eight in all – were in the employ of the Indies Government, ranging from the Resident himself through to the humblest clerk or warehouse keeper. A further seventeen were listed as small traders and artisans – and four as sailors – and nine were military personnel, mostly retired. A further nine individuals were engaged in the indigo industry, and three were said to be without employment and/or on poor relief.[8]

The ethnic breakdown of this group, in so far as the data allow, reveal that only one-third of the Europeans were born in Europe and the majority in Asia, and that the parents of the latter category were often also born in Asia. Those who came from Europe were retired military, some shop keepers or otherwise engaged in trade, and higher ranking civil servants, and owners of indigo factories. However, although this demonstrates that there were Europeans of mixed descent in middle-status positions and Caucasians (i.e. individuals born in Europe) in low-status positions, nearly all high and middle-status positions were in the hands of Creoles or Caucasians. The majority of the low-status jobs and almost all the unemployed were Indies born and of mixed descent (i.e. *mestizo*) while none of whom later held a high status position. Between 1819 and 1823, four of the five senior Government officials employed in Pekalongan either as Resident or Residency Secretary, had been born in the Netherlands, and two owners of indigo factories were probably both of European extraction. [9] Together with a number of Creoles employed as *Controleur* [district officer] and other ranking government officials, they constituted the tiny provincial elite of Pekalongan's European community.

Their female partners – whether in marriage or less formal cohabitation – tended to be predominantly Creole or *mestizo* in origin. 'A wife born in the Indies' was a commonplace of the era, but not necessarily a sure or very informative guide to social reality. The Caucasian Otto Carel Holmberg de Beckvelt,[10] for example, who was the Dutch Resident of Pekalongan towards the end of the 1820s, had married a woman – Henriette Smissaert – who was born in Amsterdam but who had Indies-born ancestors, and was herself brought up in the Indies from earliest infancy. Whether such a woman was Caucasian, Creole or *mestizo* is largely a matter of social usage: given that she belonged to the elite, no doubt she considered herself white. She and her husband, who had himself arrived in Java as a very young man in 1817, and whose family had long connections with the Indies, formed part of an incipient Indies bourgeoisie of government officials, sugar manufacturers (many of them state Contractors) and business people whose intricate networks of kith and kin were to form the dominant elite in the colony throughout the mid-century decades (and beyond).

The *Cultuurstelsel* and Its Impact on the European Community in Pekalongan

In the 1830s, the *Cultuurstelsel* 'arrived' in Pekalongan (as we have seen), together with a little band of individuals contracted to the Indies Government to manufacture indigo and sugar from raw materials supplied to them – this was the essence of the *Stelsel* – through the forced labour of the local Javanese peasantry (whose land was also commandeered for that purpose). In the case of sugar, what this meant over the following two or three decades for the Residency's colonial European elite can be summarised fairly briefly: it meant a small influx of new people, but relatively little change in its existing (and, as always, evolving) character. At the elite level, the arrival of the Cultivation System, and with it a handful of European Contractors in both sugar and indigo certainly caused tensions among the provincial Caucasian-Creole elite where the Resident and his ranking officials had previously been unchallenged in their social assumptions as well as political hegemony. Early in the 1830s, for instance, one infuriated official complained to Batavia, in respect to one the indigo Contractors, 'that the manufacturer Thompson's expectation is, and always was, that the Resident of Pekalongan should be the overseer of his indigo plantations' and that the fellow's machinations 'weigh down on me in my office and make my private life as well as my public position well-nigh unbearable ...'.[11] Around the mid-century, tensions among the elite were further exemplified in the well-publicised dispute between the then Resident and the leaseholder of the Simbang sugar-growing estate, J.E. Herderschee (on whom, see below).[12] Nonetheless, conflicts of this kind (and in reality there was far more accommodation than conflict) did not signify any profound disturbance of the social order among the Residency's European community.

In the first place, the state Contractors and other capitalists involved in the sugar industry who established themselves in Pekalongan Residency in the 1830s and 1840s were newcomers only in the most literal sense of the word, and they constituted scarcely more than a handful of individuals. The first to arrive (in 1837) was Hermanus van Blommestein, a retired sea captain whose previous employment had been as harbour master at the port of Semarang. His years there had brought him close contact with that city's Chinese business community, contacts which he evidently maintained at his Batang (Kalimatie) sugar factory, a few kilometres to the east of Pekalongan town. After his death in Java in 1864, the factory passed into the hands of his son Adrianus, who had previously been a 'front man' for Chinese sugar interests in the adjacent Tegal Residency (where he was the nominal owner of the Pagongan sugar factory) and who, when in financial extremis two decades later, was expected to be bailed out by his good friend Be Biauw Tjoan, the Chinese Captain of Semarang and one of the richest Chinese business men in the colony.[13]

Typically Indies connections of this kind were reinforced, as in the case of the Van Blommestein family, by a number of factors. Hermanus van Blommestein (1791–1864), the family patriarch and a Caucasian in terms of crude ethnic identity, had married *Jonkvrouw* Catharina Johanna van Braam (1795–1878) the daughter of an aristocratic Dutch colonial naval officer and an Indies-born mother. His wife's pronounced Creole-mestizo ancestry and family ties linked the Van Blommesteins firmly into the network of elite Creole families in Batavia and elsewhere in the Indies.[14] Their position within the Indies bourgeoisie of the mid-century decades was further cemented when the couple's nineteen-year-old daughter Maria Cornelia became the wife of *Controleur* Eduard Rochussen, son of the Governor-General.

Further west along the coast, at the Sragie sugar factory, the owner, virtually throughout the mid-century decades was Louis (or maybe Ludovico) Vitalis, a former high official of the Indies government who had already been domiciled in Java for more than two decades when he took over there in 1841. Vitalis, born in Aix-en-Provence and probably a scion of the well-known Greek merchant family of that name, 'repatriated' to Paris in the 1850s and died in Antwerp twenty years later. His immediate kin, however, had impeccable Indies connections. He was married to Francina Rieman, the Java-born daughter of a Java-born, *mestizo* mother and a Caucasian father.[15] In turn, one of their offspring, Emilie Vitalis, married Barend Herderschee, younger brother of Johannes Eliza Herderschee,[16] leaseholder and sugar manufacturer on the so-called Simbang Estate ('*het Land* Simbang'), a large tract of rice-fields and forest in the eastern lowlands of Pekalongan, some twenty or so kilometres east of Sragie. In turn, the elder of the Herderschee brothers was another Caucasian so long established in the Indies, and so intermarried with the Indies clans, as to be virtually indistinguishable from a Creole. None of these people, in short, were representative of a new wave of colonisers who might be expected to overturn the existing social order of the colonial European communities amongst whom they found themselves.

Nor was such a threat posed – for all that it might ostensibly appear to have been one – by the general managers (*administrateur*), engineers and other skilled operatives whom the sugar industry brought in its wake. Undoubtedly, such people tended to be new arrivals in the colony, and to lack the family connections or long prior domicile in the Indies of Pekalongan's mid-century sugar owners. At Wonopringo, for example, an older *administrateur* (Johannes Stokhekker), inter alia a one-time warehouse keeper and long-settled in Java, was replaced at the mid-century by the technologically proficient Thomas Jeoffries Edwards, an Englishman who had been in the colony for no more than a decade (see Knight in this volume). His assistant there was the German technician (*machinist*) Robert Kampf. At Klidang, a fairly small sugar-making enterprise carried on in the eastern part of the Residency by a Batavia lawyer and his (probably) Chinese business partners, two newcomers in succession (Jan T. Halkema and Thama C. Simonet) were brought in, presumably because of their ability to handle the new machinery. On the Simbang Estate, Barend Herderschee appears to have been replaced (possibly after his brother's death in 1862) by the newly arrived and Dutch-born IJsbrand van Dijk, assisted by the German *machinist* Johannes Wiert. After the departure of Louis Vitalis in 1852, the management of Sragie devolved upon another fairly recently arrived Dutchman, Petrus Meijer.

Nonetheless, the social implications of this development are far from straightforward. Most of these men (as far as can be judged) took Indies wives or co-habited with locally born women – and established essentially *Indisch* families of a kind with which the existing colonial European communities had long been familiar. Edwards, for example, lived for twenty years or more with a *mestizo* woman, formally 'recognised' (that is to say, conferred a 'European' legal and social identity upon) his children and himself died in the Indies, leaving a 'widow' and descendants who were still living in the colony in the early twentieth century. His successor at Wonopringo, J.C. Heijning, although a member of a Dutch patrician family, had been born in Asia and then educated in Holland. He had returned to Java with a Dutch-born wife sometime in the 1840s.[17] At the nearby Sragie sugar factory, *administrateur* Meijer, on the other hand, was married to a Java-born woman, albeit the bearer of English forenames and a Dutch surname: Helen Jane Bremner. *Administrateur* Van Dijk of Simbang was married to the likewise Indo-European Paulina Klein, while the manager of Klidang, Thama Simonet, had married a Java-born but apparently Caucasian woman.[18]

The expanded provincial elite of mid-nineteenth-century Pekalongan was not confined, of course, simply to the owners and key employees of the sugar (and indigo) factories. The local representatives of the Indies state's evolving bureaucracy were also key figures, notably the Resident himself, the *Secretaris* and the handful of *Controleurs* who played a crucial role in the supervision of the production of raw material – with sugar cane increasingly to the fore – on which the *Cultuurstelsel* was based. Famously, however, the number of Dutch officials in the Residencies of Java scarcely increased between the 1830s and 1860s, and in Pekalongan, at least, the Resident himself was a largely transient figure: in the three-and-a-half decades concerned, no less than fourteen individuals held the office (compared to nine in neighbouring Tegal).[19] Within this context (although the subject merits further investigation) it looks very much as if the social characteristics of Dutch officialdom in the Residency remained much as they had been in the 1820s: that is to say, they were either European-born Caucasians or Indies-born Creoles, with the former tending to predominate in a situation where training – although not birth – in the Netherlands was increasingly becoming a prerequisite for high-ranking officials.[20]

Europeans of the Lower Class and the Problem of Unemployment

Within this context of a provincial colonial community whose elite was enlarged but scarcely transformed in the mid-nineteenth-century decades by the arrival of the *Cultuurstelsel* and its attendant sugar industry, the most interesting issue was in many ways what happened to the lower class of colonial Europeans of mixed ethnicity. *Mestizo*, virtually by definition (see above), they comprised the bulk of the Dutch community in Pekalongan as elsewhere in Java. While the history of the elite is often traceable in patrician genealogies and family histories, the lower-class has been largely neglected. In this respect, the most striking feature of the 'census' data from 1855 is not only the increase in lower class numbers but also the extent of their ostensible pauperisation. At first glance, at least, it looks as if the 'Indo Problem' – the existence in the towns and cities of Java of a large economically and socially marginalised group of soi-disant 'Europeans' – had arrived in Pekalongan a full half-century before it made its appearance in colonial and metropolitan discourse. In fact, as we shall suggest, this was probably a misreading of the situation, but a misreading that, on the evidence of statistical data alone, is comprehensible enough.

The most immediately striking feature of the information about the lower class of Pekalongan's mid-century European colonial community, as revealed in the 'census' of 1855, was the percentage of adult males recorded as unemployed. Some twenty-four people, more than one-quarter of the male population (not including 'retirees' – mostly ex-military), were said to be without jobs and, as such, the recipients of poor relief. This contrasts markedly with the reconstruction of the situation some three decades earlier,[21] when a miniscule proportion – three adult males out of a total of over 60 – were recorded as unemployed.

Table 4.1: Employment of Adult Male Europeans in Pekalongan, 1819–1855.

Employment	1819–1823	[1828–1835]	1855 'Census'
High Ranking State Officials	5	3	3
Middle Ranking Officials(e.g. *Controleur*)	–	3	4
Lower Ranking Officials (e.g. *commies*)	12	13	14
Low Ranking State Employees (e.g. warehouse staff)	11	8	9
ALL STATE OFFICIALS/ EMPLOYEES	28	27	30
Indigo Manufacturer	2	6	–
Employee/Overseer Indigo	–	–	6
Leaseholder	7	2	1
Sugar Factory Owners & Administrateurs	–	–	8
Sugar Factory Employees	–	–	16
ALL INDIGO & SUGAR	9	8	31
(Retired) Military	9	8	11
Artisans, Small Traders, Entrepreneurs	17	4	6
Unemployed/Poor Relief	3	13	24
Grand Total	66	60	107

Source: *Verslag Residentie Pekalongan 1819 and 1823, Nominatieve Staat, NA, MvK, inv. nr. 3113.*[21]

A partial explanation of the high unemployment figure for 1855, it might be suggested, was that the running down of the state's indigo industry had meant a loss of jobs for the Residency's non-elite Europeans who had previously found employment in the industry as supervisors. The concomitant growth of the sugar industry had not compensated for this, it might be argued, because the employment that it offered required a level of technical expertise that the lower-class Europeans of Pekalongan did not possess. There is some truth in this, but as an explanation of the high degree of unemployment recorded in 1855, it is scarcely satisfactory: the indigo industry never seems to have provided employment for more than a handful of the European community's lower class, while the 'replacement' sugar industry did not entirely exclude such people. Indeed, in the longer term, from the 1870s onwards, lower class Europeans could hope to find employment in the sugar industry as field supervisors, where their presumed conversance with the mores of the Indonesian workforce compensated for their lack of formal qualifications.

An altogether more likely hypothesis is that the available data on employment is seriously at fault. First of all, the data of the various census reports are not consistent with each other. As has been observed elsewhere, there was a tendency not to count poor Eurasians in the first registration of 1819 to 1823. With the arrival of European education and religious services, the European society became more inclusive towards its poorer elements. They became counted as Europeans. This could also explain why, twenty years later, the adult male European population of Pekalongan could almost double.[22] Second, definitions of what is work and employment change over time and that authorities became increasingly sensitive towards the problem of economic marginalisation of European descendants. Notionally that data describes a situation, around 1820, when one-third or more of Pekalongan's non-elite Europeans – seventeen in all – had jobs as shop keepers and artisans (as opposed to 1855 when only six such people were recorded). This seems an improbably high figure in so small a community, not least because Pekalongan town was already on record as having a large and thriving Chinese community (see above), whose members would be expected to occupy the bulk of such functions in any colonial town in nineteenth-century Java. It certainly raises questions about what being a 'shop keeper' or 'artisan' actually meant for the members of the European community in 1820. Did being a 'shop keeper', for instance, mean anything more than the (occasional) sale of a few trade goods to neighbours? If this hypothesis is correct, it could mean that the margin between employment and unemployment was very slight indeed – and that, for many lower class Europeans, being without any substantial occupation was not just a feature of the mid- (and late) nineteenth century but was a predicament already experienced at a considerably earlier date. It was a predicament, moreover, on which the arrival of the sugar industry after 1830 had a relatively minimal short-term impact. It neither provided much local employment, nor did it significantly take it away.

Christian Worship and Community Dynamics

The real dynamic of provincial colonial communities like those of the town of Pekalongan, it might be suggested, was to be found elsewhere. One crucial facet was the issue of religion and, very closely connected, that of 'European' identity. Visiting Pekalongan during the course of a tour of Java in the late 1840s, the polemicist and *predikant* (clergyman) W.R. van Hoëvell noted both the absence of place of Christian worship and the community's agitation to have a church build for them by the Indies government. As Robert Ross has pointed out in the parallel (although very different) case of the Dutch communities in southern Africa, the practice of the Christian religion was an important, possibly even critical factor, in the perpetuation of European identity.[23] Writing about the Dutch community in Pekalongan, Van Hoëvell reported that they were very keen to build a church and that they were particularly anxious that in its absence their *children* might miss out a proper Christian upbringing. Van Hoëvell went on to report that he had helped the community draw up a petition to a hitherto indifferent or hostile Indies Government about both the church and the provision of a resident clergyman.[24] Regular Christian observance, it may be imputed, was an integral part of these people's understanding of what it was to be a European, and to the ranking among Europeans that entailed. Where you were seated in church, for example, both reflected and reinforced standing within the community outside its walls. Understandably, therefore, the European inhabitants of Pekalongan were anxious about their Christian status – presently somewhat weakly sustained by a preacher visiting from Batavia twice a year to celebrate communion, carry out baptism and sanctify marriages. Equally understandably, they were even more deeply concerned that their children should be seen as Christians.

For the small European elite of mid-nineteenth-century Pekalongan, the absence of church and clergyman did not necessarily pose problems, for it seems likely (although the point would bear further investigation) that they were able to compensate for the absence of a formal place of worship by the organisation of regular devotions within their own households, under the guidance of the *pater familias*. Among Protestants at least, this practice was widespread in parts of northwest Europe by the mid-century. For the lower class Europeans, this option was probably not available, and in any event their position, so 'dangerously' near the margins of European society in the colony, would have inclined them to seek recognition of their – and their children's – status in visible, public forms of Christian worship. The fear, in particular, that their children would not grow up as Christians was something to which xxx specifically alluded. They feared that the bi-annual visit of a clergyman from Batavia was not sufficient to preserve the Christian-European nexus. By the mid-1850s, however, the European community at Pekalongan had obtained both a Church and the services of a *predikant*-schoolteacher.[25] The implication, following the argument that has just been made, is that this was concomitant with a shoring-up of European identity, particularly, it may be suspected, among the community's lower-class members.

If the issue of formal Christian worship points to one dynamic within the colonial European community of mid-nineteenth-century Pekalongan, the evidence of the 1855 'census' points to several others with quite different implications. One such dynamic stemmed, it would appear, from the absence of local employment opportunities for young adult lower-class males and the considerable degree of out-migration that this caused. The other, presumably a direct consequence, was that the difficulty evidently experienced by young women of the community in acquiring marriage partners – or indeed partners of any kind – within the European population. Most immediately, the combined upshot was a community always 'threatened' by transience and by a weakening of (formal) social bonds. An important underlying factor, however, was the European community's nexus with the local Chinese and Indonesian populations of Pekalongan town and its surroundings.

A Community in Flux

Fragmentary as it is, the evidence suggests that this was not a new, mid-nineteenth-century phenomenon but, rather, that a substantial part of the European population in the Residency had been in a state of flux for some decades prior to the 'census' of 1855. In 1819 just twelve of the 62 adult men in Pekalongan had been born there, while nearly half were arrivals from Europe. For Caucasians, the average duration of their stay in Pekalongan in the early decades of the nineteenth century was less than five years, a fact largely accounted for by the fact that they were elite-level officials who moved on as a matter of course to other and hopefully better positions elsewhere. A comparison of data from 1819 and 1823 points to the fact that in this five year period, there was an out-migration of some twenty-two people or around one-third of the total adult male population (nine other individuals died). This attrition, meanwhile, was only partly balanced by the arrival of some sixteen or so newcomers.[26]

In the early 1850s mobility was also very high as shown in table 4.2. Few men stayed for long periods, as only a quarter of the adult males had lived in Pekalongan for at least ten years.[27] No less than 52 of the 116 adult males in 1855 had arrived during the last three years, while 33 men had left since 1852. Of these 52 arrivals, 10 men were return migrants, most of them unemployed, probably returning to their family. Many of these immigrants did not stay long:

no less than 19 had already left within five years. During the period immediately after 1855 the process of migration continued. By 1860 no less than 32 men had left while 22 have arrived (Table 5).[28]

Table 4.2: Migration of European adult males in Pekalongan, 1852–1860.

In/Out	Civil servants	Sugar industry	retirees	Other	Unemployed	Total
IN 1852–1855*	13	15	5	4	5	42
OUT 1855–1860	9	3	3	3	12	32

*Returned migrants not included.

One of the most marked aspects of this degree of transience was the relative absence of young adult males in Pekalongan's European community. In the cases where the father was Caucasian or Creole – and hence a member of the elite – the absence of male children of fifteen years or over was virtually complete: they may have found a job elsewhere sooner because of their family connections or, more probably, they had gone to school either in Batavia or in the Netherlands. This latter was one of the mechanisms through which the elite maintained metropolitan ties vital to its long-term position in the colony.[29] Young men with a *mestizo* father seem to have remained in Pekalongan somewhat longer, but by their twenties a significant proportion of these, too, had left the town.[30] We do not know where these young *mestizo* men went: they moved away from Pekalongan after the age of fifteen – many were over twenty – and had at best only an elementary education, a result of the fact that most of their fathers had low wages or were living on pensions. In contrast to Caucasians – and to the Creoles of the colonial Batavia-oriented elite – few if any of them participated in the colonial migration circuit between the Netherlands and the Indies. It must be presumed that, in so far as they found employment at all, they got jobs as overseers on plantations, or as clerks in offices elsewhere in the colony. Rather surprisingly perhaps, only a very few local youths took up low-level positions in the Residency office in Pekalongan itself, where the majority of such positions were filled by outsiders.

There were, to be sure, a handful of *mestizo* families in Pekalongan who were long-settled in the town. Indeed, half of the European population of Pekalongan had been born in the Residency itself, and most of them, in turn, had parents who had also been born in the colony. Some families had been living in the European community for over a quarter of a century, and there was a considerable degree of intermarriage between them. In 1855, at least one in five of the town's European inhabitants was a member of the Anthonijsz, Pechler, Jansz, Toorop, Westhoff and Meijer families, and 80 percent of these had been born in Pekalongan itself. The twenty-year-old Johannis Th.A. Westhoff worked in the Residency office together with his father and his older brother. The family Anthonijsz also had a father-son combination working there. The only other locally born man to have gained employment as a clerk, Jacobus Springer, was married to the daughter of the Javanese woman Piah and the former *Kommies*, Urbanus Samuel Jansz, a particular favourite of Resident Preatorius (1834 to 1837), purportedly on account of the fact that his family had supplied fish on a daily basis to the Resident's household.[31] Three other members of these 'core' families found work in the 1850s in the sugar industry. The availability of local employment may well explain why three of the families boasted a more or less equal ratio of men to women: the other three, however, demonstrated the same marked tendency for the out-migration of young males that characterised the community as a whole.

The consequent, pronounced imbalance between the sexes among people of marriageable age within the European community in Pekalongan is a marked feature of the data available for 1855. One of the most striking features of that data is what it demonstrates about the inverse ratio of women to men [or vice-versa?] of marriageable age. It might be expected in community of this kind that the age cohorts were more or less equal as to sex, and became smaller gradually with advancing age. This was not the case however: in the age group sixteen to thirty there were twice as many women as men.

Unsurprisingly, this imbalance had a considerable impact on the incidence of marriage in the community. Some *mestizo* women found husbands higher up the social scale, among the Caucasian and Creole elite. The most eminent example was when Dirk A. Varkevisser, at that time Dutch Resident in adjoining Tegal, took as his wife Wilhelmina C. Antonijsz, daughter of one of Pekalongan's biggest *mestizo* families. But that was in 1838, and by the mid-1850s no similar marriage across social lines had taken place in Pekalongan for a decade or more.[32] A subsequent 'success story' was that of Surabaya born Louisa Besenthé, who at the age of nineteen gave birth to the first child of Jacob Graswinckel, the 28-year-old Caucasian employee at the Wonopringo sugar factory. Although Jacob initially did not acknowledge fatherhood (see below), their partnership was sealed with a marriage in 1865. By 1870 Louisa had reached the top of local society when Jacob had been appointed *administrateur* at Wonopringo. For the most part, nonetheless, locally born European women married partners from their own milieu (local *mestizo* men never married newcomer women). Many of these women, however, did not marry at all – or married in accordance with rites other than those of the Christian church.

One factor at work here, already alluded to, was that there were too few adult European males in the community to provide them with husbands. Another factor, however, was an evident propensity, among what adult males there were, to form informal partnerships with women from outside the European community. In 1855 only just over half of the adult members of Pekalongan's European community had been 'Churched' – or married, that is to say, in accordance with Christian rites, and unmarried partnerships were common. Indeed, 37 percent of the 472 'acknowledged' children born in Pekalongan, were the children of unmarried partners: children, that is to say, who had been acknowledged and formally registered by their European fathers (and who thereby gained the social and legal status of Europeans)[33] but whose mothers in many cases were not themselves classified as Europeans.

Either way, through the paucity of men or male preference for 'native', Chinese or 'unacknowledged' and hence unclassified Eurasian women, many of the lower class women of the European community seem to have had little chance of finding a husband in their own cohort – even assuming that they wanted to. Marriage into the Chinese and Indonesian – largely Javanese communities – whose mid-nineteenth-century presence in Pekalongan was briefly observed at the outset of this chapter, was a very real if hardly documented option: late nineteenth-century sources, for instance, support the idea that significant numbers of 'recognised' *mestizo* women of the lower class of the colony's European communities found partners 'in the *kampong*' or among Java's Chinese communities.[34]

The net effect is to underscore how porous were the borders between the different communities and how potentially misleading in this circumstances simple notions of 'identity' might be. As such, they were quintessentially *Indisch*, to the extent that *Indisch* (literally 'Indian', but here in the sense of Indo-European) delineated a cultural construction of ethnicity particular to colonial Java: one that encapsulated a high degree of social and cultural hybridity. A crucial dynamic of such communities was grounded in what Cooper and Stoler have referred to 'the interstitiality of colonial lives' – the connecting tissues that interleaved the daily existence of Caucasians, Creoles, *mestizos*, Chinese and 'natives'.[35]

Towards a Conclusion

In the context of a brief discussion of the arrival of the colonial sugar industry in mid-nineteenth-century Pekalongan, something which began in the 1830s and only reached its 'mature' form after 1850, this chapter has sought to investigate the extent to which the industry impacted on the colonial European community that had come into existence there nearly a century earlier. Composed, as was the case throughout Java, of people who were seen or who saw themselves as Caucasian (*totok*), Creole and *mestizo* – the distinction between the latter had as much to do with class as with ethnicity – the European community was not untouched by the arrival of a new and technologically advanced form of Western enterprise. Its elite was enlarged and experienced by a degree (not to be exaggerated) of intra elite conflict, while Europeans of the lower class appear to have experienced the arrival of sugar in largely negative terms, in so far that it failed to provide the employment which they needed. In broad terms, however, and allowing for continuing problems relating to employment and its categorisation, the dynamic of colonial European society in mid-nineteenth-century Pekalongan was probably to be found elsewhere: in the provision of formal Christian worship, with its potential for consolidating a distinct European identity and – paradoxically enough – in the extensive out-migration of adult males, the prevalence of unmarried women and high rate of illegitimacy. A further and yet to be fully explored facet of the community was the interface, in these circumstances, between the European community and those of the local Chinese and Indonesians with whom it coexisted in the urban area of mid-nineteenth-century Pekalongan.

Notes

1. For major recent discussions of the *Cultuurstelsel*, see Elson, *Javanese Peasants and the Colonial Sugar Industry*; Elson, *Village Java under the Cultuurstelsel*; Fernando, 'Peasants and Plantation'; Knight, *Colonial Production in Provincial Java*; Suryo, 'Social and Economic Life in Rural Semarang under Colonial Rule in the Later Nineteenth Century'; Van Niel, *Java under the Cultivation System*; Van Schaik, 'Colonial Control and Peasant Resources in Java'; Van Schaik, 'Bitter and Sweet. A Hundred Years of Sugar Industry in Comal'.
2. See, for example, Taylor, *The Social World of Batavia; European and Eurasian in Dutch Asia*; Houben, 'De Indo-aristocatie van Midden Java: de familie Dezentjé'.
3. Bosma and Raben, *De Oude Indische Wereld 1500–1920*.
4. The authors are deeply indebted for their assistance to Leo Janssen and Peter Christiaans of the Indische Genealogische Vereniging, and to the staff of the Arsip Nasional Republik Indonesia, Jakarta.
5. In the entire Pekalongan Residency around 1820 there was reportedly a community of some 2250 *peranakan* (i.e. acculturated, *mestizo*) Chinese men (668), women (658) and children (928), predominantly employed as traders, agricultural entrepreneurs, manufacturers and artisans. About half of them lived in the town of Pekalongan itself. See 'Statistiek Pekalongan 1821', B/2, NA, The Hague, Collectie Schneither, 90. Some twenty-five years later the *peranakan* Chinese population of Pekalongan town apparently amounted to 1,900 souls; see Bleeker, 'Fragmenten eener Reis over Java', 266–67.
6. Van Hoëvell, *Reis over Java, Madura en Bali in het midden van 1847*, 90.
7. The following description of Pekalongan town in the first half of the nineteenth century is primarily derived from: Bleeker, 'Fragmenten eener Reis over Java', 266–67; Van Sevenhoven, 'Java, ten dienste van hen die over dit eiland wenschen te reizen', 333; Nagel, *Schetsen uit mijn Javaansche portefeuille* [see Mitchell Catalogue]; Ong Tae Hae, *The Chinaman Abroad*, 11–12.
8. Verslag Residentie Pekalongan 1819 and 1823, Nominatieve Staat, NA, MvK. 3113. The term 'adult males' here is reserved for those over fifteen years old.
9. They were circa 1820 Robert Scott Douglas (died in Pekalongan 1822) and the altogether more shadowy figure of Charles du Pont.

10. For a detailed account of De Beckfelt and his family, see Knight, 'The Contractor as *Suikerlord* and Entrepreneur'.
11. Resident Pekalongan to DC, 17.10.1833, Exh. 28.10.1833/3357 ANJ AC 586, ANRI.
12. On Herderschee's clashes with officials of the Indies Government, see in particular *De Zaken van het Land Simbang nader toegelicht*, and Netscher, *Regt en Onregt of Den Toestand der Gewestelijke Besturen in Indie*.
13. See [extract] NHM Batavia Factorij to Amsterdam, 22.7.1881. 'Dossiers Cultuurzaken (…) Wonopringo & Kalimatie', NA, NHM. Be was for 'nearly half a century (…) the doyen of the *cabang abas* [i.e. the leaders of the Chinese business community] of central Java'. On Be Biauw Tjoan (1824–1904), see Rush, *Opium to Java Revenue Farming*, 77–78, 93–96.
14. See the entry in *Nederland's Patriciaat*, 1969 (53), which also details the many other branches – in the Indies and the Netherlands – of this very extensive family.
15. On Vitalis and his family, see *Indische Navorscher* 1, no. 4 (1934), 16, 32.
16. On J.E. Herderschee (born in Amsterdam 4.2.1813 died in Batavia 16.5.1862 see *Indische Navorscher, New Series 7*, no. 4 (1994), 205. He was already in Batavia at the age of twenty-one in 1834, when he married the daughter of an old Indies family, Johanna Clasina [Langenberg] Kool (born 3.1.1820 died in Batavia 1.5.1870).
17. On Johannes Cornelis Heijing (1808–1866) and his wife, Jannetje Swerver (1812–1896), see the entry on the family in *Nederland's Patriciaat* 1990 (74), 242–46.
18. See, variously, *Regeeringsalmanak*; Janssen, *De Burgerlijke Stand van Pekalongan*; L. M. Janssen, *Onuitgegeven materiaal van de burgerlijke stand Pekalongan*, n.d.
19. Between 1825 and 1860, Tegal had nine Residents, and considerable continuity: P. van der Poel 1824–1833, D.A Varkevisser 1836–1846, J.A. Vriesman 1846–1857. Pekalongan has fourteen Residents and pronounced discontinuity: F.H. Doornik (1837–1843) lasted longest; the rest lasted no more than two or three years, with the exception of G.J.P. van der Poel (1852–1857) – but he was seriously ill in the last two or three years of his tenure.
20. The highest positions were held by those who were born, or at least educated in Europe, (like Secretary Vijzelaar, Acting-Resident Canneman). Even where high-ranking civil servants were born in the Indies, they were the Creole sons of parents who were born in Europe (like Resident G.P.J. van de Poel, and the *Controleurs* A.T.H.L. Raaff, J.W. van Rijck, A.A. Sluijter – all of Batavia – and K.A.L.J. Jeekel).
21. *Verslag Residentie Pekalongan* 1819 and 1823, Nominatieve Staat, NA, MvK, inv. nr. 3113. Figures for 1828–1835 and 1840–1847 (in italics) are estimates, based on all names mentioned for those years in the birth and marriage registers of Pekalongan (Janssen, *Burgerlijke Stand*; Janssen, *Onuitgegeven materiaal*). Therefore, the number of positions of persons who were replaced within these years may have been overestimated. 'High government' staff are (assistant) Resident, secretary, inspector; 'low government' staff are overseer, warehouse master, teacher, postmaster-publican, schoolusher.
22. See Raben and Bosma, *De oude Indische wereld*, 220.
23. See the chapter on 'Christianity, Status and Respectability' in Ross, *Status and Respectability in the Cape Colony, 1750–1870*, 94–124.
24. See Van Hoëvell, *Reis over Java*, 90–94. Van Hoëvell remarked that the community has raised money to build a church, but has run into problems with the Indies Government over permission, about which he is advising them. It appeared that Indies Government regulations prohibited building of a church 'op plaatsen waar geen leeraar gevestigd is', where there was no guarantee that the building can be properly maintained. Van Hoëvell has largely been read for his opposition to the Indies Government's system of forced-labour cultivations, and for his incidental remarks about the 'condition of the [native] peoples'. What he had to say about Christianity in mid-nineteenth-century Java and what it 'meant' has largely been ignored.
25. The Church was built in 1852, and accommodated both Protestant and Catholic congregations. See 'Algemeen Verslag Residentie Pekalongan over het Jaar 1857', 67, Arsip Daerah, Arsip Nasional Republik Indonesia.

26. Residentie Pekalongan 1818 and 1823, NA, MvK, inv. Nr. 3113. For nearly all men the place of birth was given. In 1823 there were twenty-seven new names, but eleven of these were boys, sixteen to eighteen years of age, who were not counted in 1819. Since only men were accounted for in the standard statistics or list of residents at the time, we are far better informed about males than females.

27. *Regeeringsalmanak* 1835, 1845.

28. All calculations on migration are based on *Regeeringsalmanak* 1852, 1857, 1860, and the 'census' of 1855 (which also provides ethnicity, age and occupation). Because the *Regeerings Almanak* only provides the occupations of civil servants, it is not possible to give these for the emigrants in 1852 to 1855 and immigrants 1855 to 1860.

29. In the age group under 16, there were 21 boys with a European father and Indo-European mother, and 48 boys of whom both parents were Indo-European. In the age group 16 to 30 the numbers were 4 and 26 respectively.

30. Among the largest Indo-European families long residing in Pekalongan (Anthonijsz, Pechler, Jansz, Toorop, Westhoff and Meijer, all with more than ten members present) there may have been a survival strategy in their migration pattern. Three of them had members working in the sugar local industry and the number of adult males and females was about equal. The other three families had at least twice as many adult females compared to males. This suggests an emigration of male members of the families, who had not obtained a job in the local sugar industry.

31. See 'Memorie van klagten tegen den tegenwoordigen Resident van Pekalongan, Praetorius, September 7, 1837', in Arsip Nasional Republik Indonesia, Bt. 7/9/1837–16.

32. The marriage register of Pekalongan (1829–1856) also mentions Johanna A. Kleijn marrying Assistant-Resident J. de Jongh Hemelrijk Tak in 1835 and Susanna Cornelius marrying the widower Jan T. Halkema, sugar manufacturer in 1844. See Janssen, *De Burgerlijke Stand van Pekalongan. Geboorteregisters (1821)(1828–1868)*.

33. At the same time and in the same town there were children of European fathers who were physically indiscernible from the 'official' children, but not acknowledged, and therefore not included in any statistics of Europeans. Their number is unknown. Some of them were acknowledged later, usually when the parents eventually decided to marry.

34. Van Marle, 'De groep der Europeanen in Nederlands-Indië', 118.

35. Cooper and Stoler, *Tensions of Empire*, 34.

5

SUGAR AND DYNASTY IN YOGYAKARTA

Ulbe Bosma

Today, thousands of tourists swarm Yogyakarta's palace, which is the Sultan's *kraton*, buy silver souvenirs for which the city is famous and visit the miraculous Burubudur. Guides may tell them that the Sultan's modernist court played a central role in any transitional phase of modern Indonesia, but they probably say very little about the sugar colony that underpinned its power. By contrast, I will focus on how a select group of planters made their fortune and developed their sugar factories from the 1860s onwards.[1] Less than twenty-five years later the production of the Principalities – Yogyakarta and Surakarta together – made up 17 percent of the total Java sugar export.[2] Sugar helped to sustain the splendour of the palace of the Sultan of Yogyakarta (and for that matter of adjacent Surakarta), which was restored after the *kraton* had been plundered in 1812 and had then deteriorated during the Java War (1825 to 1830). My narrative concentrates on a few important nineteenth-century Yogya families, who were considered to be Europeans under law, but usually had Javanese grandmothers or even mothers and were members of the Sultan's entourage. This racially mixed group of entrepreneurs of Yogyakarta were understandably treated by the Sultan as beloved members of his entourage as they guaranteed his fortune.

My history of the emergence of the sugar industry in Yogyakarta between 1830 and 1910 calls into question an historical orthodoxy. It is a well-known fact that in 1884 sugar prices plummeted world-wide, marking the beginning of a rapid concentration of ownership of sugar estates in the Dutch East Indies.[3] It has been widely accepted that after 1884 metropolitan banks took over the old Indies sugar factories and refurbished them into modern capitalist enterprises. The present argument, however, is that the year 1884 as a moment of rupture has been overstated. There was undeniably a rapid development of the Java sugar industry in the final decade of the nineteenth century, but much of this revolution was the result of a continuous process of innovation from the 1830s onwards.[4]

The image of the pre-1884 Indies planters as orientalised landed gentry, whose careless lifestyle was supplanted by white efficiency after 1884 needs to be revisited. The image is so widely held because it is so plausible. It is supported by the assumption that the opening of the Suez Canal brought the blessing of large numbers of expatriates and, in particular, white women's civilisation to the Dutch East Indies. The image of white saviours depicts the already present society of often racially mixed planters falling prey to the relentless march of reason in the age of imperialism. But the simple fact is that neither expatriates nor their female kin came in large numbers before the First World War. The proposition that metropolitan capital appropriated the sugar industry after 1884 has never been put to test. The historiographical orthodoxy simply assumes the metropolitan take-over as a cornerstone of the master narrative of European colonial expansion.[5] On closer examination, this assumption proves to be misguided.

This Euro-centric bias is not very different from the one that considered the plantation holders in the West Indies or Caribbean as conservative to the bone and with a strong distaste for innovation. For sure, the image of the traditional, Seigneurial planter is not entirely unfounded. For Java it goes back to the time of the Dutch East India Company and the British inter-regnum, when land around Batavia was sold or given as a fief to their high servants. The State Cultivation System, implemented in 1830s, was meant to ease out this type of landlord, whom Governor-General G.A.G.Ph. Van der Capellen had called 'a parasite plant' in 1823: curling like a liana between the Javanese peasantry and colonial government, tapping off precious resources from both.[6] The Cultivation System was not, however, extended to the semi-independent Principalities Surakarta and Yogyakarta, leaving room for an emerging local planter class. This planter class was racially mixed, European in outlook but at the same time very familiar with life at the courts.

Yogyakarta's sugar economy was financed through family capital that was accumulated through the production of indigo. Only in the course of the nineteenth century this product was replaced by sugar. But before dealing with this transformation into a true Sugarlandia, I shall outline how the social and family culture of this plantocracy was inscribed by its Javanese aristocratic environment, and the way in which economic and political interests and values determined perceptions of ethnicity and tradition. I will occasionally refer to Surakarta to contextualize the experience of Yogyakarta. I will furthermore argue that 1884 did not constitute a rupture in Yogya's Sugarlandia. The final part of the chapter will address the issue of the singularity of the history of Yogyakarta's planter class and argue that a Creole planter class was not a phenomenon unique to the area. Indeed, it was paralleled elsewhere in the colony, including areas where the Dutch had ruled directly and the Cultivation System had held sway. Furthermore, it was also able to survive throughout the nineteenth century.

The Principalities

No doubt the landleasers of the Principalities were perfect 'nouveaux riches'. The affluent plantocracy originated from a small European community, which consisted of no more than 113 adult men and their families at the end of the British inter-regnum in 1815.[7] Some of them were retired military men from the Surakarta and Yogyakarta garrisons, others served the Sunan of Surakarta or the Sultan of Yogyakarta as officers of their guard, trumpeters or coachmen. The majority, however, made ends meet as petty traders, shop keepers, clerks, schoolmasters, surgeon-vaccinators, blacksmiths, barbers, carpenters and so on.

Their lives thoroughly changed under the administration of Resident H.G. Nahuys van Burgst (1816 to 1822, 1827 to 1830). In the eighteenth century the princes had sometimes leased small plots of land to their European employees or relatives to grow vegetables, but Nahuys used his connections with English trading houses in Semarang and Batavia and with the princes to negotiate large scale contracts for leasing land. He practically acted on his own account, which explains the ire of Governor-General Van der Capellen when he learned how English capital and Chinese and Eurasian landleasers had nestled into the politically highly volatile semi-autonomous Principalities. However, his attempt to turn the clock back and root out what he considered to be speculative excesses turned out to be one of the causes of the Java War (1825 to 1830): a devastating jihad led by the Yogya prince Dipanegara. The colonial government soon came to realise that 'parasite plants' were not entirely useless in the Principalities and hence the landleasers were allowed back in 1827. One of the richest and most famous was Johannes Augustines Dezentjé (1797–1839), the son of a French officer and a Javanese mother.[8] During the war he recruited his own army of Javanese soldiers and captured some rebels. It was enough for the grateful Resident Nahuys van Burgst to arrange for him so many leases that he would come to single-handedly produce one third of the coffee in the Principalities. In addition, Dezentjé produced some sugar and, probably, tobacco. He refurbished his house in Ampel as a palace in the style of the Javanese grandees and he installed an impressive *gamelan* (a Javanese orchestra) in his mansion. He never went out without a retinue of *prajoerits* (Javanese soldiers), and fashioned himself as a caring father for his people. Adding to his oriental reputation was his wedding in 1835 to a princess from the Sunan's court and his knowledge of the language and customs of the local population.

Dezentjé was nonetheless a shrewd entrepreneur, who was keeping up appearances to attract labour to the thinly populated hills where he wanted to grow his coffee. He was also the first in the Principalities to invest in large-scale sugar production. Via his business partner, Gillian Maclaine, he signed a three-year contract with the NHM (Nederlandsche Handel-Maatschappij) involving a formidable advance payment of 1,181,000 guilders, of which 840,000 had to be invested in sugar production.[9] He soon got into deep financial trouble. One may immediately think of his lavish style, as Dezentjé's partner Gillian Maclaine explains, in his letter to his brother in Scotland of 1837: 'Dezentjé is an extensive coffee and sugar planter, with a gross income of upwards of [pounds] 30,000 a year, and yet I can't keep him out of debt. His failing is an all-too-common one to require any particular description'. But from the same letter it appears that Dezentjé was no longer in charge of his financial situation: 'I have however put him on an allowance, and he has given me carte blanche to do as I think fit ...', wrote Maclaine.[10] The real cause of his financial difficulties was that sugar required enormous investments, which did not immediately yield benefits. This was probably the conclusion of the representative of the NHM who saw Dezentjé in dire need, but gave him the benefit of the doubt.[11] To complete the disaster Dezentjé himself died in 1839 amidst a coffee crisis, which brought his coffee empire to the brink of collapse. Gillian Maclaine departed for Scotland a year later, a journey that ended tragically as he and his family found a grave in the Indian Ocean in 1840. Dezentjé's heirs would have been penniless and condemned to an anonymous existence in a Surakarta *kampong* (indigenous neighbourhood) contending themselves with a career as clerks or messenger boys, if friends and relatives had not succeeded in returning the estate to the family after buying it at an auction for a very small price.[12]

This brings us to the dynastic character of the estates in the Principalities, as they developed within a European community that was already living in this area in the days of the East Indian Company. Moreover, the plantation economy was kept together by an intricate web of family ties. Unintentionally, the Indies government had done its part to create this closed shop as it decided to exclude Chinese and foreigners (non-Dutch) after the Java War. The colonial government followed its national interest and wanted only Dutch landleasers.[13] Also barred were the European smallholders who were not able to produce export crops, of which coffee (in Surakarta) and indigo (in Yogyakarta) were the most important until the 1860s.[14] Interestingly enough, however, the so-called provisional regulations of 1839 also stipulated that the landleasers in the Principalities had to behave themselves as Javanese noblemen. Although it was quite impossible to match the exuberance of Dezentjé, adapting to local mores would not have caused too much hardship to the landleasers.

Yogyakarta and Surakarta were both marked by a dynastic business history in which ethnicity was defined in terms of entrepreneurial culture. Another marked feature was that it was not based upon an influx of metropolitan capital but upon local accumulation. I shall deal with each of these features (dynasty, ethnicity and capital) separately in the following sections of this chapter.

The Napoleon of Yogyakarta and His Relatives

The Yogyakarta entrepreneurs followed the landleasing regulations of 1839 to the utmost satisfaction of the Indies government. In that respect, Yogyakarta was in a far better position to produce a stable, locally based and racially mixed plantation society than Surakarta. The available area for landleasing was much smaller and there was a highly accessible court whose Sultan personally knew all the landleasers of his realm. That the Yogya planters remained a closed circle can be demonstrated by looking at the lists of registered landleasers. Taking the list of 1865, for example, I can attribute 42 of the 53 plantations to families, who lived in the Principalities during the British inter-regnum (1811 to 1815). The position of the Yogyakarta old families was stronger than that of their kin in Surakarta, where only 65 of the 102 estates were still in the hands of the same families.[15] The old Yogyakarta planters' families, who all had Javanese blood ties, were closely intermarried. The undisputed leader of this clan was George Weijnschenk (1811 to 1878), whose photograph betrays his almost Napoleonic arrogance, and who was well connected to the court and, via his brother and sisters was directly related to the other important Yogyakarta families: Baumgarten, Dom, Raaff, Stralendorff, Kläring, and Wieseman.

This relationship between the landleasers and the *kraton* became part of the court protocol in the course of the nineteenth century.[16] The landleasers had to attend the important events at the Yogya court, i.e. the *garebag puasa* (the end of Ramadan) and the birthdays of the Sultan and the crown prince. These festivities commenced with a tour in carriages around Yogya city: first the Sultan and the Resident, followed by the princes, the Sultan's elephant, the Resident's staff and the landleasers. The ceremony was concluded by toasts to the well being of the usual imperial figureheads. When the glasses were emptied, the entire entourage sat down to play cards. This gathering gave the appearance of being informal but was in fact a strictly regulated event. In the Resident's presence the fixed stakes for the card games did not exceed twenty-five guilders, but after his withdrawal the Sultan and the landleasers raised the stakes to a 100 guilders and continued to play cards for a few more hours. In the old days, the entire Sultan's entourage went to the Resident's house to have dinner, leaving the Sultan's elephant strolling in the Resident's garden amidst the Buddha statues. In the 1890s, when the colonial state was almost at its apex, this part of the ceremony was apparently dismissed as too casual and not in accordance with the court's dignity.[17]

Needless to say, this public display was to ritualise a colonial order that was indisputably new. The legitimacy of this order depended upon the ability to demarcate European and Javanese spheres and to unite them simultaneously. The principle of distinct spheres was embodied in the practice of interpreters, who translated the toasts and speeches at public events. It symbolized the colonial assumption that relations between the European colonial sphere and indigenous traditional sphere could not exist unmediated. But the landleasers and courts of the Principalities did not need intermediaries. Scarce fragments of George Weijnschenk's correspondence, for example, demonstrate that he had an intimate knowledge of what was going on at the court.[18] The Javanese side of the colonial binary yields abundant evidence that European con- sumption goods and knowledge of Dutch had spread over the *kraton*. Exchanges of gifts and particularly the gesture of the Sultan to house the Masonic Lodge 'Mataram' – that had been founded by the Weijnschenk clan – at the *kraton* illuminate the intimate and evolving relationship between the landleasers and the Yogyakarta court. The Lodge became a place where mem- bers of the high nobility of Yogyakarta, including even the Javanese prince Paku Alam V, met their friends.[19]

Meanwhile, many landleasers lived with and also married Javanese women, mostly of quite humble origins, which might point to the existence of a zone in which domestic service and sexual relations became blurred. In this respect Yogyakarta was not an exception to patterns in other plantation societies, where rich planters lived in concubinage. Nonetheless, it was probably unthinkable in a plantation society in the West Indies that planters' sons mar- ried after years of concubinage with their (former) domestic servants. In the second part of the nineteenth century at least twelve Yogyakarta planters mar- ried their Javanese partners. Among them were George Weijnschenk and his son George Lodewijk. This happened usually after their partners had become mothers of their children and they obviously no longer expected to find a young partner from their own milieu. A marriage was costly and it is there- fore not surprising that only wealthier members of the European society bothered to marry their Javanese or Chinese partners to make their children their lawful heirs.[20]

George Weijnschenk, in fact, married three times and his marriages demonstrate how marital arrangements were in keeping with dynastic strate- gies of the wealthiest planters. As a young man George married Maria Dorothea Baumgarten, an alliance that connected the two most important Yogyakarta Creole families. His brother and sisters were married also within the proper Yogyakarta milieu. George's first wife died within a year, after which he lived for thirteen years with the Javanese *Ramag* or *Boesoeg* (give translation), who gave birth to ten children. He married her in 1850, adver- tising his wedding as an act to legalise his children.[21] George survived her and subsequently married Wilhelmina Krämer, the widow of his deceased brother, who gave him one son. Even though the couple became legally separated within a year after their marriage, the Weijnschenk empire was preserved as a family enterprise.

A summary of George's marital career does not, however, present the full picture. European visitors to the Indies had stories about wealthy planters who maintained harems.[22] Although we do not have any records to prove this in the case of George Weijnschenk, we can deduct from his will that he had four children who had been legally adopted by his brother-in-law Pieter Dom. These children carried the surname Weijnschenk-Dom and each of them received upon George's death a house and 100,000 guilders.[23] Polygamy was not a secret thing in Java and probably fairly unproblematic in an over-whelmingly Muslim environment. By contrast, the planters daughters were expected to marry a white newcomer. They were well educated at private schools, which were available for them in the major cities of the Indies, including Yogyakarta. Officers of the garrisons, medical doctors and representatives of trading houses seemed to be preferred to candidates from their own milieu. As a result the Yogyakarta landleasers' clan both shared the Javanese grandees' way of life and maintained their links with the metropole.

Ethnicity and Enterprise

In nineteenth-century Java, *mestizo* and 'Creole' were still semi-official categories, distinguishing between respectively 'coloured' and 'white' Indies-born persons. In the plantation society of the Principalities we should not, however, read them as racial or even ethnic or cultural markers, but primarily as assessments of entrepreneurial achievements.[24] Hoetink and Mintz might help us to understand better the more or less unconsciously, but strongly culturally, and I would add economically, determined perceptions of racial difference in which white/non-white was the underlying polarity.[25] In the Principalities – and elsewhere on Java for that matter – the white and non-white polarity was translated into Creole and *mestizo*, which constitutes of a demarcation line within the existing social stratification. Moreover, we have to take into account that during the nineteenth century, as Stoler has rightfully observed, more than 80 percent of the Indies European population was born in the colony. Hoetink's famous observation that 'within certain limits of physiological features, white populations are demarcated by economic, cultural and social achievements rather than by racial purity' can aptly be applied to Javanese life.[26]

There is strong support for Hoetink's concept of 'somatic norm image' – that originated from his research in the Caribbean – in reports of the colonial civil servants based in Java's Principalities. According to them, Yogyakarta was a well-organised Creole plantation society, whereas the society of their close relatives in Surakarta was far less disciplined and markedly mestisized. Interestingly enough, European society in Yogyakarta was even more mixed in racial terms than Surakarta. How should one explain this incongruity? The perceptions of civil servants who reported on a regular basis about the social and economic behaviour of European subjects are consistent with the different agricultural mappings of the two Residencies. The agricultural estates of Surakarta were scattered over the Residency and their total acreage was three times as large as that in Yogyakarta, which was far less dispersed and therefore easier to control. Moreover, the production of coffee – the dominant crop in Surakarta – was less thoroughly organised than that of indigo. This explains why in 1860 the Resident praised the diligence of the Yogya indigo planters and their control over production and labour.[27] Surakarta counted many large estates, but also small and marginal planters, who in fact lived from share-cropping and whose wives, usually Indonesian, had to make ends meet by small trade. Quite a few of these marginal planters were not born in the Residency, but had adapted themselves to local life. Observations and comments on the way of life of less successful planters colour the reports of the civil servants on Surakarta: 'A consort, *wayang*, and *gamelan*, neglect of family values following the example of the Javanese grandees [in other words, maintaining a harem] are used to give them prestige which make their estates however prosper less than those of 'orderly' Europeans'.[28]

The observations made in government reports reveal a general pattern of opinion, namely that a Creole is someone who knows how to grow crops for the world market and a *mestizo* is an economically marginalised individual who has trespassed the constructed divide between the colonial and indigenous sphere. Again, these observations can be at variance with the actual degree of racial mixing. To underwrite my contention about the applicability of the concept of 'somatic norm image' in the Javanese context, it might be helpful to say something about the observers, in this case, the Dutch civil servants, a substantial minority of whom were also born in the Indies, and most of them of mixed origin. Hence, the Indies-born wealthy planters might only experience in Europe what it meant not to be labelled white. Indeed, much to his surprise, one of the Yogyakarta landleasers discovered during a trip on the Rhine that he was met with some reservation by the polite society on board.[29] It all depends, of course, upon the perspective and the colour of the observer's yardstick.

Recycling Capital

C.L.R. James reminded us forty years ago how the dazzling fortunes generated by Saint-Domingue in the 1780s created the economic basis for the French Revolution. It was against the grain of the general assumption that the development of plantations was financed from metropolitan sources.[30] Like their counterparts in the Caribbean region, the emerging sugar estates in the Principalities were not the result of metropolitan capital moving overseas to make itself productive through colonial exploitation, but founded upon local accumulation of capital.

Export agriculture in Surakarta and Yogyakarta commenced with Chinese and English capital that had been accumulated in the opium trade in Asia.[31] By the late 1830s the semi-governmental Nederlandsche Handel-Maatschappij (Netherlands Trade Society) became active in these Residencies, but that was only for one decade. After the collapse of the Dezentjé empire, the NHM retreated from the Principalities. The small rivulet of capital that came from the metropole when the Cultivation System was nearing its end, in the early 1860s, was insignificant in comparison to the capital that was in the estates of the Principalities. How then was the development of export agriculture in the Principalities financed? The question is hard to answer, because of the lack of nineteenth-century administrative records of the estates in the Principalities. In the absence of a conclusive answer, however, I tend to agree with Vincent Houben when he points out that central Java succeeded in meeting its own capital demands.[32] Obviously, family relationships played an important role in pooling business profits from good years. Finally, one must assume that the ascendancy of 'King Sugar' was based upon earlier profits made in crops that were less capital intensive. It is known for example, that just before the introduction of sugar in Yogyakarta, in the late 1850s, the indigo planters made huge profits because of the indigo uprising in Bengal. In the same period the Surakarta coffee found favourable markets.

The Semarang banker G.L. Dorrepaal (1816–1883) became a genius at pooling business profits. Son of a ship-owner, who was sailing to Java from at least 1814 onwards, he arrived on Java in 1840. Although his Dutch shipping background may have provided him with some means, a more important share of his starting capital might have come through his marriage a few years later with Ludovica Manuel (1817–1896), who was a member of an influential and wealthy family. Her sister was married to Johan Frederik Arnold, founder of the Arnold trading house and connected to the heir of the incredibly wealthy Augustina Michiels, daughter of Major Jantji, the West Java landlord. Ludovica's brother lived on Peterongan, in the vicinity of Semarang, with his Chinese wife and a small harem. It must have been these connections that provided Dorrepaal with the starting capital to materialise his visionary ambition. After thirty years of hard work he had become by far the most important man of central Java, seconded by George Weijnschenk, who was epitomised as the Napoleon of Yogyakarta. When Dorrepaal died in 1883, his bank could boast about having a clientele of 22 sugar, 38 coffee and 53 tobacco and/or indigo estates, most of which were located in Surakarta and Yogyakarta. In addition, Dorrepaal owned, or participated in, two dozen estates in the Principalities.[33]

When from the early 1860s onwards the State Cultivation System became gradually replaced by private enterprise, the Principalities were ready for a transition process towards the production of sugar. Thanks to Dorrepaal's active role, but also strongly endorsed by the Sultan and the Sunan, the first railway of Java, connecting the port town of Semarang with the Principalities, was under construction to reach its destination, Surakarta, in 1870. Whereas in Surakarta the railway brought many new plantations (quadrupling to 192 estates from 1855 to 1875, declining again to 133 in 1900), developments in Yogyakarta were far more stable, as the total number of plantations stayed between 43 and 60. The simple explanation is that there was no room for further expansion in that Residency. Dorrepaal, for example, did most of his acquisitions in Surakarta and only four in Yogyakarta. The old Yogyakarta families carried on with their indigo, the profits of which indubitably enabled them to enter the sugar market at their own pace. Whatever the differences between Yogyakarta and Surakarta, the railway had been crucial for the development of the sugar industry: to bring in the equipment and to transport the sugar to Semarang .

In the beginning of the 1880s, the twenty-seven sugar factories in the Principalities were good for 17 percent of the Java sugar production. Aggregate figures must suffice as reports on the family plantations, let alone their administrations, of the Principalities are practically absent. But it is known that the landleasers of these Residencies were considered to be the leading entrepreneurs in the Indies export agriculture in the 1870s and 1880s. Surakarta and Yogyakarta organised the first Indies Agricultural Congresses. In the early 1880s their sugar producers began to organise themselves and tried to establish a sugar research station. Just before the sugar crisis of 1884, the Indies government granted a concession to connect twelve Yogya sugar factories (practically all of them) by horse trail with the railway station.[34] Meanwhile, the sugar producers of the Principalities had managed to reduce the production costs of their sugar below the average costs of Java.[35] Whether or not this should be attributed to low labour costs – low in comparison to other Residencies of Java – is not entirely clear.

Labour Regime

Elsewhere in this book Sri Margana deals extensively with the relationship between the expanding sugar economy in Yogyakarta and the local population. The point to be made here is that these landleasers' exploitative attitudes towards the local population were not mitigated by the fact that they were sons or grandsons of Javanese women. They were probably not as brutal as slaveholders, who went down in history as sadistic masters. The old nineteenth-century planters of Java are usually depicted as relatively benevolent, although autocratic rulers. One should, however, not make too much of this benevolence, as the landleasers considered the local Javanese of their estates primarily as a cheap labour force. Growing indigo is exceptionally labour intensive and burdensome for the local population. From the onset, the landleasers did not tolerate any interference of the Civil Service, the help of which was often invoked by the local Javanese, as Margana argues, in their affairs. Two Yogyakarta Residents, R. Fillietaz de Bousquet and H.F. Buschken had lost their position as a result of a conflict with a landleaser; another, C.P. Brest van Kempen, was supported by the colonial government in Batavia, but went insane because of all the obstruction and social ostracism.[36] Peasant resistance was met by the landleasers taking the law into their own hands, flogging unwilling peasants with a stick or locking them in a wooden block. The records suggest an intensifying struggle between landleasers, government officials and the peasant communities in the second half of the nineteenth century. Through this struggle the image of the landleasers as autocratic but fatherly rulers over their people became tarnished. This also happened to George Weijnschenk in 1873 when newspapers reported that he put a *bekel* (village notable and tax collector) in his private prison, after peasants on his lands had put up a massive resistance against the *corvée*.[37]

Different racial backgrounds of the planters, in other words, did not produce different plantation regimes. It seems that white arrogance as the source of colonial brutality is still a key historical orthodoxy, but that can only be based upon a very selective colonial reading. Brazil's historiography takes for example a completely different position, since Gilberto Freyre wrote his famous *The Masters and the Slaves*, in which he made planters' sadism and miscegenation the foundational categories of nineteenth-century Brazil.[38] The combination of white and ruthless was an old colonial myth in Asia, which became reinvigorated in the early 1990s, when a renewed interest in the harsh labour regimes of tobacco estates in east Sumatra went hand in hand with a shift of focus from political economy to social constructions of colonial domination based on notions of racial superiority.[39] This shift, of course, was part of the general discursive, or linguistic, turn in studies on colonialism. Sure, an important difference between the lot of migrant labourers in Deli and that of peasants of the Principalities is that in the latter case village and family structures were still in place, and that, unlike the coolies in Sumatra, the villagers of the Principalities could migrate. But by focussing on some of the most salient aspects of the labour regime itself, it is difficult to see the difference between the private prisons, which have been described by J.L. Th. Rhemrev and brought to light again by Jan Breman, and those in the late nineteenth-century Principalities.[40] The basis of sugar factories was their total control of scarce labour and water, which might explain their display of naked power instead of the conspicuous consumption shown in the past by Dezentjé. Coffee and tea was usually planted in scarcely populated areas uphill, to which labour could not be forced but needed to be attracted. The crops made the difference, not the personal background of the planter, as the comparison between Yogyakarta and Surakarta has already demonstrated.

Hence, I would suggest that objective economic and geographical factors receive proper attention as determinants of labour relations, whereas social constructions of race should not be dissolved from the political economy. The struggle to control labour was what determined business culture, including the planters' relationship with colonial authorities. In Yogyakarta, as well as in the tobacco districts of eastern Java and east Sumatra, the entrepreneurs were high-handed and treated colonial authorities with utter contempt. Whether the entrepreneur's mother was Javanese, Dutch or German, does not seem to have been of much relevance.[41]

Crisis, What Crisis?

In fact, the argument about the irrelevance of racial mixing with respect to the behaviour of the local planters' clan of the Principalities, is just one of the pieces of the main argument against the overstatement of the rupture of 1884. Another important part of that argument is my contention that the impact of white Europeans and overseas capital by the end of the nineteenth century has been generally overstated. Elsewhere in this book G. Roger Knight and Arthur van Schaik argue that the racial composition of the sugar industry staff did not substantially change over the nineteenth and early twentieth centuries. Machinists and other technical staff for the sugar factories had travelled from Europe to Java from the early nineteenth century onwards. As for the role of overseas capital, I have already argued that it hardly played a role in the genesis of the emergence of estates in the Principalities. Did this change after 1884?

To answer that question, one needs to establish what happened in 1884. It was primarily a banking crisis, caused by a sudden fall of the sugar prices, which bankrupted trading houses. The agricultural banks were practically bankrupted too when they tried to rescue the planters by buying up their sugar and had to be restructured. The Semarang house of Dorrepaal, which was just in a restructuring process after its founder had died the year before, ran into trouble relatively late and found the money markets, at least in the Indies, depleted of capital.[42] It was the only bank that disappeared from the scene, but it is questionable whether it would have survived its founder anyway. In late 1886, the Yogyakarta sugar producers and clients, Dorrepaal Raaff, Weijnschenk, Kraag and Kroemer, did not wait for the bankruptcy of their bank but went to the Nederlandsche Handel-Maatschappij. The great sugar planters of the Principalities survived the crisis, but were not interested in keeping alive the bank that had served them so well since the 1850s.

So, what did really happen? Did 1884 bring a victory of metropolitan commercial interests over Creole sugarlords? Did these banks annex these family enterprises and reconstitute them into PLCs (Public Limited Company) as is generally believed? The picture is far more nuanced and needs to be considered in the context of the relationship between the planters and their suppliers of capital during the entire nineteenth century. Let there be no misunderstanding about who came out of this crisis as a winner. The Nederlandsche Handel-Maatschappij did. It tightened its inspection regime over sugar factories to which it supplied capital, and even appointed its own managers to the estates of its clients if the occasion were there. This example was followed by other banks. But supervision over a production process is not the same as taking over in terms of property. Yogyakarta is a particular point in case.

In the 1870s and 1880s, the founders of the Yogyakarta estates left their estates to their children. What we see is a gradual transition from individual property to family-owned estates. The crisis of 1884 came after the second generation had taken over from the successful generation of landleasers of the 1850s and 1860s. In the 1880s the PLC was still only one of the options to secure family ownership, and only few used this one. The sons of George Weijnschenk, for example, responded quite differently to the 1884 crisis. A few years before in 1879, at the death of their father, all 'legitimate' children had got their share. The two eldest sons had already succeeded their father in business and had started to buy out their sisters and younger brothers. The 1884 crisis forced them to stop their instalments. They persuaded their brothers and sisters either to accept a redemption or have a share in the estates.[43] The example of the Weijnschenk brothers is important as it points both to a transitional phase between the patriarchal landleaser and corporate capitalism, and to the possibility of considering this corporate capitalism as an extension of family business, which would simply erase the entire idea of a 'rupture' at the end of the nineteenth century.

Let us have a look at this. From the *Regeeringsalmanak* it appears that in 1880 fourteen of the 33 estates were registered under joint family ownership.[44] How and when did these family enterprises become PLCs? The case of the Lipoero Sugar factory, owned by the Berends family, is a very interesting one in this regard. In 1897, it was one of the first Yogyakarta estates that were transferred to an estate company (PLC), with a capital of 600,000 guilders. But its capital was divided in ten shares of 60,000 guilders each and its board of governors consisted of members of the Berends family, which strongly suggests that Lipoeroe was still a family-owned business. Now, most striking is that the overwhelming majority of the PLCs of Yogyakarta were established after 1902, when the sugar market was rapidly improving. The *centrals*, which began to dominate Yogyakarta's Sugarlandia in the same period, might have been the result of better prospects for Java sugar.

Why, in spite of evidence that suggests continuity, does historiographical orthodoxy still confronts us with an image of rupture in the 1880s? I shall first deal with the question of how this idea of rupture came into existence and then proceed with my case for continuity.

Seigneurial Nostalgia

The cultural style of the Creole planters' families has been an important reference point in the memories of the Indies community. An overspending
lifestyle, with many servants – and until 1860 domestic slaves,[45] huge houses
and hunting, appear time and again as essentials of the Indies way of life. Its
archetype is the grand seigneur, the *toean besar* like Dezentjé, which continued to exist even in the later days of George Weijnschenk. This lifestyle is supposedly contradictory to modern capitalism and modern imperialism, and
hence not resistant to the exigencies of the world market and Western efficiency. In spite of their claims to the contrary, followers of cultural studies
tend to emphasise rather than debunk the passive role of the orient. As a
result the picture of white colonial presence as relentlessly efficient has even
been reinforced over the past decade. In the case of Java's Sugarlandia this
tendency to 'privilege the colonial discourse' is particularly strong, because of
a selective reading of the cultural legacy of the old Creole colonial society.

First, the Indies past appears through statues to remember wealthy
planters, reinforced by the searches for aristocratic heritage amongst planters'
families, and the numerous stories about mild patriarchal lords who cared for
their subjects as if they were their children. But this does not point to tradition per se but to a tradition that, if not invented, was at least partly constructed, and for good reasons. The history of Java's plantation society is one
of historical emptiness and its heroes were almost without exception of humble origin. In less than 50 years a large-scale sugar industry emerged that was
able to compete on the world market and made Java the second largest sugar
producer behind Cuba. Hence, rapid change invoked the need for strong traditions. And these began to play a new role after the First World War, when
immigration from Europe strengthened white domination. The Indies life of
tempo doeloe (the old days) became a *topos* for Creole writers and journalists
to preserve a domain of cultural and historical integrity. Quite a few important Indies families asked professional genealogists to investigate and map
their pedigree. In the case of the Weijnschenk family, the genealogist Lach de
Bère did his job to the fullest satisfaction of the family and produced a nice
patrician pedigree with a family coat of arms. But even though the name Weijnschenk suggests a background of vineyards in Württemberg, grandfather
Leopold was born in Sankt Pölten, probably in a shoemaker's house.[46]

Second, fin de siècle novelists contributed to the image of the decaying
Indies Creole society at the beginning of the twentieth century. The most
famous novel is Louis Couperus's *Stille Kracht* (1900) (Hidden Force), a title
that brings us immediately into the animistic world of Java. Couperus intro-
duces his readers into the world of the De Luce (Dezentjé) family and depicts
an atmosphere of decadence and inertia. The grandchildren of the legendary
Dezentjé were, however, solid entrepreneurs and owners of the biggest
estates in Surakarta. Couperus was a novelist and enjoyed his freedom to

construe an atmosphere, which he expected would intrigue his readers. It did and continues to do so. The book turned into a film and was broadcast on Dutch television in the 1970s! The same atmosphere of decay permeates another novel of *tempo doeloe* by P.A. Daum, who, contrary to Couperus, was dedicated to literary naturalism. His *Ups and Downs in het Indische Leven* (1892) (Ups and Downs in Indies Life) narrates the story of the sons of a wealthy West Java landowners family that is prone to misery and decline because of their breathtaking financial escapades. But these stories are part of the fin de siècle pessimism about survival chances of the white race in a tropical environment. This discourse was just a part of the pseudo-Darwinist fairy tale of the infertility of mixed-bloods.

Other – indubitably more boring – sources are needed for an insight into what happened to the Yogyakarta estates between 1884 and the First World War. These are the 43 estates of 1865 that were owned by the old Yogyakarta families, thirty-six survived the full period between 1865 and 1916. They are found in the *Regeeringsalmanak*. To these one may add three other estates founded by members of these old Yogyakarta families between 1865 and 1880.[47] The transformation from indigo to sugar had been completed in half a century as the diagram below shows:

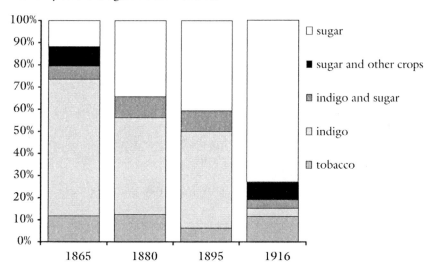

Figure 5.1. The Advance of Sugarlandia in Yogyakarta as a percentage of the Old Yogyakarta Family Estates

Of the 36 estates of 1916 that already existed in 1865, five had been merged with other estates. Only three of the remaining estates had persons as registered owners, the other 28 were transformed into PLCs. The *centrals* had put their stamp on Yogyakarta too. In 1865 there were 11 sugar mills, 14 in 1880, 16 in 1895, and 15 in 1916. However, by 1916, an additional 9 estates delivered their sugar to the factories, and had become satellite estates.

Meanwhile, the congruence between the names of the estate owners of 1865 and those of the governors of 1916 is striking. Let me exclude the estates, which grew indigo, tobacco or coffee, most of which were owned by the *Klattensche Cultuurmaatschappij*, the heirs of Dorrepaal by 1916. Of the fifteen sugar factories six can be identified as still belonging to the old families (Weijnschenk, Berends, Broese van Groenou, Pijnacker Hordijk (two factories) and Enger). The nine satellite estates are owned by members of the Baumgarten (2), Weijnschenk (4, Dom and Enger (1) families. Another one belonged to the Klattensche Cultuurmaatschappij of the Dorrepaal heirs. The two sugar factories of the Raaff family might still be in their hands around 1916. The Kläring and Kraag families apparently sold or lost their estate to the *Cultuurmaatschappij der Vorstenlanden*, and the Kraag/Van Prehn family to the *Klattensche Cultuurmaatschappij*. These transfers of property, however, took place after 1904, which suggests that these families had seized the opportunity to get a good price for their estates, now that prospects were improving. In other words, not the crisis but the good prospects for sugar after the Brussels Sugar Convention (1902) led to a rapid concentration of power in the hands of a few families, and to the secular intertwining of their interests with those of the metropolitan banking capital, which was represented by the *Cultuurmaatschappij der Vorstenlanden*. One man, J.M. Pijnacker Hordijk – brother of the Governor-General, brother in-law of Broese van Groenou, and son in-law of Wieseman, stands out as a powerbroker. He was governor on the board of four out of the fifteen Yogyakarta sugar factories, one in Surakarta and three in the neighbouring Residency of Banjumas.[48]

The old Creole family network of Yogyakarta had not disappeared. Details on the staffing of the sugar factories are scarce, but even if we may expect that technical staff was recruited from Europe, there were also many Creole employees, and the managers on the spot mostly belonged to those families that already lived in the Principalities in 1815. One of these was running the large sugar estate and factory 'Tantong Tirto' of Wolter Broese van Groenou, brother in-law of J.M. Pijnacker Hordijk. A picture of the staff of the factory of the latter, 'Bantool' shows us a group of employees of whom most were members of old Yogyakarta families.[49] A few years before the First World War, a visitor described the estate as a complete village of houses for the European staff that had been constructed amidst the Buddha statues. During the sugar campaign each day eight railway wagons took the sugar to the station of the Nederlands-Indische Spoorwegmaatschappij (Netherlands Railway Company), which carried it further to Semarang.[50]

How Did the Principalities Fit into the Larger Picture of Java?

The question is whether this Yogyakarta network was unique in the way in which it survived the 1884 crisis. Since Furnivall's seminal *Netherlands India* (1944), one is inclined to believe that the agricultural crisis of 1884, which was caused by a sudden and drastic fall of the world sugar prices, inaugurated a comprehensive reorganisation of the Java sugar industry. Basing himself upon an earlier analysis by the historian of the *Javasche Bank*, Furnivall concludes: 'The general effect of all these reconstructions was to place [Dutch guilders] f 30 to f 35 million of new capital from the Netherlands at the disposal of the credit institutions in India.'[51] This line had its reverberations in almost every text on late nineteenth-century colonial Indonesia: Dutch banks provided the means for a take-over of the sugar industry from an obsolete largely Creole sugar plantocracry in order to transform it into a modern and efficient agricultural enterprise. On this reading, the Nederlandsche Handel-Maatschappij imposed its system of management, laboratories (*proefstations*) from the late 1880s onwards, putting the sugar industry effectively in metropolitan hands.

This perception is flawed for a number of reasons. First, as I argued for Yogyakarta, one needs to differentiate between managerial control and ownership, between banks and estate ownership. The second objection is that one should always be careful to tag a particular nationality to capital. The 30 million guilders that were involved in the restructuring of the agricultural banks from 1884 to 1885 were not entirely from the Dutch government. Indeed, an important part of this capital came from savings that had been made in the Indies. Third, the millions Furnivall mentions were not new capital, but capital to recover the losses and strengthen the capital base of the agricultural banks. Fourth, it was part of an ongoing process of profits and losses. Just a few years before the agricultural crisis of 1884, in the tobacco crisis of 1876 to 1881, about 26.5 million guilders had been written off.[52] In spite of all these losses, the overall pattern was one of net capital outflow from the Indies to the Netherlands. Between 1870 and 1900, dividends from the Indies were probably so large that capital imports from the Netherlands were not needed, and in addition a net capital outflow from the Indies was generated.[53] Apart from the early years of the Cultivation System, in which the Netherlands made serious investments via its Nederlandsche Handel-Maatschappij, there has been a consistent net capital outflow from the Indies to the Netherlands.[54] These macro observations square nicely with the findings for the local history of the Principalities. I argued that the emerging Yogyakarta sugar industry financed its own entrance into the global sugar economy by using the profits of indigo production to convert their estates into sugar. It was also unique because of its strong financial base, and for that reason, Dorrepaalsche Bank had not been as active here as it had been in Surakarta. If one takes Pekalongan, well researched by G. Roger Knight and Van Schaik, one has by and large the same group of sugar factories in 1910 as around 1880. If these sugar factories are related to families and later to members of the boards of the PLCs, three factories (Adiwerna, Djatibarang, and Kemanglèn) remain tied to the families of the first contractors, O.C. Holmberg de Beckfelt and T. Lucassen. Other Residencies did even better in terms of continuity. In 1910, 9 out of 15 factories in Cheribon and 18 out of 40 in Surabaya were still tied to families of the owners of 1880. These are just rough indications, which should invite for more research into family enterprises in the late nineteenth and twentieth centuries in Sugarlandia. Preliminary findings for the 177 sugar factories that existed in 1910 suggest that half of them, 88, can be directly linked to the old families. In addition, another 22 factories can be linked to Chinese families. The 88 factories that could be linked to old Indies families were not marginalised but developed at the same pace as other factories. There is not much variation in factory output, ranging between 50,000 and 150,000 *pikul*. The average size of the 88 factories that could be linked to the old families was close to 113,000 *pikul* (1 pikul = 61,76 kilograms).[55] In 1910 only 37 of the 177 sugar factories were directly owned by the large *cultuur-banken*, the Nederlandsche Handel-Maatschappij (6), the Nederlandsch-Indische Landbouw Maatschappij (6), the Handelsvereniging Amsterdam (8), the Koloniale Bank (7), de Cultuurmaatschappij der Vorstenlanden (4), and Hoboken (6). Together these companies owned 21 percent of the factories on Java and were good for 23 percent of the production of Java sugar.[56]

There is unmistakably a shift over the period 1880 and 1910, but not as dramatic as one might expect. In 1880, only six factories were directly owned by a metropolitan enterprise, most of them by A. van Hoboken in Rotterdam. The powerful Nederlandsche Handel-Maatschappij had been very reluctant to become directly engaged in sugar production, expecting that beet sugar and Mauritius were looming large and threateningly over any prospects for the Java sugar industry. In 1910, just a few years after the Brussels Sugar Convention (1902), prospects had improved and in the few years before many new investments and many family enterprises – clearly visible in Yogyakarta – were transformed into PLCs. However, there is no such thing as a take-over of sugar estates by metropolitan firms on the scale that Dorrepaal had been taking over plantations in Surakarta in the 1860s and 1870s. In fact, it appears that the sugar landscape was rather consolidated in the early 1880s. One should not underrate the fact that quite a few family-owned factories were in a rather junior position beside the powerful *cultuurbanken* – the Ament sugar factories in Cirebon were largely owned by the NHM as was the Gonsalves sugar factory, Tersana, for example[57] – but this is balanced by the histories of other families, who were still very much in control of the factories, and even became power-brokers, like J.M. Pijnacker Hordijk and P. Eschauzier.

Another important feature is the absence of any geographical differentiation between old and new capital. This in marked contrast with Cuba, where the western part became the area where the large, often American owned firms were operating, or Puerto Rico, where the northern part of the island was dominated by local Creole and/or Spanish entrepreneurs, whereas the northern part was for American investors. Neither was there a sharp difference as in the West Indies, where Trinidad became a location for heavy outside investment and dramatic concentration of ownership within little more than a decade. Here the number of estates declined from 90 firms in 1887 to 39 in 1898, and of which 30 were in the hands of just six enterprises.[58] In contrast, the old sugar families of Java were rather evenly distributed over the entire island: Holmberg de Beckfelt/Hoevenaars, Ament and Gonsalves in Pekalongan/Tegal and Cirebon, Etty/Pereira in Pasuruan and Besuki; Eschauzier in Surabaya, Thurkow/Voute/Dorrepaal in Semarang; Weijnschenk and Wieseman/Broese van Groenou/Pijnacker Hordijk in Yogyakarta. The latter enlarged their field of operations to the adjacent Residency of Banjumas. In the eastern part of Java, plantation agriculture evolved around the Rotterdam group of A. van Hoboken & Zonen and its satellites Reijnst & Vinju, Anemaet & Co., Van Delden, Van Haeften, and the Birnie family.

The question is, why has this continuity not been noted so far? Part of the explanation could be that the leaders of the colonial plantation economy were usually retired managers of plantations. In order to find out who they are, one has to look at their genealogies, instead of their place of residence, as all these rich families were constantly moving within a migration circuit between Java and the Netherlands. Another bias is that research into colonial financial power focuses upon social capital instead of actual production figures. A recent study into the composition of this class by Arjan Taselaar, which aimed at mapping the 'colonial lobby' between 1914 and 1940, selects only companies with more than 3 million guilders of social capital, whose boards of directors were based in the Netherlands.[59] This approach is deeply problematic, as the general policy of family enterprises, which were converted into PLCs, was to keep social capital low. One could even say, the richer the families, the lower the social capital of their estates.

This is not the place to correct Taselaar's in many respects important and excellent study, but if it were done, one would not be surprised if it turned out that the children and grandchildren of these famous Indies *grands seigneurs* had firmly entrenched themselves in what has generally been perceived as the form of metropolitan high finance that allegedly came to dominate the Java sugar industry. The centre of gravity did not change, but the Indies planters' families changed their modus operandi, making themselves less visible behind the anonymity of PLCs.

In less than a century, sugar dominated Java, making itself felt through enormous pressure on the people of Java's countryside and a powerful lobby in the mother country. The way in which these colonial *nabobs* took possession of imperial politics has been so sharply observed by Hobson with regard to the British Empire that I borrow it for the Dutch case:

The South and South-West of England is richly sprinkled with these men, many of them wealthy, most of them endowed with leisure, men openly contemptuous of democracy, devoted to material luxury, social display, and the shallower arts of intellectual life. The wealthier among them discover political ambitions, introducing into our Houses of Parliament the coarsest and most selfish spirit of 'Imperialism', using their imperial experience and connections for their private benefits, and posing as authorities so as to keep the yoke of Imperialism firmly fixed upon the shoulders of the 'nigger'.[60]

Notes

1. This article is partly based upon a joint research project by the author and Dr. Remco Raben, which has been published as: Ulbe Bosma and Remco Raben, *De oude Indische wereld 1500–1920*. (Amsterdam: Bert Bakker 2003.)
2. Mansfelt, *Exportcultures van Ned.-Indië 1830–1937*, 30.
3. The same process occurred in Cuba. Scott, *Slave Emancipation in Cuba*, 208–213.
4. Knight, 'The Visible Hand in *Tempo Doeloe*; Leidelmeijer, *Van suikermolen tot grootbedrijf*; Bosma and Knight, 'Global Factory and Local Field: Convergence and Divergence in the International Cane-Sugar Industry', 5–7.
5. *Volkstelling 1930*, 19; *Jaarcijfers voor het Koninkrijk der Nederlanden 1912*, 17; Post, 'The Kwik Hoo Tong Trading Society of Semarang, Java'.
6. Ottow, 'De oorsprong der conservatieve richting', 238.
7. *Regeeringsalmanak*, 1815.
8. Bosma and Raben, *De oude Indische wereld 1500–1920*, 104.
9. NA, inv. no. 2399, Letter of the President of the Factorij to the President of the NHM, 10 May 1841, no. 7 and 25 May 1841, no. 8, secret.
10. Ardtornisch Papers, Gillian Maclaine to Angus Maclaine, 19–12–1837: this reference was obtained thanks to Roger Knight.
11. Archive NHM, inv. no. 4398, 'Notulen van de directie der Factorij', 12 November 1839.
12. Houben, *Kraton and Kumpeni; Surakarta and Yogyakarta, 1830–1870*, 286.
13. In fact, this policy was also applied to those areas of Java where the Cultivation System was implemented.
14. 'Reglement betreffende de huur en verhuur van gronden voor den landbouw in de rijken van Soerakarta en Djocjakarta', GB 21–12–1857.
15. A reconstruction was made on the basis of the register of estates in the Principalities in the 'Staat der partikuliere landbouwondernemingen', *Regeeringsalmanak*, 1865, 137–45, and Christiaans, *Het gereconstrueerde huwelijksregister van Djokjakarta 1817–1905*.
16. Margana, *Kraton Surakarta dan Yogyakarta, 1796–1874*, 76–109, 288–375.
17. Engelbert van Bevervoorde, 'Eigenaardigheden en bezienswaardigheden', 142; Stark, *Uit Indië, Egypte en het heilige land*, 96.
18. Letter of G. Weijnschenk to H.P. Beresteyn, 11–1–1864, coll. Beresteyn, National Archive, The Hague.
19. Stevens, *Vrijmetselarij en samenleving in Nederlands-Indië en Indonesië 1764–1962*, 39, 184, 215; Bosma 'Citizens of Empire'.
20. Van Marle, 'De groep der Europeanen in Nederlands-Indië', 317.

21. Jean Gelman Taylor cites this announcement, commenting upon its far from delicate wording. See Taylor, *Smeltkroes Batavia*, 180.
22. See for example De Haan, 'De laatste der Mardijkers', and De Haan, *Priangan. De Pre-anger-Regentschappen*, 291.
23. Will of George Weijnschenk, in: Ph. Lach de Bère, *Genealogie van het Nederlandsch Indische geslacht Weijnschenk*, 16–17.
24. Ann Stoler argues: 'The contestations over métissage suggest nothing linear about these developments. Rather, class distinctions, gender prescriptions, cultural knowledge, and racial membership were simultaneously invoked and strategically filled with different meanings for varied projects', see Stoler, 'Sexual Affronts and Racial Frontiers', 521.
25. Mintz, 'Ethnic difference, plantation sameness', 38–41.
26. Stoler, 'Sexual Affronts and Racial Frontiers', 515; Hoetink, *Het patroon van de oude Curaçaose samenleving*, 107.
27. De Resident van Djokjakarta Brest van Kempen, 'NOTA betrekkelijk de landverhuur in de Residentie Djokdjokarta', Bijlage IJ 'Verslag van het beheer en de staat der Oost-Indische bezittingen over 1860', Bijlagen HTK, (1861–1862) 735.
28. Politiek verslag Residentie Soerakarta 1855, 10. inv. no. 111, ANRI.
29. Opstel F.C. van Vreede-Broese van Groenou, coll. KITLV.
30. James, 'French Capitalism and Caribbean Slavery', 47–61.
31. Van Enk, *Britse kooplieden en de cultures op Java*.
32. Houben, *Kraton and Kumpeni*, 263.
33. *Regeeringsalmanak*, 1875, 287–94.
34. *Soerakartasch Nieuws- en Advertentieblad*, 6–9–1884.
35. Van den Berg, *Over de productiekosten van de Java-suiker*, 1.
36. Houben, *Kraton and Kumpeni*, 274–75, 277; National Archive, The Hague, Coll. R. Fillietaz de Bousquet, inv.no. 5
37. *De Vorstenlanden*, 17–5–1873 and 8–7–1873.
38. Freyre, *The Masters and the Slaves*.
39. 'Foreword by Ann Stoler' in: Clerkx and Wertheim, *Living in Deli*.
40. Breman, *Koelies, planters en koloniale politiek*.
41. The comparison with Deli has already been made by Wim Wertheim. See Wertheim, 'Conditions on Sugar Estates in Colonial Java', 274.
42. De Bree, *Gedenkboek van de Javasche Bank*, II, 243.
43. *Mataram*, 25–1–1935.
44. *Regeeringsalmanak*, 1880, 341–43.
45. In the Dutch East Indies slavery was abolished on 1 January 1860.
46. Christiaans, *Het rooms-katholieke doopregister van Semarang 1809–1929*, 2.
47. These were the following estates: Bandjararja, Bedodjo, Barongan, Padokan, Gedjajan, Magoewo, Gesiekan, Kadirodjo, Tantong-Tirto, Wanoedjaja, Moedja-Moedjo, Wioro, Randoegoenting, Sorogedoeg, Siloek Lanteng, Bantol, Lipoero, Poendoeng, Pisangan, the indigo estate of W.T.T. Semster, Tjebongan, Boeloos, Wringing, Demakidjo, Sedajoe, Sonosewoe, Klatjie, Rewoeloe, Medarie, Tempel, Doekoe Pisangan, Kebongagoeng, Sewoegaloor, Ngemplak, Pleret, Kenallan.
48. *Handboek voor cultuur- en handelsondernemingen*.
49. Picture of KITVL collection published in Bosma and Raben, *De oude Indische wereld*, 289.
50. Stark, *Uit Indië, Egypte en het heilige land*.
51. Furnivall, *Netherlands India*, 196–97.
52. De Bree, *Gedenkboek Javasche Bank*, II, 174.
53. Bosch, *De Nederlandsche beleggingen in de Verenigde Staten*, 78.
54. Maddison, 'Dutch Income in and from Indonesia', 26; Eng, *The 'Colonial Drain' from Indonesia*.

55. Transformation of production and property of estates that were registered in the *Regeeringsalmanak* of 1865, 1880, 1895 and the *Handboek voor cultuur- en handelsondernemingen* 5–28, 1893–1916.
56. *Handboek voor cultuur- en handelsondernemingen*, 1910.
57. Taselaar, *De Nederlandse koloniale lobby*, 58–59.
58. Dhanda, 'Labour and Place in Barbados, Jamaica and Trinidad', 243.
59. Taselaar, *De Nederlandse koloniale lobby*, 50.
60. Hobson, *Imperialism. A Study*, 132.

6

HYBRIDITY, COLONIAL CAPITALISM AND INDIGENOUS RESISTANCE: THE CASE OF THE PAKU ALAM IN CENTRAL JAVA

Sri Margana

Introduction

The historiography on peasant resistance in the Javanese countryside has by and large been focused on collective resistance like social movements, violence, cane burnings and strikes. Some of these resistance movements were inspired by a messianic ideology and hopes of a revival of Java's glorious past under the *Ratu Adil* (Just King). Sartono Kartodirdjo's *Peasant Revolts of Banten* characterised these movements as peasant village elites resisting colonial exploitation and situated them in opposition to the plantation economy and the Dutch colonial state.[1] Apart from the fact that Banten was not a particularly important area for Java's plantation economy, which makes the relationship between colonial explanation and the occurrence of peasant resistance in this poor western part of Java rather tangential, an exclusive focus on the conflict between colonial domination and collective resistance would not do justice to the role of elites. It has been argued before, by Jan Breman, that the 'Asian village' is not a homogeneous unit.[2] Vincent Houben, for instance, has pointed to 'intra-Asian' coercion and thus the role of local elites as part of this structure of violence.[3] Moreover, we need to explain why areas with similar degrees of economic oppression did not produce the same level of resistance. When, for example, a widespread labour strike took place in the central Java Principality of Yogyakarta in 1882, it did not reach every part of the Residency. This was in spite of the fact that the strike lasted for at least three months, that it was attended by heavy cane burnings, and that it involved around 10,000 workers from 30 estates in Yogyakarta. The majority of the strikers came from the sugar and indigo plantations of the three main Regencies (i.e. 'sub-districts') of Yogyakarta, Sleman, Kalasan and Bantul. The Adikarto Regency, which was part of the Yogyakarta Residency but the domain of its own princely ruler, the Pakualam, was not affected by the strikes,[4] nor were two estates (Sewu Galur and Sumbernila) that were notoriously exploitative.

Part of the explanation for the differential patterns of resistance in central Java's four Principalities, I will argue, resides in the fact that peasant resistance is not always channelled into collective action, violent resistance, and confrontation with colonial planter domination. Resistance can also be individual (and not only in the sense of diffuse 'everyday forms' or of 'moral economy') but also institutional and juridical, and it can confront colonial elites as well as their native allies (who were not always easy to tell apart). The Principalities of inner Java present an extraordinary context where colonial plantation production came face to face with precolonial institutions that either remained functional – or were given new life by peasant reivindication.

The position of the Principalities was unique in Java, for they enjoyed a semi-autonomous status under Dutch colonial government. While less impacted upon in some respects than areas under direct Dutch rule, the Principalities' villages were hardly static and homogeneous; it was an environment characterised by rapid social transformation, inequality and competition.[5] Above all – and the Principalities are a case in point – peasant resistance unfolded in an environment where plantation capitalism had been grafted unto ancient agrarian taxation systems, in an intensely hybrid situation perhaps unmatched anywhere in the sugar plantation economies of the era. Conflicts were often framed in terms of legal struggles around the application of the old taxation system to new social realities, where villagers invoked norms and interpretations that could run in their favour. The peasants not only resisted the heavy burdens of the plantation economy, but also tried to use the political structures of the colonial government and the plantation to settle scores among themselves.

In this study I will ground my argument on the archival documents of the Pakualaman administration, one of the four Principalities of central Java. These archives have only recently been opened for research, and only now do historians begin to grasp the level of opposition against, and the intense negotiation with, the plantation economy.[6] The intervention of both plantation interests and colonial government led to an intensifying legal discourse of social relations at the village level. For 1899 alone, the *pradata* (judicial records) of Yogyakarta mention 355 agrarian disputes, a number which rose to 519 in 1911. In 1899, 60 disputes were about tax and compulsory services, 54 about *bekel* (village notable and tax collector) dismissals, 51 about other *bekel* related issues, 55 about house taxation disputes, and 50 cases about land taxation.[7] On the basis of these judicial records, one can bring the various actors in these struggles, and their perceptions, to life. I will draw upon a few cases from the late nineteenth-century sugar estate Sewu Galur and the indigo estate Sumbernila, both located in the domain of the Pakualam.

The Social Basis of the Colonial Plantation Economy in the Principalities

In the Pakualaman, as elsewhere in the Principalities, European estates leased *apanage-land*s from members of the royal families. Large sugar plantations, complete with state-of-the-art sugar factories, were established in these *apanage* lands under long-term contracts. In a sense, the estates became part of the *apanage* system, although they also promoted considerable changes in it over time. Let me first sketch briefly the situation before the arrival of the European plantation holders.

The age-old *apanage* system fused specific Javanese forms of landholding, vassalage, *corvée* labour, sharecropping, and taxation. *Apanage* was based upon the assumption that all the land belonged to the king, who distributed it to the *priyayi* (royal families and officers). At the apex of the Pakualaman principality stood the monarch (Prince Pakualam). The monarch delegated the daily administration of his realm to his *patih* or chief minister, who, as it happened, was in the service of both the Javanese ruler and the Dutch colonial government. The elite of the principality consisted of the *sentana* (the royal family) and *priyayi* (aristocratic officials). The royal domain had to provide for the income of the ruler and his immediate relatives, whereas the *apanages* provided the income of the extended royal family and the high-ranking Javanese officials. *Apanage* holders, or *patuh*, had to surrender two-fifths of the agricultural produce of their estates and supply a certain number of statutory labourers to the palace. The *patuh* were entitled to choose their *bekels*. In practice, the *bekel* did not only collect taxes but gave out the land to several *sikeps* or *kuli* (peasants who cultivated the land) under the *maron* system (yield division). The *bekel* was entitled to one-fifth of the harvest, two-fifth went to the *patuh*, the remaining two-fifth was left to the peasant. The *apanage* taxes were paid in kind, with the product of the harvest. They were collected twice a year, namely just before the *Garebeg Maulid* (the celebration of the birth of prophet Muhammad) and the *Garebeg Puasa* (fasting time).

The landless people or so-called *ngindung* played an important role in this agrarian structure. They often worked for the *sikep* and did the compulsory work for the *patuh*. Although they were landless they were often provided with a house and *pekarangan* (its premises), which as a matter of fact made them eligible for house tax too. The amount of the tax or the volume of work that a *ngindung* had to carry out was related to the size of his house and its premises, which was usually around 78 *cengkal* (140 m²). In many cases *ngindung* shared houses, which made them eligible for only half of the house tax, but they were still considered to be a *cacah* (household unit) and therefore subject to that particular tax.[8]

Concepts of ownership and property hardly apply to Javanese agrarian relationships. According to narratives that were also religious and mythological, the ruler of each Principality conquered the land from the original native inhabitants and then relinquished the right he had won to his vassals. The distinction later claimed to exist between *ingkang andarbe* (the owner) and *ingang manggoni* (the occupier of the land) is artificial, since only the prince could be regarded as landowner. The distinction between *ingkang andarbe* and *ingang manggoni* cannot be put on equal footing with the European distinction between property and possession. Javanese agrarian relationships are largely fiscal, and involved certain rights over a piece of land, the value of which was determined by custom. *Jung* and *cacah* were therefore not units of land measurement as such, but were fiscal units that combined notions of the amount of labour one person could carry out, the size of the plot of land, and its productivity. Since one *cacah* was equivalent to the size of a rice field that could be cultivated by a single household, it was the central notion in the trinity of land-labour-productivity.[9]

When the plantations emerged in the Principalities in the early nineteenth century, the role of the *bekel* had already developed from being a simple tax collector to being a 'petty king' of the village who performed a range of administrative – including religious – duties.[10] Although the *bekel* clearly belonged to the village elite, he or she was not the village head, as *apanage* units were usually smaller than village units, and might be located in more than one village. The position of *bekel* was usually auctioned, and its price was the *bekti* to be paid to the *patuh*. The new *bekel* got a *piyagem* (letter of appointment), which indicated the size of the land under cultivation, the amount of tax to be paid, and the compulsory work (*kerigaji* and *gugurgunung*) to be carried out. If the *bekel* failed to deliver, she or he would be declared *kether* (careless) and the *patuh* could replace her or him.[11]

In this system the European landleaser came in, positioning himself between the *patuh* and the *bekel*. He was considered to be a '*super-bekel*' by the *patuh* but in his relation to the *bekel*, the landleaser took over the role of the *patuh*. Perhaps not in the immediate beginning, but gradually, it became clear that the population of the Principalities was worse off under the European leaseholder, because he took the best land and increased the labour services. Fundamental to this was the heavily increased demand for labour at the time of the cane harvest (in particular), since this was generally carried out without recourse to seasonal migrant labour from other districts, unlike other parts of Java.We can safely assume that the position of the *sikep* generally deteriorated, as the plantations increased the number of *sikep* to enlarge their labour force. As a consequence *sikep* land was reduced to a size that was just sufficient to sustain the people on the plantation. I therefore do not subscribe to Houben's view that the number of *sikep* fell while the number of wage-labourers rose. It was true that *sikep* could become *ngindung*, but one should take into account that *sikep* could also perform wage labour to earn some additional income. Moreover, in the twentieth century, when the colonial government finally succeeded in reforming the agrarian system in the Principalities, its social conditions were often compared to serfdom.[12]

Government Regulations and Judicial System in the Principalities

The changes in the agrarian structure of the Principalities that were brought about by the plantation economy were attended by continuous government interventions to prevent the planters from establishing a kind of *hacienda* system within the *apanage* system. Governor-General G.A.G.Ph. van der Cappellen was the first to take drastic measure and abolished the landleasing in the Principalities altogether, with disastrous results, as his decision is generally considered to be one of the main causes of the Java War (1825 to 1830). Van der Capellen's successor reversed this policy, and allowed landleasing from 1828 onwards, after which landleasing increased rapidly to a maximum of 251 estates in the 1870s. The first regulation on landleasing (1839) was particularly aimed at excluding Chinese and European foreign entrepreneurs, stipulating that leaseholders in the Principalities had to be either Dutch or Indies born Europeans.

Governor-General J.C. Reynst and the resident of Yogyakarta J.I. Sevenhoven, were among the greatest critics of the system in the 1830s and 1840s.[13] However, the plantation leaseholders were well connected to the courts, and were able to resist many attempts to encroach upon their power. The government contended itself with regulating existing practices to mitigate the social ills of the plantation system and to make it serve Dutch colonial interests.

In 1857 social unrest in the Principalities was such that the government in Batavia announced new regulations on landleasing. This met with stiff resistance from the European leaseholders, who were able to block further restrictions on their enterprise for the rest of the nineteenth century. The *Pranatan Bekel* (Bekel Regulations) was only introduced in 1883 and authorised the administrator to give a legal punishment against the *bekel* who did not hold the *piyagem*, but did not stipulate any sanctions against administrators if they did not issue the required *piyagem* to the *bekels*. The most important consequence of the *bekel* regulation was the increase in *bekel* dismissals, as it enabled the plantation administrators to fire *bekels* for every failure to provide the required workforce, small thefts, or not showing up at the night watch and so on.

The Administration of Justice

Whereas the power of the landleasers over the village authorities, in particular the *bekel*, increased over time, the situation with regard to the administration of justice was more balanced. While the plantation administrator began to control more and more of the lower echelons of the police and administration of justice in the Principalities, the Resident controlled the higher echelons. This jurisdictional arrangement was important, since it meant that peasant-planter conflict was unlikely to remain confined to the estate concerned. There was a higher authority to which recourse could be had.

The local judicial-administrative institution was the *pradata distrik* (district court), headed by the *wadana polisi;* this official was appointed by the Javanese regent. However, in the plantation areas it was usually the administrator who nominated the *wadana.* Javanese who had a dispute with the plantation management therefore went to the *pradata kabupaten* (regency court, or so-called *Landraad Kabupaten*). The *pradata kabupaten* was led by a *bupati polisi*, who was appointed by the Prince Pakualam in consultation with the Dutch Resident. Finally, there was the *pradata ageng* or the *politeirol*, led by the Prince of Pakualam; if Europeans were involved in a court claim, it was presided jointly by the Prince and the Resident.[14]

The Area

The estates of Sewu Galur and Sumbernila, the location of this case study, were situated in the Adikerto regency. This regency had about 4,000 *cacah* (households) dispersed over 56 villages, in an area of 12,250 km^2. Adikarto was in the lowlands and was perfectly suited to the cultivation of paddy rice, indigo, tobacco and sugar. Sewu Galur was founded in 1881 by E.J. Hoen, O.A.O. van den Berg and R.M.E. Raaff as a Public Limited Company with a capital of 750,000 guilders.[15] In 1883 this factory leased 5,289 *bahu* of land from the Prince Pakualam and his close relatives (see appendix 2).[16] The plantation was good for 34 percent, or 50,400 guilders, of the Pakualaman's yearly tax income.[17] The *bekti* was established at 750,000 guilders. *Bekti* was an advance payment made by the landleasers when the lease was formalised, or when it was renewed (usually for twenty years). The production capacity by the end of the nineteenth century was about 70,000 to 80,000 *pikul* [1 pikul = 61.8 kilograms]; thus Sewu Galur was a middle-range sugar factory.[18] Sumberlina, an indigo estate, occupied an area of 6304 *bahu* (see appendix 3) in the west of Adikerto. It was founded in 1880 by Prince Pakualam and was administered by an Eurasian, J. Hofland. Its first capital was supplied by the bank of *Internationale Crediet- en Handels-Vereeniging* (Internatio Rotterdam). Pakualam transferred his rights to exact compulsory work and to appoint village officers to Internatio.[19] While the sugar estate Sewu Galur was owned by the Creole planters of Yogyakarta, belonging to the well-known Weijnschenk clan, and the indigo estate was owned by the Pakualam, the daily management in both cases was entrusted to Creole administrators.[20] The direct role of Prince Pakuluam, in partnership with an Amsterdam financial house, suggests the complexity that *apanage* relationships reached at their summit. But the local level was no less complex.

The Administrator and the *Bekel*

To illuminate the tension between the *bekel* (the tax collector), who was losing his or her strong position as village notable, and the administrator who tried to manipulate the *bekel*-ship into the lower position of *mandoor*, I will narrate a story from Kalikopek, a village under the administration of the Sumbernila esate.

On 27 September 1883, Ngabehi Mertadikrama, a *paneket* (village head) of Kedungdawa summoned Secodikrama, a 59-year-old widow and *bekel* of Kalikopek to come to the office of Sumbernila's administrator J. Hofland. Secodikrama came and kneeled on the verandah waiting for the administrator to come. After having waited for half an hour, Ngabehi Jagaprakosa, the police officer of Tambak, came over to her with a message from Hofland. He told her that the administrator had decided to fire her as a *bekel* of Kalikopek and that he himself would take over her position. The reason conveyed to her was that she had apparently been unwilling to provide the compulsory workforce for the indigo plantation – an allegation that Secodikrama vehemently denied. After a while Hofland came out to the veranda and stood right in front of Secadikrama. Then, he called Nagawirya, a *jugul* (vice *bekel*) of Secadikrama to testify against her. Nagawirya confessed that the area under her supervision was twenty-seven *bahu* but that only a workforce sufficient for eighteen to twenty *bahu* came out to fulfil its obligations. Secodikrama insisted that she had been meeting her obligations. Hofland became outraged and walked over to her while she was still kneeling; he kicked her right on the face and cursed: 'bangsat, oblo, lonthe aku ora caturan karo kowe' (bastard, whore, hooker, I am not talking to you). Secadikarama fell unconscious for a while. Then she rose up and said that she would not accept this treatment and promised to bring the case to court.[21]

Two weeks later, on 15 October 1883, she wrote to the Resident about her case. She filed a complaint against the abuse and contested her dismissal as *bekel* of Kalikopek. The Resident referred the case to the *Landraad*. In

court, she argued that she had the right to defend her position as *bekel*, a position which she had been holding for a long time since the reign of Pakualam
II (1829 to 1858). At that time her terrain was wasteland, which she had
made fertile. But the seventeen witnesses summoned to the court were
against her and testified that she should be regarded as *anglempit bahu*
(unable to provide the proper workforce) for *intiran* (compulsory work).
They corroborated the accusation that she had twenty-seven *bahu* but made
a workforce available that was equivalent to just eighteen *bahu*. In addition,
she had allegedly relieved six *kuli juguls* (landless peasants) from their task of
preparing the indigo seed. In brief, she had allegedly acted in clear violation
of the *Pranatan Bekel* (*Bekel* Regulations) and her dismissal was justified. The
court decided accordingly but it also found Hofland guilty, although not for
his physical abuse but for his rough language. His behaviour was considered
to be inappropriate for a 'white and honourable' gentleman and hence in violation of the Landleasing Regulation of 1839.[22] Secodikrama had not much
support among other members of the village, and some were clearly looking
to their own interests. Ngabehi Martadikrama, for instance, testified that
Hofland only raised his foot to frighten her, and actually did not touch her
face. But he was the village head man, who took over Secodikrama's position
as *bekel*.

Transforming the Apanage System:
Weakening the Position of the *Bekel*

Secodikrama's case is a micro-history of the ongoing struggle between the
bekels, the 'little village kings', defending their economic positions, and the
administrator who increasingly considered his *bekels* as his *mandoors* or foremen. Secodikrama could base herself on *adat*, in which tax and tribute had
been central. But for the landleasers the recruitment of labour was of para-
mount interest and therefore Hofland based himself on the *bekel* regulation.
Most of the taxes of the *apanage* system were replaced by the obligation to
plant crops for the plantation or to do other work to maintain the plantation
infrastructure. The *bekel* was appointed and fired by plantation administrators,
who had obtained the right to issue the *piyagem* or letter of appointment.[23]
It is this very *piyagem*, which became a rich source of conflict. The plantation
administrator was often late or negligent in issuing the *piyagem* to the
appointed *bekel*; for the administrator preferred to see the *bekel* as just a *mandoor* in charge of the recruitment of compulsory labour, and was not interested in formalising his or her position.

On 10 August 1916, Mangun Sentana, a villager of Panjatan village filed
a complaint[24] against the administrator of Sewu Galur because his *bekel* land
would be transferred to Suradiwirya, the *bekel* of Genthan village. He claimed
that he had held the position of *bekel* for fifteen years. He had been appointed

by Van der Plas, the head of overseers of Sewu Galur to which Ngabehi Wongsodimeja, the police chief of the district of Galur, had been standing witness. Although Mangun Sentana had no *piyagem*, his position as *bekel* had never been contested by other villagers or by plantation management. But according to Suradiwirya, Mangun Sentana was just a *jugul* or *vice-bekel*. Fifteen years ago he had first tried to have Prawiradana from Tayuban to become as *jugul* or *vice-bekel*. But this was rejected by Van der Plas, the administrator. Then, Suradiwirya tried to give this office to another villager, but again the administrator rebuffed him. Eventually, the administrator himself appointed Mangun Sentana as *jugul*. Sentana did not receive a *piyagem*, because he was just a *jugul* and for this position a *piyagem* was not required.[25] Yet, Mangun Sentana had met all the *bekel's* obligations and hence felt that he ought to be treated as a *bekel* and receive a *piyagem*. Clearly, Suradiwirya had settled his scores. Others had experienced the same uncertainty about their legal position. For instance, Mertawijoyo was *bekel* in Tanggul for twenty-five years without a *piyagem*. Ali Mustar, *bekel* in Gesikan village, worked 30 years without a *piyagem*.[26] They were not exceptions to the rule, as the regent of Adikarto reported in 1909 that in Sewu Galur, 202 *bekels* had not been granted their *piyagem*.[27]

What was going on? According to the *bekel* regulation, the *piyagem* included the size of land and the amount of compulsory labour to be delivered. If the *bekel* agreed with the *piyagem*, he or she would be appointed. Clearly, the administrator and many of his *bekels* could not agree on the specific amount of compulsory work to be delivered. No wonder, as this was precisely the subject of unabated struggle between administrators and *bekels*, a struggle in which our Secodikrama, kicked in the face, was one of the participants. Not having a *piyagem*, however, seriously weakened the position of the *bekel* and in practice undid the government ordinance of 1868 determining that the position of *bekel* was hereditary.

Transforming the Police

To achieve full command of labour, the plantation administrators deliberately stripped the *bekel's* position of its formal legal character. Moreover, the administrators put the local district police at their service. The local police was initially established to provide security for European residents in the area[28] but it gradually became a tool to ensure the supply of labour to the plantation. The police officers were provided a house, some land, and a salary by the plantation. Their task was to monitor the attendance of the labour force. Although the European administrator did not have the right of appointment, in practice he appointed and dismissed police officers.[29]

In November 1886, Hofland filed a request or *anggantung* in order to fire Kartodipura as the police officer of Kulwaru, and proposed to transfer the duties to Satirta. The policeman was considered *kether* (in abandonment of his duties). First, he did not report that three out of six *bekels* he was monitoring did not meet their obligations. Second, Hofland also discovered that one of his *bekels,* Santadikrama, never stayed in his village and never reported to him. Hofland also reported that Katodipura had ignored his order to bring the *glidigan* (wage labourers) to the field.[30] Here we see two mechanisms in play. The police was not only used to enforce labour but also to recruit new workers. This was a difficult task, as peasants for obvious reasons were quite reluctant to do increasing amounts of compulsory work. The rural officer knew that his salary would be cut or that he would be sacked if he did not provide the labour. An instance of this took place in Genthan village. The administrator fired the *bekel* because of his failure to harvest indigo. In return, Kartodipura's salary was reduced by as much as the price of the indigo that was supposed to be harvested.[31]

The Administrator and Village Religious Affairs

The administrator gradually transformed the *apanage* institutions, which were basically fiscal, into instruments of labour recruitment. But he extended his power even further by intervening into civil or governmental matters in his territory, even if these had no direct relation with plantation interests. His interventions could easily reverse decisions made by the civil authority in villages. Most remarkably, the administrator challenged or reversed decisions by religious authorities. This was what happened in Dundang village. Here, Kyai Muhamad Ngapiya was a *naib* (local Islamic official in charge for marriage affairs). In 1886, there was an eligibility test for this position. The *penghulu kabupaten* (local Islamic official in charge for marriage affairs) decided that Ngapiya did not pass the test. Therefore, he had to be replaced. He then proposed his son, Kasan Munawar, as his successor. After the test was carried out, his son succeeded in replacing him. However, the *penghulu* refused Ngapiya's request to appoint his son in Dundang village because the *penghulu* had chosen another man, namely Muhamat Sangit. Munawar was relegated to another village, but requested Hofland to overrule the *penghulu*'s decision. Hofland gave permission to Munawar to be *naib* in the village because his father had always served the plantation well.[32]

On 7 July 1889, Hofland dragged Karyadi, a villager from Kulwaru Wates to the police because he lived in the house formerly occupied by his father Ali Muhamat, a *kaum* of the village who had been in Blitar, East Java, for three years, to study religious teachings. For living in the house he had to pay 13.75 *rupiah.* He was also told to hand over his house to Kasan Ngumar, who was given his position by the plantation fifteen months earlier, but had not yet occupied the house yet. Ali Muhamat's absence was never reported to the *bekel* and village police and the position of *kaum* in the village remained vacant. Almost three years after Muhamat's departure, the villagers nominated Kasan Ngumar as the new *kaum*, an appointment that was approved by the administrator. As a new officer, he was granted a *krayan* (the house formerly occupied by the older *kaum*). Karyadi did not want to hand over the house to the new *kaum*, claiming that his father had put him in charge of his house. The administrator however did not accept that Karyadi lived in this house for three years without paying or doing compulsory work.[33] Even in the appointment of new a *kaum* the plantation management intervened as they considered this too primarily as a labour issue.

Compulsory Work and Peasant Resistance

Part of village administration, the police force, and even religious appointments at the village level fell under the jurisdiction of the administrator. The only power outside was the colonial Civil Service and the higher echelons of the administration of justice. The amount of compulsory work was high and often too high. According to *Heerendienst-besluit voor Suiker en Indigo Ondernemingen*, as issued by the Resident of Yogyakarta J. Mullemeister in 28 June 1886, the villagers in sugar cane and indigo plantations had to perform *kerigandiensten*, *gugurgunungdiensten*, and *wachtdiensten*. *Kerigan* was compulsory work done once in every five days (according to the Javanese day system) or seven days, from seven o'clock to half past eleven in the morning. The tasks included the reparation of roads, bridges, and digging ditches. *Gugur-gunung* was done once in 30 days. All villagers had to clean the areas where they lived. The *wachtdiensten* was an activity of watching the factory and houses of plantation administrators from six in the evening to six in the morning.[34]

The local archives show that the plantation management grossly exceeded the parameters of tradition-based entitlements to compulsory labour, and that villagers tried to evade these burdens. As stated in the Resident's regulation, mentioned above, *kerigandiensten* had to be performed once in every five or seven days, but sources reveal that actually these tasks were performed every day of the week.[35] The same was true for the indigo plantation areas in Tambak. *Gugur-gunung* was supposedly done only once a month, but in fact was required once in every five days according to the Javanese calendar. In addition, peasants were required to do *kerigan* work, including keeping watch over sugar cane or indigo crops and planting them, starting with preparing the land and seeds, planting the seeds, then maintaining the fields until harvest. The table below shows that that such work was conducted throughout the week.

Table 6.1: Kerigan-services in Bugel and Wanadadi under Sewugalur, 25 September–1 October 1901.

Date	The Whole Number of Workforce	Numbers in Attendance (Bekel)	Numbers in Attendance (Sikep)
25 September 1901	5,341	438	1,645
26 September 1901	5,341	416	3,368
27 September 1901	5,341	3,757	1,516
28 September 1901	5,341	3,783	1,443
29 September 1901	5,341	3,755	1,390
30 September 1901	5,341	3,749	1,122
1 October 1901	5,341	3,703	546

Resisting the *Corvée*

The judicial records are full of cases where peasants tried to escape from taxes and compulsory labour. However, they risked serious fines or imprisonment. On 30 June 1891, G.C. Spaan reported two *bekels* from Kedundang, namely Leda Sentana and Sadikrama as well as a *kuli*, Mertasetika, to the police because they had neglected their duties. Leda Sentana and Sadikrama had agreed to finish a job of digging an irrigation canal but did not meet the deadline. They were put in jail for five days. The *kuli* Mertasetika was punished more severely, with ten days in jail, as he had asked a little boy, who was clearly unfit for this heavy work, to do the job.[36] In other cases too, heavy fines had to be paid. By the end of 1896, Wiradrana, a villager of Beran village, was reported to the police as he refused to plant sugar cane, and had not paid his house tax and police-watch tax for eleven months. He was sued for non-payment of housing tax for eleven months amounting to 3 guilders, police-watch tax for 16 months of 3.20 guilders, lawsuit fee of 9 guilders and *pausur* 3.20 guilders.[37]

The large fine accords with the amounts to be paid in the *glidig*-system, which allowed villagers to pay off the *corvée* in the sugar or indigo fields. The planting alone took many days and if a *sikep* wanted to be exempted from these tasks altogether he or she had to pay 109.10 guilders for *wang glidig*. Most peasants did not have these amounts and police records give evidence of many peasants taking serious risks to escape from this work. On 5 June 1891 for example, Setradimeja, a *bekel* from Kecubung, was reported to the police by G.C. Spaan, an administrator of an indigo factory, because he had dared to charge ten *dhuwit* to twenty-nine villagers in his area to bribe an overseer of Sumbernila factory. Setradimeja had tried to arrange his task of planting of indigo so that it would be near to his dwellings. The overseer, however, refused the bribe and reported him to the plantation supervisor. Setradimeja was fired from his position and put in jail for fourteen days.[38]

In other cases, villagers tried to get rid of an overseer they disliked. For example, G.C. Spaan reported Sawitana, a *bekel* in Kaligintung to the police on the allegation that he slandered an overseer named Kasan Talib. The event started with Sawitana's dislike of Talib, whom he tried to replace by asking 56 villagers to demand Talib's succession. Rebuffed, he tried a different approach. Since Talib was planning to build a house, Sawitana visited him and offered four *rupiah* for a loan. After the money was lent to Talib, Sawitana told the factory supervisor that Talib had extorted four *rupiah* from him. The supervisor confronted Talib with this story, and Talib immediately reacted by returning the money to Sawitana. However, Talib had already spent some of the money, so he was able to give back only part of it; he promised to pay the full amount later on. But Sawitana reported to the police only that Talib did not return the entire sum, hoping that this would be sufficient for Talib's dismissal. Eventually, the plantation management was fed up with Sawitana's manipulations and put him in jail for fourteen days.[39]

There was, however, one matter in which the administrators showed leniency: these cases were usually related to water supplies and food production. For instance, on 17 October 1882, J. Hofland asked Sogan police to free four *kulis* from Bendhungan, Jawikrama, Ranakarta, Kartawikrama and Citrataruna villages, who were caught by the Kartodiwiryo overseer because they stole water for their farms. But Hofland felt that the factory did not need that much water during daytime. He knew that sufficient food supplies were vital to keep the labour force intact. This offence was not serious enough remove peasants from the labour process by jailing them.[40]

If no other options were left, however, villagers moved to another village, preferably outside the estate concerned. Not only did landless peasants move around to find work elsewhere; even landowners left their belongings behind to escape from the heavy burden of compulsory labour. The planter would respond by bringing in new *sikeps*. This could lead to new legal problems if the original owners came back to their villages and found their lands and farms occupied by new *sikep*. Whereas migration was more or less an individual act, *seleh* (literally give up), i.e. surrendering compulsory work altogether, was an act of collective resistance. *Seleh* was similar to a strike, but included the labourers returning the houses and land that they had been granted to the plantation. This happened in the village of Kecubung. R. Marteen, a supervisor of the Sumbernila factory, panicked because Sumawirya, *bekel* of Kecubung, together with eighteen other peasants, declared *seleh* and returned all the houses and farms to force the plantation to reduce the burden of compulsory work.[41]

Merging the Household

At the beginning of this article, I mentioned that 55 out of 355 cases for the Yogyakarta courts were about 'house taxation disputes'. Since a household was one of the taxation bases, one option was to join two houses to split the burden of these taxes. The tribulations this might involve are illustrated by the following story. On 15 of November 1887, J. Hofland, the administrator of Sumbernila, reported Jamunawi, a villager of Genthan, to the police of Adikarta. Jamunawi was accused of joining his house[42] with Mustam's, his neighbour, and refusing to carry out the compulsory work. Nor did he pay his *intiran* (a compensation in cash for his regular duties as night watch man, and other compulsory work for the plantation). Jamunawi claimed to be exempted from his duties, as he was now part of the Sewu Galur administration and no longer part of Sumbernila's. And, he continued, the house where he lived was granted to him by A. Vroom, the former administrator of Sewu Galur factory. This house was known as a *krayan* (official house), and corresponded to his position as a *kaum* (person in charge of religious affairs) of Genthan village. His argument seemed to be quite convincing as he could show his *piyagem* (letter of appointment) as a *kaum*, which was signed by A. Vroom.[43]

Actually, the roots of the dispute dated back to the time when Genthan village was rented by the sugar factory Sewu Galur. The village was an *apanage-land* belonging to Kanjeng Ratu Sepuh, one of the Pakualam's royal families. The range of land was 5 *jung* (1 jung = 2 to 4 *bahu*) and divided into two parts; the first 2 *jung* was granted to Demang Mertawijaya, the other 3 *jung* to Demang Mertataruna. Later on, Sewu Galur leased half of the former land (1 *jung*) The remaining 1 *jung* was still *apanage-land* and soon leased out to the indigo plantation of Sumbernila.[44] Twelve households were involved in this transfer, including Jamunawi's, who was then appointed by A. Vroom as *kaum* in Genthan. The problems began when his house was divided into two parts; one part was under Sewu Galur's administration and the other was under Sumbernila's. Jamunawi's house was transferred into Sumbernila's administration, while he was still employed as *kaum* under Sewu Galur's administration.

The transfer to Sumbernila entailed Jamunawi's assignment to compulsory work at the indigo plantation. He refused to work, claiming that his house was now only the equivalent of half a *bahu* or workforce, and that the other half of the work obligation corresponded to Demang Mertawijaya, who occupied the other half of the house. Jamunawi negotiated with Mertawijaya to take over his duties every other year in return for 6 *wang* per month. Mertawijaya accepted this proposal, performing every other year his duties and paying his part for the other year. Then, Demang Mertawijaya was replaced by *bekel* Nitimeja, who shifted his part of the work to Mustam, a villager who also had just half a *bahu*. But after a few years, Mustam felt overburdened and asked Jamunawi to substitute for him in planting indigo every year, for which he would pay him 6 *wang* monthly. After Jamunawi refused, Mustam returned half of the house to Nitimeja, who asked Jamunawi to give back his house to him. Jamunawi, however, insisted that as a *kaum* he had every right to live there.[45]

Conclusion

The level of resistance – a term that needs to be understood in the context of the foregoing argument – and its legal, indeed judicial, nature in Pakualaman is striking. Such resistance was, however, the consequence of the hybrid character of the plantation system in the Principalities. It was the taxation system in which the *bekel* had traditionally been playing a central role, as farmer, village notable and tax collector, and where the household was the basis for taxation. By the end of the nineteenth century, agrarian laws in the Principalities were a peculiar blend of tax and labour regulations. Whereas landleasers and their administrators considered social relations in their plantation domain as labour relations, the villagers considered the administrator to be a *patuh* who violated the *adat* by excessive taxation. Continuous government intervention gave both sides the idea that they were right. Thus, Hofland, could escape from being sentenced for physical abuse through bribing and probably intimidating witnesses but was sentenced for violating the 1839 regulation which stipulated that he should behave as a Javanese nobleman towards his *bekel*. Secodikrama lost her position as a bekel, because she did not comply with a *bekel* regulation that had taken away part of her autonomy.

There is no reason to assume that labour relations in the Principalities were less vexed than in the outer regions, as Wertheim suggested.[46] The difference was, however, that village elites in the Principalities could resort to *adat* and European legal institutions, which still recognised their position as taxpayers. Above all, they were not indentured labour and could migrate.

Let us be clear about one thing: Asian or European capitalism is irrelevant as regards the level of oppression or resistance. Indeed, Pakualam's indigo plantation experienced more social conflicts than the Sewu Galur sugar plantation.

Recourse to the Principalities' higher echelons of legal administration (perhaps a safety valve) was so frequent that the Civil Service became annoyed about the amount of work it involved. In 1902 Yogyakarta's Resident, J. A. Ament (1896 to 1902) complained about the peasants' growing awareness of legal mechanisms and in particular the piling up of small criminal cases at the *Raad Kabupaten,*(regency courts):

I remind you once again that according to Article 83 of *Angger Recht-Organisatie,* some small cases such as negligence in maintaining houses, walls, roads, canals, unattended night watches, or improperly conducted night watches, stealing trivial items such as one or two bunches of bananas, one or two bunches of fruit, or one or two cents no longer need to be handled by the *Raad Kabupaten*.[47]

Ament's proposal to have the police officers deal with these petty offences would have put the villagers even more at the mercy of the administrator, as the police officer was in effect an employee of the administrator.

Yet the European administrator, in spite of his combined *bekel-patuh* power, was neither slaveholder nor employer. The lands were not his lands and the people were not his servants. Hofland had to appear at the court, and probably gave bribes and used his power to appoint *bekels* to win his case. Police force was used to put people to work, to confine them and so forth, but the administrator had no right to take things into own hands, even if he often did so. The people on his estate knew when he violated the law. In particular, the *bekels*, the village notables, were well aware that the administrators did not control the regency courts and the *Landraad*. Around 1900, almost every day, a villager from Yogyakarta took his or her case to the court.

Notes

1. Kartodirdjo, *The Peasant's Revolt of Banten in 1888*. The author had enlarged this study in *Protest Movement in Rural Java: A Study of Agrarian Unrest in the 19th and Early 20th Centuries*.
2. Breman, *The Shattered Image: Construction and Deconstruction of the Village in Colonial Asia*.
3. Houben, 'History and Mortality: East Sumatran Incidents as described by Breman'; see also his broader studies in Houben and Lindblad, *Coolie Labour in Colonial Indonesia*.
4. Djoko Utomo, 'Pemogokan Buruh Tani di Abad ke-19: Kasus Yogyakarta'.
5. Breman, 'The Village on Java and the Early Colonial State'.
6. An enormous amount of indigenous documentation dealing with the peasant and agrarian world of the nineteenth and early twentieth centuries can be found in the Widya Pustaka's office, of Pakualaman Palace Yogyakarta. This collection is now under reconstruction and reservation and open for public. The archive's number indicated in this paper is temporary and could be changed as part of this reconstruction.
7. Van Vollenhoven, *Adatrechtbundels*, Serie D, No. XXXIII, 206.
8. Van Vollenhoven, as note 7, above, 213–15.
9. Houben, *Kraton and Kompeni: Surakarta and Yogyakarta, 1830–1870*, 309–10.
10. Suhartono, *Apanage dan Bekel: Perubahan Sosial di Pedesaan Surakarta, 1830–1920*.
11. Margana, 'Soerorejo versus Kartosudiro: Bekel and Bekel System', 186.
12. Houben, *Kraton and Kompeni*.
13. Concerning the political debates about the landleasing in the Principalities area, see Houben, 'Private Estate in Java in Nineteenth Century: A Reappraisal'; see also Houben, *Kraton and Kompeni*, 268–78.

14. With regards to the judicial system in Javanese Principalities, see Van den Haspel, *Overwicht in Overleg: Hervormingen van Justitie* etc.
15. *Handboek voor cultuur- en handelsondernemingen*, 1888–1940.
16. PA, 2705.
17. Poerwokoesoemo, *Kadipaten Pakualaman*, 316.
18. *Handboek voor cultuur- en handelsondernemingen*, 1888–1940.
19. In addition, the contract stipulated that in return for a yearly advance of 60,000 guilders to pay for the planting of the indigo, upon which 9 percent interest had to be paid, Pakualam would relinquish one-third of the estate's profits to Internatio. In 1886, Pakualam indicated that he felt that these conditions were unfair and after long and unfruitful negotiations the plantation was sold. PA, 860.
20. Concerning the relation between Weijnschenk clan and the Javanese ruler in the principality of Java, see Bosma, 'Sugar and Dynasty in Yogyakarta'.
21. PA, 4156.
22. PA, 4156.
23. 'Pranatan Bekel' in Hunger, *Javaansche wetten, verordeningen, regelingen, besluiten*, Vol. 1.
24. PA, 4868. From the local archive I found that people who had complaints against the plantation authorities usually went to the village police, then the police assisted them to write the letters of complaint, addressed both to the local official (usually *Bupati Pulisi*) and Dutch Resident. Usually the local official would only pay attention to the matter after the Dutch resident urged him to intervene.
25. 'Pranatan Bekel' in Hunger, *Javaansche wetten, verordeningen, regelingen, besluiten*, Vol. 1.
26. PA, 322.
27. PA, 2602.
28. I haven't found the exact time when this police institution (called *gunung*) was established. In the Surakarta region, it appeared after the Java War (1825–1830).
29. The police was formally appointed by the local Regent, though upon the Resident's recommendation and with the approval of the European administrator.
30. PA, 318.
31. PA, 318.
32. PA, 30.
33. PA, 4128.
34. Gortmans, *Het Landhuur-Reglement*, 24–28.
35. PA, 2705.
36. PA, 4577.
37. PA, 4869.
38. PA, 4577.
39. PA, 4577.
40. PA, 4868.
41. PA, 285.
42. The term 'house' includes the *pekarangan*-land (a piece of land surrounded the house), however such merging could only be done between the pieces of land and houses which were next to each other.
43. PA, 4869.
44. PA, 4869.
45. PA, 4869.
46. Wertheim, 'Conditions on Sugar Estates in Colonial Java'.
47. Resident Ament to Rijksbestuurder and Wadana Pakualaman, 13 February 1902, in: Van Bevervoorde, Assistant-Resident of Jogjakarta 1903, *Nota over het Rechtswezen in de Residentie Jogjakarta*, appendix III, 106–107.

7

'A Teaspoon of Sugar ...': Assessing the Sugar Content in Colonial Discourse in the Dutch East Indies, 1880 to 1914

Joost Coté

The title of this chapter alludes to the debate about the role of sugar in the process of colonialism: did the sugar industry epitomise the blessings of European colonialism and could it be the agent of acculturation, as some colonial reformers suggested; or was it the oppressive force of European imperialism and the obstacle to indigenous development, as others claimed? In a volume concerned to raise these questions anew, it is of interest to review the ebb and flow of contemporary debate in one corner of the greater Sugarlandia. Although, as some critics of postcolonialism have argued, retracing colonial debates may do little more than privilege colonial discourse, raking over the embers of colonial debates, will, hopefully, uncover the complex of interacting threads of debate that ultimately shaped the late colonial state against which the nation struggled.

As other contributors of this volume show, the sugar industry everywhere played a central role in the colonial process of 'taking possession', of physically appropriating the territories colonialism claimed while remaining central to the evolving discourse upon which colonialism rested. Because of the significant profits it generated for both the expatriate capital market as well as for settler planters, and its propensity, as a multi-dimensional industry, to transform the natural and social landscape, sugar had significant political clout in the construction of colonial policy and practice. More generally, the dramatic impact of its technology in the rural landscapes it dominated in the nine-teenth century, lent it an aura of 'progress' and 'modernity' that seemed to transform it into the perfect metaphor for European colonialism.

This chapter attempts to retrace the contemporary colonial discourse in the Dutch East Indies from the latter part of the nineteenth century to the middle of the first half of the twentieth century in which the sugar industry was variously presented as the fulfilment of European colonialism.

The discursive significance of sugar as a metaphor for colonial capitalism takes it beyond a question of its local economic, political or social impact. Although the various influences of the sugar industry played out differently in different colonial constellations and changed over time as circumstances changed, it was everywhere a key component of a broader discourse on race that infused all late colonial thinking. For instance, although strikingly differ-ent in many respects in the adjacent Dutch East Indies and British Australian colonies, sugar played a crucial role in legitimating European colonialism in both. In the latter, sugar cultivation in sub-tropical Australia was central to a discourse defining an exclusive 'white nationalism', ultimately generating a key argument confirming white superiority. In the Dutch East Indies, sugar remained a constant theme in legitimating a role for European colonialism to act as mentor and nurturer for a 'developing' indigenous population.[1]

In the latter decades of the nineteenth century an identifiable discourse on colonial policy was emerging in the Dutch East Indies, which can be termed 'progressive'.[2] While its origins can be located in the self-interest of colonial settler entrepreneurs and their Dutch investors, it carried clear overtones of a broader political debate about relations between the imperial centre and its settler colony. Quintessentially taking a 'liberal' position, its colonial and met-ropolitan advocates distinguished it from an earlier 'laissez-faire liberalism' in its attempt to seek a compromise between the interests of capitalism and those of labour, represented in the colonial context by European commercial agricultural interests on the one hand and Javanese labour on the other.[3] It was undeniably 'progressive', not only in its belief in the possibility of mate-rial improvement, but also in its optimistic prognosis of the psychological transformation of traditional society, in its belief in the redemptive power of state institutions and in its stated concern for the 'welfare' of the disadvan-taged. It was, however, no less colonial for that and indeed came to represent the core of a twentieth-century debate about 'moral colonialism'. As a dom-inant discourse, the sugar industry also was caught up in its articulation, with advocates variously arguing that sugar either promoted or disadvantaged the colonial mission to bring welfare and progress.

The most articulate advocates of a new liberal discourse – and in this dis-cussion an attempt is only made to identify some key protagonists and themes – can be identified as 'intermediaries', men who managed to straddle metro-politan and colonial constituencies. They were Dutch trained, European pro-fessionals who made their careers in the colonies, identified with colonial interests but looked beyond its self-interests. Journalists, lawyers and engineers, dominated the 'intellectual' media in the colony, representing neither planter, nor colonial bureaucracy, European capitalist nor metropolitan electorate. These individuals, whose views are largely described in the discussion that follows, although they hardly constituted a group, can be likened to the 'new class' identified throughout the turn of the twentieth century in Europe and America as the instigators of a reformist discourse.[4] As Peter Wagner has argued more generally, the liberal 'crisis' in the 1880s in Europe derived from the growing recognition that although the nineteenth-century liberal 'promise' of individual autonomy had never been open to mass society because of the fear that such openness would threaten existing society, now 'the contours of such a contained, restricted liberal society' would be violently breached, if not carefully managed. The reality of ethnic difference in a colonial state sharpened the disparity between the universality of the liberal notion of the individual and its limitation, along racial lines, in practice.[5]

They were in this case 'intermediaries' since they were able to successfully convey 'the best interests of the colony' to the metropolitan electorate, and in the case of the most prominent of them, Henry van Kol and Conrad van Deventer, to the heart of the political centre. However, it is not their ownership of the discourse that is the focus here but how the sugar industry came to be taken up in its many variants. This chapter discusses the role of sugar in this discourse on the nature of the colonial project as it evolved in the Dutch East Indies between the 1880s and the First World War. It argues that the rapid expansion of colonial capitalism by the turn of the twentieth century quickly problematised any naive assumptions that capitalism, state controlled or private, could provide a total solution as initially posited by some. Drawing increasingly on socialist assumptions as well as broader cultural critiques of both European civilisation and modernity more generally, diverse critiques of colonial practice developed in the last years of the nineteenth century questioning both the claims of European leadership and its ability to transform the native and his environment. By the 1920s this critique had effectively dissipated, in part because a progressive discourse had been absorbed into a broader consensus celebrating the evident success of the colonial project; in part because such a critique now appeared to form part of a much more dangerous discourse that was increasingly dominated by the logic of anti-colonial Indonesian nationalism. Throughout, as Bosma has shown, the sugar industry remained the actual as well as the metaphorical touchstone for this debate.[6]

Sugar and Colonialism

While the association of sugar with European settlement in Java goes back to the beginning of the eighteenth century,[7] its association with a discourse of what I have defined as a 'progressive colonialism' dates from the latter part of the nineteenth century. It was at this juncture, with the demise of the colonial *Cultuurstelsel* policy of government monopolisation of the commercial production of agricultural exports, and, more cogently in the wake of the world-wide depression, that the debate about a 'modern colonialism' began to develop. The roots of this polemics can be found in the liberal philosophy of an earlier generation of colonial critics.[8] But, where earlier critics had argued that the task of civilising Java was the responsibility of a reformed colonial government – Multatuli believed the *Cultuurstelsel* could be a major instrument of Javanese *opvoeding* and was a harsh critic of *vrije arbeid* (free labour) – a new generation of post-*Cultuurstelsel* 'progressive' liberals needed to respond to a new economic environment where colonial capitalism had gained a prominent foothold in both the colonial economy and its politics. They saw their task as defining the role of private colonial enterprise in the broader context of colonisation.

Towards the end of the nineteenth century, the need to fund scientific research facilities and experimental stations to develop better varieties of sugar cane which in turn justified the investment in new technologies promoted the organisation of the industry. The demands for increased investment, improved technology and management skills required the sugar lobby to advance and protect its interests. Initially instituted in the 1870s,[9] by the time of the sugar industry conference held in Semarang in 1889, industry leaders recognised that government surveillance of an industry that had such a direct impact on the welfare of the indigenous population, was inevitable. Until 1894 sugar factory owners remained more or less free to negotiate the appropriation of land with village headmen or, in the Principalities, with the *apanage*-holders of the royal courts – a process fraught with opportunities for fraud, coercion and exploitation – but these relations now increasingly came under much closer government inspection. In that year, the government issued the first series of regulations intended to control relations between sugar factories and village landowners. Covered by these new regulations were such key aspects as the amount of village land that factories could command, the amount of compensation to be awarded for loss of productive land, the division of water resources between the needs of *sawah* (irrigated field) and sugar cane fields, and the level of wages to be paid to day labourers and carters.

Four years on, in 1899, further changes were introduced that effectively inserted the colonial government between factory owner/manager and the Javanese villagers.[10] Astute members of the industry recognised these changes for what they clearly were: the provision of a stable basis for the industry to deal with what had hitherto been an unreliable and arbitrary relationship with indigenous landowners and workers. The regulations in fact assisted sugar investors to fuel their ravenous appetite for land in order to offset declining prices by larger outputs[11] but did little to protect the Javanese farmer.[12] Between 1896 and 1913 the area of Javanese agricultural land hired by factory owners for the cultivation for sugar cane in Java doubled from 104,267 hectares to 205,397 hectares.[13] As a result of the expansion of land under cultivation and the doubling of the production per hectare. production rapidly increased from 400,000 tons in 1890 to 744,000 tons in 1900, to 1,278,000 tons in 1910.[14]

The extent of the sugar industry's penetration of Javanese farming land, and its crucial role in the colonial economy, as well as the political power that the sugar lobby could consequently muster, meant that sugar could not but be central to the preoccupations of colonial politicians. But equally – and importantly because of this – the industry was central to the question of the relations between colonial and indigenous society, and, from the perspective of colonial reformers, to the question of native welfare. Resolving the question of colonial relations was the issue that preoccupied colonial reformers.

The Political Discourse: Colonialism as Mentor

The principles of nineteenth-century colonial reform derived from progressive liberal discourse that can clearly be recognised in the writing of the journalists Carel Eliza van Kesteren and Pieter Brooshooft. Both were metropolitan-born journalists, who employed their journalistic skills to set out what they saw as an agenda for modernisation. Following the decision to withdraw the colonial government from monopoly control of the colonial economy, these men (and others) were concerned to 'normalise' colonial society, to establish what might be termed a 'colonial civil society', one built on private enterprise, whose government reflected the economic interests of all members of society, and one in which public life was conducted in a proper 'civilised and modern way'. Theirs was an argument for a rational political economy that would ultimately be in the best interests of colonial capital, but simultaneously emphasised that these interests could only be achieved if an arrangement were made with the colonised masses of native society. This required that the self-interested politics of colonial capital be curtailed by a commitment to a higher moral objective, one that amounted to a European mission to civilise.

The essential progressive elements of this discourse lay in the emphasis on *opvoeding* – the inclusive Dutch term incorporating both the concept of education and training and the notion of nurturing and raising up. This concept implied, first, that the Javanese individual existed as a subject of concern of the colonial state – that his economic and political existence was a matter to be taken seriously. Second, that he was susceptible to the educative influences of inherently civilising institutions.[15] While the question of how this influence was to be exercised included some reference to the provision of formal 'native education', more typically it was treated in more general terms, as the need for the 'modernisation' of the indigenous population. This was, as one exuberant contributor to the *De Indische Gids* put it, something that had to be of concern to 'all those who work hard and energetically together to achieve the glorious goal to raise the native peoples to a higher level of development and culture.'[16] Government inaction or irrational action – action contrary to the advancement of state and society – would have a deleterious impact on native welfare and (consequently) would damage the authority of the state and Dutch prestige.[17] The other strand in this discourse suggested that as the longer-term local needs were best understood by local interests, greater autonomy from metropolitan control was essential. Thus the question of a settler politics came to be intimately bound up with the question about the best way to achieve a *modus vivendi* between native labour and colonial enterprise.

Van Kesteren dedicated his new journal, *De Indische Gids* (published in the Netherlands and directed at imperial policy makers) to the achievement of such a new colonial era. In its first edition, in 1879, he set out the fundamental principles of the journal's charter:

> The general and healthy development of the Indies – necessary for Dutch trade and industry and, what is more significant, a moral obligation towards the indigenous people of the colony – is impossible without (a) the co-operation of European capital, European enterprise and European expertise; (b) the assurance to the native that he will gain the fruits of his labour; (c) the rational, intellectual and moral education of the native who is now demoralised by opium, lack of security and other causes; (d) modifications to a number of economic conditions which obstruct his economic progress. [18]

Over the next decade he argued in numerous leader articles that the modernisation of the colonial state depended on the enactment of rational government regulation. Good government required accurate surveys and the preparation of statistics without which effective policy could not be developed or efficiently implemented.[19] But above all, as he reiterated in articles in almost every edition of his journal, colonial legislation needed to be assessed in terms of its impact on the welfare of 'the native'.

Van Kesteren's position was most coherently outlined in a long critique of colonial policy published in 1885.[20] His definition of a progressive colonial political economy marked a clear break with 'economic' or free trade liberalism and conservative politics generally.[21] While accepting the essential role of private enterprise capitalism, Van Kesteren argued here that 'old style' liberalism was unable to resolve the complex social and economic issues of modern colonialism. In broad terms, his argument was that modern colonialism required a reconceptualisation of the nature of the colonial state.[22] Central to his recipe for 'progress', however, was the support for modern European industry since it was through the example of efficient European enterprise that 'useful knowledge, and a positive attitude to order, diligence, thriftiness and contentedness', the hallmarks of the productive social virtues, would be disseminated amongst 'the natives':

> whatever else may be contested concerning the Netherlands Indies, the pre-eminence of European over native industry ... [including] agriculture, cannot be. The superiority of the European compared to native industry is like comparing greatness to inferiority, development to stagnation, a dynamic, powerful and uplifting intellectual energy to a spiritually deadening or at least spiritually incapacitating training. European industry alone can provide the means to bring this country to its fullest potential; European industry alone can raise the carrying capacity of the people sufficiently to ensure that the financial burden which the European administration imposes will cease to be a concern.[23]

Left unspoken in this salute to colonial capital, was the prominent position of the sugar industry in Java. What followed, in Van Kesteren's view, was the necessity of an effective 'European administration' to provide the essential infrastructure for the modernisation of colonial economy and society: the development of irrigation works; extension of the railway transport system; the regulation of labour and land hire regimes; the maintenance of 'security' and rule of law; and above all, education. Van Kesteren's was a call for a more interventionist and scientific approach to colonial government, an argument that mirrored the greater reliance on technological and scientific upgrading that was taking place within the plantation economy. Most of this agenda fitted well with the interests of the sugar industry but it pointed well beyond the self-interest of the industry to paint a broader picture of a modern polity.

The argument for colonial reform in the 1880s was developed against a background of the emerging 'new imperialism'. The political interests that the expansion of imperial trade brought with it ensured that colonial practices increasingly came under the scrutiny of the international community, and hence the sensitivities of a metropolitan state. Thus, as Van Kesteren emphasised in his polemic, the Netherlands was accountable to 'civilised Europe' for the way it governed in its colony:[24] 'our good name, our moral authority, our future [depends on the] way in which we fulfil our task in the East.'[25] Alluding to the generally held view that colonial policies of an earlier era were no longer acceptable, Van Kesteren urged that proper colonial management and 'a somewhat broader view of our task as colonial power' would ensure that the Netherlands could 'regain a seat of honour in the gallery of nations'.[26] Implicitly, therefore imperialism called out a new nationalism by recognising a greater national responsibility. The contemporary nation and its govern-

ment, Van Kesteren stressed, was also accountable to the glorious history of
the Netherlands' past. Compared to Britain which was

> so thoroughly saturated with a sense of solidarity and community spirit; [where]
> patriotism glows in the heart of each ... [our] love of fatherland all too often is dif-
> fused into a misty kind of cosmopolitanism or is overwhelmed by mean-spirited
> energies or personal egotism and we have become flat and slothful and listless.[27]

Van Kesteren's agenda was broadly taken up by his colonial newspaper, *De
Locomotief*, under the editorship of Pieter Brooshooft. It was Brooshooft who
was later credited with coining the term, 'ethical policy', which characterised
Dutch colonial policy of the early twentieth century.[28] In the literature associated with this aspect of colonial history his name is usually put forward as
the founding voice of a reform movement.[29] It is within his writing career,
however, that one can most clearly see the rapid shift from a progressive liberal position, such as that of Van Kesteren, and as initially reflected in
Brooshooft in the 1880s, to a much more critical and pessimistic assessment
of the possibility of productive colonial relations as expressed by some colonial critics, including Brooshooft, a decade later. It was, however, this earlier
'progressive liberalism' that was to provide the rationale for twentieth-century
colonial policy, and in particular, a rationale used to legitimate the operations
of the sugar industry.

In a major statement envisaging a new colonial era, *Memorie over de Toestand in Nederlandsch Indië*, published in 1888, Brooshhooft like Van
Kesteren framed his argument for normalising relations between Europeans
and Javanese within a discourse of national self-interest. For Brooshooft, however, the demand for colonial reform was lodged more specifically within a settler demand for greater autonomy. His report was one of a series of petitions
in the 1880s to the Dutch parliament urging support for rebuilding the shattered economy. But for Brooshooft, any demand for greater autonomy – any
notion of a proper state – could not be based merely on the self-interest of
colonial planters. Like Van Kesteren, Brooshooft's key argument was that the
achievement of longer-term future was irrevocably linked to native welfare.

More thoroughly than in Van Kesteren's writing, Brooshooft made it clear
that he viewed the Javanese farmer as 'the other actor' in a colonial political
economy, as both a productive unit and as a citizen in the colonial state. Both
Javanese and European economic interests, his report emphasised, needed to
be safeguarded and advanced, and both were entitled to government protection. On the other hand, the report implied that only if the Javanese were
brought within the parameters of a Euro-centric world would they learn to
take advantage of the 'free labour market' and the 'market value' of agricultural land, as advocates of a colonial capitalism suggested. Only individual
landownership and recognition of the monetary value of labour would lead to
the modernisation of traditional social relations and culture as well as the

improvement of the farmers' economic potential and material quality of life.[30] Only then would a productive relationship between indigenous and settler agriculturalists evolve. The circumstances that proved this for Brooshooft was the infamous 'Ciomas affair' when a landowner crushed a revolt that occurred on a private estate causing the death of 50 and injury to hundreds of workers. In a series of twenty-one articles in *De Locomotief* of 1887, Brooshooft concluded that that the events and the regional civil unrest it led to were directly due to the years of systematic mistreatment of villagers who lived on the estate owned by and who worked for the European estate owner.[31] This event exemplified what capitalist self-interest would lead to and proved the necessity of a more humane and statesmanlike colonial politics. Brooshooft's report the following year represented a blueprint for a colonial state and demonstrated a statesmanlike solution to the question of colonial relations upon which, ultimately, *rust en orde* (peace and order) as well as prosperity would depend.

Thus, as both advocates of colonial reform urged, the real interests of colonial capitalism lay in resolving 'the native question'. At the beginning of the era of the expansion of private colonial agriculture, as sugar increasingly began to encroach on the heart of Java's *sawah* lands, these liberal reformers were pointing out the inherent dangers of narrow self-interest and the practical implications of an 'enlightened' colonial policy. If villagers were not protected from the inordinate demands of sugar factories, Javanese farmers could refuse on their part to rent out their lands for sugar production when they realised that to do so was no longer compulsory under the terms of a liberal 'free enterprise' colonial regime.[32] In a 'free economy' it was therefore essential that 'the native' come to recognise that his participation in the sugar industry was in his best economic interests. Recognising the importance of this mutual interdependence was crucial because, as Van Kesteren warned in the aftermath of the financial crisis the colony had just survived, 'the entire economic structure [of the colony] will in fact falter if given the slightest jolt.'[33] In the final analysis, if the economic situation of the Javanese farmer was not addressed, there would be revolution since, as in the French Revolution, *'tout ce pays et infecté de rentes* [the whole population is affected by taxes].'

Assessing the Mentor

The critique of colonial policy that evolved in the 1880s alongside the first flush of colonial capitalism was tempered by the impact of the world-wide depression. This as Van Kesteren hinted, had brought the colonial economy, near to a crisis. In Semarang, the financial and administrative centre of central Java, the young colonial legal officer, Conrad van Deventer, wrote to family in Holland that the colony was on the edge of bankruptcy due to 'the sugar crisis'.[34] The Koloniale Bank and the Nederlandsch-Indische Handels-bank, important sources of capital for colonial plantation companies, had, he reported, plunged by 40 and 50 percent. Local rumours hinted that the Semarang branch of another major financial institution, Maclaine Watson and Co., was on the verge of going under. Local observers, Van Deventer wrote, were predicting the end of the sugar industry.

> Millions and millions had been invested to refurbish sugar factories with newer, more efficient machinery. It promised a magnificent future, the sugar industry in Java promised better profits than anywhere else in the world ... [but then] the harvest of 1883 lost no less than 26 million [guilders].[35]

Van Deventer was to become the leading figure in metropolitan Netherlands in steering a vision of a new colonial policy through the highly fractured Dutch political environment in the first two decades of the twentieth century. While his account may well have exaggerated the actual situation, it unquestionably reflected the concerns of the small urban colonial enclave and left an indelible mark on the young lawyer. As a small-time colonial investor, and in his capacity as a lawyer, in a leading Semarang law firm, he was directly in touch with bankers and plantation managements on a daily basis. On the other hand, as his private correspondence reveals, he deplored the standards of colonial 'society' and its culture[36] – much as did the contemporary writer, P.A. Daum – and regularly contributed articles on 'high culture' – the highlights of European stage and opera – for Brooshooft's paper. Despite his intimate involvement in colonial affairs during his twenty years in the colony, Van Deventer remained attuned to contemporary Europe and it was precisely this conjunction that underpinned his advocacy of reformist liberal colonial policies.

Van Deventer came to share the views articulated by Brooshooft in the colony's leading 'progressive' newspaper. Privately he admitted that Brooshooft expressed publicly what he himself had been privately mulling over, although clearly recognising their radical implications. In his view, Dutch colonial policy of the *Cultuurstelsel* policy had transformed Java into an ordered and prosperous landscape – in contrast, for instance, to British India under British laissez-faire liberal politics – but this was now being threatened by unregulated private enterprise. Whereas, in Europe, government control of capitalism – to the point of nationalising key resources – seemed to offer a solution, to prevent a potential socialist revolution, the essence of a successful modern colonialism also lay in ensuring that 'the people' benefited from economic development. While not willing to publicly advocate what he termed a 'realisable socialism', he recognised the relevance of Brooshooft's 'radical' solution, which was clearly differentiated from both the self-interest of a colonial planter lobby and from the policies of the dominant conservative (i.e. Liberal) faction in the Dutch parliament that supported colonial capitalism.[37] At the same time, he sensed (as he reported in his private correspondence) in Brooshooft's solution for a modern colonial political economy, a pre-emptive political intervention against both indigenous revolt and the influence of 'the socialists' on the political front.

Other issues impacted on the articulation of a demand for reform in this crucial period. If colonial society was vulnerable economically, so too was its physical security. The continuing failure to conquer Aceh and the colonial army's initial defeat in the conquest of Lombok in 1894, also raised questions at the time about the integrity of the colonial boundaries. These heightened emotional investment in the debate on colonial policy and Dutch imperialism. Internally, fear of a possible native revolt circulated in the colonial capital in the mid-1880s. The *Java-Bode* reported on 29 September 1885:

> The words heading this article [*Prang Sabil* – civil war], which signal so much danger of which our readers are only too aware, describe what in the not too distant future will occur in certain regions of Java if the government does not take action ... Who would have thought, after what we had believed was the long-forgotten Aceh war, that in our main stand, in the very heart of our possessions, where for three centuries we have established ourselves and where almost everywhere European rule has been introduced, that such a possibility might have to be considered. Things must have come to a sorry pass.
>
> ... The fanatical movement in Sukabumi on which we briefly reported is much more serious than we had thought ... In Sukabumi today, including the mosque, there are five places where religious organisations gather. Apart from this in almost every *kampong* such an organisation can be found.

These themes were also addressed by Van Kesteren and Brooshooft, the former having already warned in the first edition of *De Indische Gids*:

> A sense of community is developing amongst the native population with a desire to participate in public issues to which the Government can no longer close its eyes without damaging consequences ... Not the least suggestion of disturbance in the most isolated corner of the archipelago, not a single revolt against our authority occurs, no defeat of our armed forced is experienced, without them rushing to announce the fact. They are gradually extending a network over the entire Indies and, where this is already in operation, its effectiveness as a means of communication is dramatic, as was evidenced in Java during the first years of the war against Aceh.[38]

These immediate and fundamental threats to the security of colonial society gave impetus to the search for a longer term solution which, as the advocates of 'progressive' reform were suggesting, could only be found in establishing a more secure basis for colonial relations. Even so, there were those who questioned the moral capacity of colonial society to perform the role of mentor. The newspaper editor, P.A. Daum, alongside his daily tasks as newspaper editor of a leading colonial daily, in which he regularly voiced his criticism of colonial policy, also found the time to write a series of twelve novels about colonial society in Java. In his novels Daum exposed the colonial planter society as morally corrupted, and colonial society as a whole as a spiritual wasteland. The plots of his novels demonstrated how the colonial economy was not only at the whim of the fickleness of the international market and the natural elements but also vulnerable to the moral weakness of its administrators. Towards the end of his long melodramatic novel, '*Up's*' *en* '*downs*' *in het Indische Leven* (serialised in his newspaper in 1890) one of the group of failed second-generation planters is finally forced to recognise:

> no, it was not the land that had let them down! The land had always been good to them and had always been a joy to them, and it still was; it was not the land, he now realised for the first time, it was the people themselves.
> Besides those with private means and in government employment, there only existed two kinds of thieves, the public ones, who were put behind bars and the secretive ones, who, while enriching themselves also made a good name in the world.[39]

Daum's constant theme was that colonial society, fractured by race, ignorance and immorality, had squandered its inheritance. It lacked the moral stature to be given the responsibility to act as guardian for an indigenous population and the wealth the Indies represented. Moreover, as the scenario of Daum's last novel, *Aboe Bakar* (1893), suggested, its nemesis lay in the culturally and racially mixed Indies-settler society that old colonial attitudes had condoned. If, therefore, a colonial society was to take charge of the colonial situation, it would need to return to the fundamental origins of a European civilisation. In the penultimate decade of the nineteenth century Daum appeared to be warning his readers that only 'real Europeans' and the spirit of European enterprise could achieve the dreams that colonial reformers had in mind.

The question of the *innerlijke kracht* – the inner moral strength of colonial society – continued to concern commentators on colonial society and the issue was most famously exposed by Holland's leading author, Louis Couperus, in his novel *De Stille Kracht* (1900) (Hidden Force). Several investigations of poor white urban society around the turn of the century, much of it focussed on the families of serving or former military, reported their lack of 'energy', the absence of vitalism, their unwillingness to work. These were Daum's characters in real life, whom the shocked investigators described as having become European paupers, and were thus hardly fit to represent Europe and act as mentors to a native society.[40]

The Socialist Turn: Railing against Capitalism

By the turn of the century, the naive optimism of liberal colonial reformers of the 1880s – reformers whose long residence in the colony enabled them to 'understand the best interests of the colony' but whose professionalism enabled them to distance themselves from the crude self-interest of the rugged settler – had increasingly to recognise the harsher realities of emerging Indonesian aspirations, European economic interests and new imperial politics. The possibility of mediating between the interests of labour and capital became increasingly more unlikely, causing the progressive discourse to split into numerous different streams. As the century drew to a close, the critique of colonial policy veered increasingly to the left and it was the New Liberals – progressive liberals, liberal democrats, social liberals, the labels varied – in the style of Van Deventer, (who had once toyed with the idea of a 'realisable socialism') whose polemics in the first decade of the twentieth century attempted to hold together, by political compromises, the spirit of Van Kesteren's and Brooshooft's 1880s liberal vision of a colonial society.

In the course of the last decade of the nineteenth century Brooshooft had shifted ground dramatically. By 1901 he had publicly abandoned liberalism declaring that colonial policy had become irredeemably capitalistic. Observing the expansion of the sugar industry into the domain of the Javanese farmer, he concluded

> that the outcome of colonial policy towards the native in terms of agriculture is that slowly but surely the *desa* (village) man is being pushed into the pool of moral and physical misery in which the disinherited of Western society are already drowned. He currently is struggling to work himself free from under the iron fist still forcing down on his head and shoulders. Should he come up from under then a bloody struggle awaits him although once resolved, a period of misery will at last have been closed. In the Indies, one is standing at the very beginning. It will be some later century which will correct the actions of an earlier era which robbed a people of its land and made it the slaves of insatiable fortune hunters.[41]

The same message that he had expressed earlier – change or else the future of the colony would be threatened – was now expressed with greater pessimism and coloured by the influential discourse of the European socialist movement, although he claimed not to be a socialist. In his criticisms of European agriculture he was to the left of his leading contemporary, Henry van Kol, a former colonial irrigation engineer and since 1896, representing the Social Democratic party in the Dutch parliament. For Brooshooft the sugar industry had become the example *par excellence* of the excesses of colonial capitalism, and in a one hundred page, *De Ethische Koers in de Koloniale Politiek* (1901), he enumerated a range of issues – and solutions – which were to provide the agenda for the later investigation into the economic circumstances of the Javanese population, the *Mindere Welvaart Onderzoek* (Diminishing Welfare Investigation, 1905–1920).

Henry van Kol meanwhile had published an analysis of the current state of colonial affairs in his his *Land en Volk van Java* in 1896. This effectively came to the same conclusion as Brooshooft had belatedly arrived at, but from a different set of premises. Beginning, as a socialist, with a declared concern for the welfare of the Javanese – whereas Brooshooft's 1888 petition had been speaking on behalf of a colonial society – van Kol argued that the inevitable result of the penetration of Dutch capitalism in Java was the proletarianisation of the Javanese. At the end of the nineteenth century he argued, that fifteen percent or 8.5 million Javanese had been transformed into *orang menumpang*, landless peasants, and had become *orang melancong*, drifters and 'ne'er do wells', to become *bujang* or wage labourers. These people were

> finding their refuge in the factories or in other employment and are beginning to form a proletarian army with which both the indigenous aristocracy as well as the colonial government will have to come to terms in the future. [42]

Alienated from the land, forced to sell their labour to factories – of which in rural Java the seasonal work provided by the sugar factory was most prominent – or to wealthier landowners, no longer able to be maintained by the support of a communal society, enslaved by capitalism and impoverished by government taxes, the Javanese were currently enduring the inevitable painful phase of capitalism.[43] The colonial government had assisted in this process of turning Javanese into the slaves of capitalism – and so it was now its moral duty of the Dutch government to soften that painful experience by reducing taxation and returning some of its stolen profits in the form of improved irrigation, training in better agricultural techniques and rice varieties to double rice yield. This was a theme Brooshooft had already developed and one which Van Deventer was able to successfully exploit in his famous 'A Debt of Honour' article of 1899. It was directed at the Dutch electorate in the leading Dutch journal on cultural and social issues, *De Gids*. Improved living standards would inevitably be the catalyst for the growth of indigenous trades and crafts but ultimately, Van Kol believed, Javanese prosperity would be brought about through the development of 'European industry', 'without which social evolution [in Java] would be stationary and Java's riches would remain unearthed'.

> Without European plantations there would be no steamships, railways, no credit facilities and almost no trade. The millions of guilders which it annually disseminates amongst the native population would never have existed otherwise. Certainly European agriculture brings with it problems … which must of course be fought against tooth and nail; but, when all these malpractices have been removed (and that is by no means impossible) then these industries should be supported as much as possible. Without the profits obtained from the sugar industry the native

would be unable to pay his land taxes, would be unable to buy out his *herendiensten* obligations. Through renting out his lands, entering into ploughing contracts, preparing fields, transporting the sugar cane and finished sugar the native annually receives large sums of money which he would never be able to earn otherwise.

Ironically, the socialist hereby embraced the central liberal assumption.[44] But Van Kol's analysis did not envisage the end of Javanese traditional society. Proletarianisation was not the inevitable end of capitalism. Rather he saw the need for the renovation of tradition: greater income could be achieved through better agricultural yields, less oppressive taxation, access to newer sources of income provided through contracts with European agricultural enterprises and non-agricultural occupations, all of which would enable the Javanese to reconstruct communalistic village organisations.

Indeed it can be argued that the real colonial concern of the commentators on *mindere welvaart op Java* (the declining welfare in Java) – as the discourse came to be officially termed – was the dissolution of Javanese socio-economic structures that capitalism produced. In part this concern expressed a humanitarian realisation of colonial responsibility but equally it stemmed from a concern that, unless Javanese society held together and was made self-sufficient, the burden of colonial responsibility for a dependent native population would overwhelm colonial resources at the expense of European capitalism. When in his pamphlet Van Kol called for *Java's grond voor de Javaan* (Java's lands for the Javanese people) he was not advocating Javanese independence but Javanese self-sufficiency. It was nonetheless an attack on the greed of 'sugar barons' and the self-interested politics of 'old colonialism'.

In a later account of his inspection tour of the colony in his capacity as a member of parliament, a journey through the record of Dutch colonialism – that included the Aceh campaigns and the new coal mines of Sumatra (which he broadly approved of) and the poorhouses, jails and famine districts of Semarang that he deplored – Van Kol documented what came to be regarded as the case for colonial reform in general and the solution to *mindere welvaart op Java* in particular. In Semarang, despite the growth trend in the value of its total imports and exports, and despite Semarang being the third largest sugar producing residency in central Java[45] drought, floods and disease had devastated the local population. Van Kol's account lingered over the details of a human disaster. He quoted a local newspaper account of 'men and women at the slaughter houses searching for the bones that are thrown away; rubbish bins are searched for fish and chicken heads to be taken home and eaten.' In 1901, Van Kol learned, 50,000 people died of cholera and fever, far more than reported in official statistics. In 1900, in the district of Grobongan alone, 72,000 inhabitants were struck by cholera or whom 5000 died.[46] The large numbers of beggars, who had been cleared off the streets for Van Kol's visit, he discovered to be locked up in sheds.[47] Here he found indiscriminately piled up together hundreds of men, women and children, the rejects of their villages, the *kere* (paupers) of the district … In the midst of a poisonous smell … in the filthy atmosphere of their sinister abode, lay the sick, the wounded, the dying, children as well, no doubt, as criminals, intermingled. The poor were thin, legs bent up, pus dripping from open wounds, yet their hollow eyes containing a gleam which I had also seen in the faces of the dying in the hospitals [I had visited] in recent weeks. Many of the dead had been carried outside and buried although I was unable to ascertain the exact number. Many a woman recounted to us how she had lost her man: and a farmer, not a beggar; many a child could point to neither mother nor father.' [48]

The local Chamber of Commerce was forced to take account of the situation because of the significant effect it had on its income due to the loss in native buyer power. It was not, Van Kol stressed, that colonial authorities had not attempted to deal with the crisis – large amounts of money, extra rice imports, and employment-creating projects had been provided. But it demonstrated what could happen on a larger scale, given one bad year of drought or floods, if the Javanese were not assisted to improve their means of subsistence. It was one of the scenarios Van Kesteren had predicted that could pull down the colonial house of cards. And it was because in the worst affected area, Grobogan, there was no 'agriculture for the European export market'.[49] With no attempt to develop new industries and no attempt to improve agricultural methods – such as the introduction of irrigation and better methods of ploughing – it had proved to be vulnerable in the face of a temporary disaster.

Although it was not caused by European capitalism, and was, if anything due to the lack of it, the contrast that became increasingly apparent between an increasingly successful colonial economy and, with the growing European awareness, Javanese poverty, generated support for what twentieth-century proponents of reform described as an 'ethical' concern for the native. The conditions in Semarang were particularly shocking because of the obvious prosperity of the European sector. Semarang was the second largest export/import centre in Java until 1909. Sugar was its main export, exports out of Semarang doubling between 1900 and 1910 from 138,692 tons to 243,054 tons, and it was this industry that was making the most obvious inroads into Javanese communities, particularly in its major production centres in the residencies of Yogyakarta and Pekalongan/Tegal.[50] And yet, in close proximity, hundreds of Javanese had died.

Modernity and the Decline of Civilisation

Apart from its economic impact – or its failure to extend a helping hand – it was the destructive impact of a heartless European capitalism on traditional life and values that concerned reformers. Implicit in the vision of a successful colonial society articulated by Van Kesteren and Brooshhooft and largely repeated by Van Kol, was a model of a Javanese agricultural community, more efficient and modernised in its practices, able to interact profitably with its European neighbours, but nevertheless culturally intact. By the beginning of the century this possibility was no longer realistic. The European economy had already disconnected large numbers of Javanese from their traditional environment. The grim image of Semarang's jails and hospitals were evidence of this. Proletarisation was taking place.

Robbery was now the order of the day; forced by hunger, people began stealing cassava; and perhaps as a consequence a race of professional thieves formed. Cattle thieving increased [from 36 in 1889 to 115 in 1901], the number of murders grew [from 7 in 1899 to 111 in 1901]; in one year there were 10 *kecu* [robbery raids] incidents. For 50 cents people were prepared to declare a false oath and in one sitting of the *landraad* [judiciary] twelve witnesses were convicted of perjury. And in the midst of this anarchy [*te midden dezer anarchie*] there existed a native administration which at all levels was less than adequate: in 1899 to 1901 a total of 43 village heads had to be dismissed.[51]

Not yet, in Van Kol's reckoning, was the growing alarm about the deliberate burning of sugar cane – the *riet branden*. Already evident in the nineteenth century, the *Mindere Welvaart Onderzoek*, reporting for the years immediately after Van Kol's journey, noted with concern – and noted the increasing concern of the sugar industry at – the significant increase in deliberate acts of arson. In central Java's Pekalongan region the number of such fires had increased from 113 in 1905 to 151 in 1908, affecting, in 1908, almost half a million *bouw* of sugar plantations.[52] The cause (or causes) – let alone the question of prevention – was a central issue in the section of the *Onderzoek* devoted to issue of policing and the law. Ultimately the Commission concluded that, like so many of the questions underlying the issue of *mindere welvaart*, deliberate acts of setting fire to sugar cane plantations related to the broader issue of security, which, in turn, was ultimately a question of economic security. As the discourse since the 1880s had asserted, the *Mindere Welvaart Onderzoek* reiterated at the heart of the native economic security issue, lay the question of the nature of the relations between the European and native economies. Moreover, on the stability in native society rested, ultimately, the social order and economic prosperity of European colonialism.

In relation to the specific question of *rietbranden* – deliberate setting fire to sugar cane – the volume editor accepted the view of the sugar industry:

Repressive measures – i.e. punishment – will not curtail the evil as long as there is no certainty of punishment, because now the majority of perpetrators remain unpunished and consequently the majority of Javanese cannot be convinced that instigating sugar cane fires can have the most unpleasant consequences, the only means whereby they would be discouraged from undertaking it. Preventative measures [alone] also cannot succeed in instilling such a conviction[53].

Since convictions for arson were difficult to uphold, sugar industry representatives giving evidence to the Commission recommended a temporary recourse to extra-legal measures, such as exile to another region where evidence was insufficient to prosecute a known instigator. But in the longer term it suggested – and the *Onderzoek* editor agreed – that a government-backed agreement between factory and *desa* representatives was needed to establish a system of canefield security guards. Even so, the prevention of such fires could only be expected in the context of a broader set of conditions, which contributed to the material and moral improvement and community development.[54]

Here then, the practical dilemma faced by sugar factory owners brought the discussion back to where it had started three decades earlier. Indeed sugar-cane-field fires were only another symptom of what colonial reformers perceived as being a much wider problem. This was the problem created by the increasing dissolution of traditional society, caused by modernisation generally, but, in the view of the *Mindere Welvaart* investigators, exacerbated by the characteristics inherent in Javanese society including: polygamy, child marriage, adultery, opium usage, and gambling. In the absence of appropriate antidotes to the 'malaise of modernity', such as schools, productive employment and trade training, the effects of a rapidly changing and materially oppressive world would be increasingly reflected in crime rates, significantly among the young.

In 1906, the *Mindere Welvaart Onderzoek* (MOW) reported, 7,116 youths were brought before police and magistrates courts in Java, 1,578 below the age of 10.[55] This according to the MWO editors, highlighted the inappropriateness or absence of proper parental guidance received by the majority of native youth. Common robbery was also everywhere on the increase. In the residency of Semarang, convictions for simple robbery (*eenvoudige diefstallen*) fluctuated between 1899 to 1904 from 831 (1900) to 1237 (1901) to 905 (1903). This however was hardly eye-catching since other towns, such as Madiun, Magelang, Cheribon, and Bandung, had as great or greater rates of petty crime. It was however immediately apparent to the compilers of the report that differences between districts and between years within districts were directly related to periods of sudden changes in normal economic conditions. The economic security of the native directly affected the everyday security of colonial society.[56]

Lack of economic security had more diverse effects. In urban Semarang itself, economic decline in the rural economy, loss of land, drought, over-population as well as the attraction of employment opportunities, brought large-scale increases both in the permanent population and in the daily arrival of itinerant labour in search of work on the wharves and elsewhere. The indigenous population of the city doubled between 1850 and 1890, and again between 1890 and 1920 from 20,000 to 53,874 to 126,628 totalling around 200,000 at the end of the colonial era.[57] New urban conditions necessitated new regulations that in turn produced new 'crimes'. The local Semarang daily, *De Locomotief*, documented the growing number of Indonesians who were being arraigned in the courts for an ever-increasing range of crimes: for jumping out of moving trams, for parking ox-carts in places where this was prohibited; for using an animal in poor condition; for riding a wheeled vehicle without a licence; for fighting on a public carriage way; for defecating in a public place. Increasingly it was observed that native as well as poor white *kampong* youths were active as *straatslijpers*, pickpockets, who attacked the upright and hardworking burghers. Changes in the law would be required to take account of the new conditions. In the countryside, also, rapid modernisation had already seen a dramatic increase in new regulations, many of them lacking a sound legal basis, so that a gradual state of lawlessness was developing. As the *Mindere Welvaart Onderzoek* noted.

> ... it is not unreasonable to assume that the practice of *prentah* [informal pressure exerted by those in authority] ... even though it lacks any legal basis, has been significantly extended in the course of the years due to the increasing demands of the traffic and of security of persons and goods, the increase in the number of government officials and of those in authority, wishing to introduce reforms, that is to say improvements, as quickly as possible, given the ease and the minimal requirements to produce such regulations, and the readiness of the native to obey them, even where it involves significant burdens or demands on his work or resting time.[58]

All in all, the number of regulations (in particular those without legal sanction) and the inability to properly prosecute (because of a lack of an adequate police force) meant that security in rural areas could not be guaranteed. Similar pressures were now becoming evident in the cities where, even more than in country areas, European commerce – indeed everyday life – was dependent on native work and affected by native tradition.

Finally, not the least significant impact of the dislocation and mobility that resulted from modernity that colonial penetration of rural areas provoked, was the growing problem of disease. Van Kol had remarked on this in general terms as one by-product of colonial intervention. Semarang, like other colonial cities experiencing an influx of rural populations, suffered high rates of mortality and regular bouts of epidemics. Deaths from cholera in the city amounted to 2,480 in 1901, 1,020 in 1902 3,163 in 1910 and 1,169 in

1911, mortality rates three or four times higher that those of Dutch and European cities.[59] A large part of the blame for this was attributed to the urban indigenous *kampongs* which were:

> Extremely smelly, filthy and squalid. The hovels are built one on top of the other, without any sense of order without taking the slightest account of hygienic require-ments. People drink from wells located right next to *slokans* [canals], the ground is damp and low-lying, the hovels damp and dark so that cholera is rife there. In 1902 ... one *kampong* was completely wiped out [by cholera].[60]

Urban *kampongs*, overpopulated by people driven off the land, produced not only the narrow, unlit streets that 'formed a veritable labyrinth ... a breeding ground of criminality',[61] but also the source of contamination of '[y]our own perceived well-being [and] the health of your loved ones', as the health and sanitation polemicist, Henry Tillema, argued to convince the electors of Semarang to support town planning reforms.[62]

The effects of modernity, both in urban and rural areas, increased the urgency and importance of, education, the central plank of the nineteenth-century reform discourse. Clearly in the case of urban health, the need to change the behaviour of rural peasants who came to the city for work, and who inhabited the cramped facilities available in the urban *kampong*, was seen as urgent. Here advocates of urban sanitation advocated a mixture of coercion and training. There was a growing perception of the need to at least institute basic education, but also of making appropriate sanitary facilities available. Ultimately *kampong* dwellers' living habits would need to be changed by rehousing them, by instituting programmes of slum clearance and town plan-ning together with a programme of educating urban natives in 'the impor-tance of a knowledge of cleanliness of body, of clothes, of property and of home.'[63]

In the countryside advocates of an 'ethical policy' also emphasised the importance of education alongside support for Javanese farmers, in particular the provision of credit facilities and irrigation, to counteract the effects of the colonial economy. Those less convinced of the efficacy of education argued for coercion. The Resident of Semarang, for instance, complained:

> Where ... one is faced with a population which hardly appreciates its own best interests, which fails to think of its future, and fails to recognise that thrift and more effort are necessary to ensure continuing prosperity; then ... [e]ncouragement, guidance and instruction in such a situation will be of little benefit. Only through exerting direct pressure on the population can circumstances be improved for the better ... So one is faced with a choice: either to ... watch a people left to its own devices take a wrong course or by imposing more direct pressure, to lead the peo-ple into a better direction.[64] .

Any assumption, it was becoming evident to practical reformers, that the native would eagerly imitate the model that European industry presented, was wishful thinking. Very quickly, as the twentieth century progressed, advocates of an 'ethical policy' were seen to be either 'simply foolish' or 'utopian' – words used to describe plans for the expansion of native education proposed by the Director of Education, Jacques Abendanon[65] – or unpatriotic. If there was problem in the educative model this perhaps had to do with the moral character of the model of European culture that colonialism offered the native. In 1912 the *Mindere Welvaart Onderzoek* expressed concern at the behaviour of '*ontaarde Europeanen*' (degenerate Europeans) in the country-side towards the Javanese, for instance demanding unpaid services or abusing Javanese women, or as factory employers in their treatment of native workers. For the *Mindere Welvaart Onderzoek* commissioners, such 'un-European' behaviour undermined 'European prestige'.[66] Or, in the words of an earlier investigation, 'in the context and unique circumstances of the European race here ... give cause for concern.'[67] Maintaining Europeanness was ultimately the best safeguard of colonial law and order, according to this analysis, which, however, totally sidestepped the much bigger issue of the dislocation of Javanese society being perpetrated by the sugar industry.

Declining Welfare and the Liberal Solution

In the process of resolving the contradictions between the aims of the nine-teenth-century 'progressive liberal' ideal and the realities that rapid modernisation appeared to be producing, one outcome appeared to be a reassertion of confidence in the European part of the equation. It had become apparent that 'imitation' would clearly not be sufficient to effect the changes in native economic and lifestyle circumstances required to achieve the modernisation of society. The *Mindere Welvaart Onderzoek* pointed out that years of social modelling had not brought the desired change to Java.[68] In its view, the evidence – urban prostitution, sugar cane fires, *kecu, orang melancong* – were all signs of a native society coming 'undone' as a result of the increased impact of colonialism. As the *desa* came into the city and Europeans fanned out into the countryside, interactions between colonial and colonised had clearly moved beyond the ability of a colonial administration to orchestrate, and the contradictions in the argument became increasingly more difficult to sustain. As one of the concluding volumes of the *Mindere Welvaart Onderzoek* suggested in 1914, it was increasingly clear that it was impossible to institute desired modifications to native society without at the same time creating real changes that would disturb the underlying nature of colonial relations. In a tone that speaks of bitter disillusionment, a MWO editor lamented:

Well yes, one wanted to do some good for [the less privileged native]: as long as they stayed within their own sphere, and, as has been stated many times, much had indeed been done for them. But in the end this did not go far enough and especially not deep enough. Certainly, who was not proud to write *verheffing* [development] and 'empowering them in the struggle of life' and 'along western lines' under this banner. But to actually implement these slogans. … Then from out of the wood-work would come the voice of experience with advice such as 'maintenance of authority', and [comments on] 'increasing forwardness' … 'there must be order' and 'the disappearance of European prestige and even that of the regents and … Much, too much remains the same. And then one can begin all over again with talk about raising up the Native etc. and more or less leave everything as it is. [69]

Liberalism had finally encountered its nemesis, as was inevitable in a colonial context. In the final resort – now (in 1914) that some reforms had been insti-tuted – it was clear that colonial and indigenous societies and economies would not work together harmoniously in a framework predetermined by colonial interests. The universal values that nineteenth-century progressive liberals assumed should and could operate under an enlightened regime did not occur. On the one hand this was because of the apparent resistance of the native to adopt 'appropriate values' along with material change, on the other because, ultimately, colonial society resisted delivering on the liberal contract – full citizenship. But it was also apparent that the nineteenth-century dis-course had maintained a kind of 'orientalism' in assuming the unchanging nature of the Javanese.[70] With some surprise, by 1914 colonials were being confronted by the first signs of modern Indonesian political organisations and signs of 'modern' resistance to the colonial regime. Again the *Mindere Wel-vaart Onderzoek* writers recognised the irony of the fact that in as far as lib-eral ideals were being realised in the transformation of Javanese society, these were now being perceived as a threat.

Even now, with more and more Inlanders calling louder and louder for the imple-mentation within their society of the modern principles which have appeared to have been so beneficial to Europeans, it seems to have had little impact [on colo-nial administrators]. Apparently because it is thought this appeal comes only from a westernised elite, intellectuals, who have little contact with the people. This writer, however, believes that it is in fact the upcoming middle class, in other words the most energetic portion of the people, that is now having its say but is also speaking on behalf of the lower classes.

No doubt many, fearing the consequences of the ethical direction – or what it is assumed to be – would now like to see the older policies (many of which remain) continue if somewhat modified. But most people recognise that too much has now changed – although of course any outburst will still need to be suppressed. But how little would now have been necessary had newer ideas been implemented on time … and had one applied one's own principles to the Native, both the ordi-nary native as well as the *priyayi*. And how long was that not being demanded, and forcefully so![71]

The publication of the *Mindere Welvaart Onderzoek* between 1904 and 1914 recorded the full gamut of reformist and reactionary ideas that swirled across the colonial debate during the decade of its work. A single 'progressive discourse' if it had ever existed, had now dissipated into numerous streams. 'Ethical', as the 'ethical' editor noted, was hardly an agreed-upon position. Nevertheless, the debate remained within the boundaries that had been established in the 1880s: the necessity to define the relations between coloniser and colonised as a basis of the modern colonial state. Even the MWO, despite its progressive orientation and sensitivities, urged the need for regulation and control. The massive multi-volume MWO report concluded that the colonial future depended on a more effective assimilation of native society in Java into an overarching colonial structure. This would require some modification of both existing colonial government and private industry practice but also of Javanese 'behaviour'. It would require more transparent and equitable bases for maintaining colonial order and greater economic, legal and social security for the indigenous population but also, ultimately, recognition of the rights of the indigenous population to have access both to the social and political benefits of modernity.

Responses to the Discourse

The sugar industry which, in the late 1890s, had made valiant attempts to clean up its act was caught in the crossfire of competing arguments. The sugar industry vehemently disagreed with those who claimed that its members exploited the natives. The sugar industry in its extensive propaganda used precisely the arguments provided by the pioneers of colonial reform in the 1880s to maintain that the industry directly benefited the native economy. According to D. van Hinloopen Labberton (ironically the namesake of the general co-ordinator of the *Minder Welvaart Onderzoek*, D.L. van Hinloopen Labberton who was a declared opponent of the sugar industry), it did so directly through monetary contribution in the form of wages but also by providing precisely those broader educational and modernising influences (encouragement for improving agricultural methods, appreciation of wage labour agreements, training in time management and future planning) that liberal reformers had been arguing for.

In an influential document regularly reproduced between 1908 and 1918,[72] Van Hinloopen Labberton defined the sugar industry as the very model of a progressive colonial influence. The critical conclusions drawn by the MWO researchers, he claimed, stemmed from a combination of that committee's (and its supporters') ignorance of economic realities and ideological bias. Specifically, he cited its failure to thoroughly check the local data that formed the basis of statistics on which conclusions were based, the contamination of the data used by the subjective views of local officials, the inability of the researchers and failure to adequately comprehend the implications of the original research questions. In general, he claimed, the MWO lacked a practical understanding of the circumstances under which the industry worked with villagers upon whom they were being asked to report.[73] In fact, van Hinloopen Labberton's own researches showed, he said, 'that the European sugar industry provided a gigantic financial advantage for the indigenous population of Java.'[74] Indeed, the entire assumption upon which the MWO was based, namely that Javanese welfare had declined, was the 'toenmaligen waan van den dag' – the politically correct fashionable attitude of the day – which could largely to be ascribed to Van Kol's publicity about the starvation in Grobogan'. This however just proved the point about the value of the sugar industry since, he concluded, this was one of the few regions where sugar factories had not been established.[75]

The complaint by the industry that white-collar investigators did not understand was repeated regularly, as was the mantra that European industry ultimately benefited the native. Constant complaints about the unfair expropriation of irrigation water by Javanese villagers were fended off by the sugar industry urging increased funding for government irrigation works. Not the least benefit for the sugar factory owners were the calming words of Van Deventer, who, in the period before the First World War, was the leading liberal mediator of the colonial debate. In parliamentary debates and in print Van Deventer set out to solve the increasingly complex problem of reconciling the interests of sugar factory owners and village landowners and labourers.[76] Van Deventer's suggestion – already mooted three decades previously – was to strengthen the bargaining position of villagers so that they would be able to negotiate more equally 'in the market place'. The times, he believed, seemed

> propitious to take measures which would have as their aim to strengthen the land hirers and labourers in what for them is usually an unequal struggle without depriving the industry of certainty [of access to land, labour and water] which they might need for the exercise of their enterprise.[77]

Achieving what in today's neoliberal parlance might be termed 'a more level playing field', Van Deventer's strategy suggestions included more careful regulation of the distribution of irrigation water, by-passing the village headman to allow direct negotiations over land hire with Javanese landowners (to avoid corruption by village heads), more explicit safeguards for both sugar factory owners and Javanese landowners in financial agreements, a requirement by sugar factory owners to contribute to the cost of protection against arson attacks. These were all proposals to ensure that the sugar industry could continue to successfully expand.

Towards the End of a Liberal Discourse

In the twentieth century, as capitalism and the media became omnipresent, lobbyists for colonial capital who had initially been resistant to the reformist demands in the 1880s, now, if they cared at all, adopted the arguments of the reformers to defend their interests. 'Ethical concern' had gained wide currency and could be as effectively employed by capitalists as easily as by 'sentimental philanthropists'. According to critics of left and right, however, an ethical concern did little to solve the problem, which remained one of how to reconcile the interests of colonial capital and advancement of the indigenous population.

Socialists to the left of Van Kol, such as the union organiser Henk Sneevliet, argued that capitalism could never be philanthropic and the only help the indigenous population could expect was through their own direct action. The liberal project of the ethicists from a Marxist perspective, undermined this momentum for 'freedom' and Sneevliet deplored the success of the colonial reformers who, he considered, had hoodwinked Javanese intellectuals by the promise of 'association'.[78] How the true interests of Indonesians were to be achieved, from a Marxist perspective, was still unclear to Sneevliet, who in 1916 was struggling to invent a 'new Marxism' applicable to the condition of a rural peasantry in a colonial context where true industrial capitalism was unlikely to create a classical proletariat.[79] Ideologically of course, his goal was not nationalism but a joint struggle of all races against capitalism.

On the right, as it were, 'practical colonialists' scoffed at the thought that Indonesians were ready for the liberal promise. As capitalism penetrated further and became more securely entrenched, attitudes hardened. The susceptibility of the Indonesian to 'become civilised' continued to be openly discussed in the colonial press, and increasing 'modernisation' it seemed, merely increased the evidence to the contrary. As one leading right-wing colonial newspaper editor put it in justifying severe punishments meted out to coolie labourers on plantations: 'If we wish to remain here than we have to remain in control. If we wish to be respected as masters, then we have to behave as masters.'[80] In this context, the critical voice of Van Kol, or continued attempts by Van Deventer (until his death in 1916) to mediate between the interests of (native) labour and (European) capital, achieved little. Indeed, where new laws and regulation were put in place but were then not equitably enforced, as the MWO pointed out, greater dissatisfaction and protest resulted.

By the First World War, the voices of Indonesian protest were becoming apparent. As Sneevliet had complained, the first generation of Javanese intellectuals had absorbed the promise of the liberal reform platform but were becoming disillusioned that it would ever be delivered. In the first direct response by a public Indonesian organisation to the colonial government at a level of policy, the Second Congress of the Sarekat Islam signalled the end of the 'contract'.[81] The colonial state had not provided conditions for improving the lives of the people and it reported that 'the ethical direction taken by the [colonial government] as its guide is not followed by many of its officials nor finds acceptance amongst the majority of Europeans'. Moreover, it concluded that

> the Native people feel deeply aggrieved about the arbitrary treatment they must endure both on the part of some officials as well as from civilian Europeans, aggrieved over the humiliating and contemptuous attitude so often held by Europeans towards Natives, unhappy at the most unsatisfactory legal status provided for native people which in its view provides them with insufficient protection.

Effectively, Sarekat Islam, which sent envoys to the Netherlands to argue its case, asserted that having failed to be adequately protected as citizens, the citizens would refuse to serve the state, specifically to support the proposed manpower and financial contributions requested to protect the colony during the war. The argument explicitly adopted the logic of the liberal discourse, which had now also become the platform for nationalist demands. Sarekat Islam's intellectuals and advisers proposed a renewal of the liberal contract in return for the support the colonial government was seeking in its new 'moment of crisis'. In its extensive list of demands, the declaration focussed specifically on the sugar industry:

> promotion of Native agriculture, industry and trade by, amongst other things, the expansion of vocational training, promotion of credit facilities and co-operatives, expansion of irrigation works and the improvement of the way water is divided between the sugar industry and the Native people; discouraging the bad practices of some *desa* chiefs and of some Native officials in the Civil Administration who act in favour of the sugar industry, act as it were as agents of sugar factories, alter legal requirements which intimately affect the Native population in particular with regard to the Ordination on the Hiring of Land so that the Native landlords are insufficiently protected against the malpractices of those indicated above, the *desa* chief [and] some Native civil servants as well as the sugar industry itself. Official regulations need to be implemented with regard to the hire of land so that from now on the [contractual] parties are no longer the sugar industry against an individual but against the entire Native community. [82]

Conclusion

In the first decades of the twentieth century, circumstances had become much more complex than they had appeared three decades earlier. The debate was now no longer simply a debate between 'conservatives' and 'progressives', or between advocates of European colonial enterprise and those concerned with 'native welfare' or even, as it appeared in the 1880s, between settler and metropolitan interests. In part the increasing complexities resulted from the fact that in the 1880s attempts were being made to put the ideas of the armchair reformers into practice. But the increasing pressure of European capital on the one hand, and the emerging demands of the Indonesian nationalist movement on the other – and the growing needs of an expanding European community – meant that by the early twentieth century, the naive optimism – if not colonial hubris – of nineteenth-century progressive liberal discourse regarding the educative value of European industry and culture could no longer be sustained. At best it was believed that results were still a long way off, that the native was not yet ready. The core concept of the discourse however, remained, that the native would benefit from colonialism. Until the First World War at least, sugar, which had been a metaphor for colonial capitalism, continued to be the standard against which such debates were measured.

Notes

1. Different demographics have traditionally been used to distinguish 'settler' from 'exploitative' colonies. However, an examination of colonial discourses shows up interesting parallels in the debates about race and power. In Australia, a policy to exclude non-European migration, resulted in the sugar industry, developed in Australia's sub-tropical northern periphery, having to demonstrate that the white race was capable of working in such 'unnatural climatic conditions', thus proving the superiority of white workers. In Java, European superiority was demonstrated in the technological superiority of this minority, thus reinforcing an argument for continued occupation. By extension, within the European East Indies community, questions of 'scientific and technological excellence' as well as cultural and moral excellence played an important role in establishing distinctions between 'white' migrants and the often mixed race settler community, and their respective ability to act as mentors for the overwhelmingly larger indigenous population.
2. I have argued this in detail in my PhD dissertation: *The 'Education' of Java: A Modern Colonial Discourse, 1965–1905*, Monash University, 1998, unpublished.
3. See the discussion of the rise of 'progressive liberalism' in the Netherlands at this time in: Stuurman, *Wacht op ons Daden: Het Liberalisme en de Nederlandse Staat.*
4. See for a recent elaboration Mrazek, *Engineers of Happy Land: Technology and Nationalism in a Country.*

5. Wagner, *A Sociology of Modernity: Liberty and Discipline*, 37.
6. See Bosma, *Karel Zaalberg, Journalist en strijder voor de Indo*, Chapter 7, on the attitude of the Indonesian nationalist movement towards the sugar industry
7. In 1710 there were 130 sugar concerns on Java. In 1745 there were 65 around Batavia. Market and local conditions suppressed the industry until it was reactivated through government support in the 1820s after which the industry became central to the *Cultuurstelsel*. (*Encyclopaedia van Nederlands-Indië*, 'Suiker', vol. 4, 148ff.).
8. Baron W.R. van Hoëvell, Dirk van Hogendorp and Edward Douwes Dekker were the key colonial voices of the mid-nineteenth-century liberal 'revolution' that initially centred on debates on the new constitution governing colonial rule. They demanded colonial representation, and improved treatment of the indigenous population. Douwes Dekker is most famous for his novel, *Max Havelaar*, 1859, a damning attack on current colonial practice that implied a denunciation of the moral character of Dutch society.
9. See Bosma and Raben, *De oude Indische wereld*, 136. The first industry conferences were held in Solo (1873) and Yogyakarta (1875).
10. As part of their settlement with villages, sugar factory owners were to pay the village land tax obligation directly to the government while colonial officials monitored wage rates.
11. East Indies sugar averaged between 15 and 16 guilders per pikol in 1884 but had dropped to 5.02 guilders per pikol in 1902, even lower than during the 1880s depression. After the Brussels Convention that banned sugarbeet subsidies, the price stabilised at around 6 to 7 guilders per pikol.
12. As Elson shows, the advantage to Javanese farmers was variable, but opposition by villagers was widespread and effectively exploited by Indonesian nationalist organisations. (See Elson, *Javanese peasants and the Colonial Sugar Industry*). Contemporaneously, the value of the sugar industry to rural Java was still being argued in 1929. See for instance Van der Jagt, *Verslag eener Reis ter Bestudeering der Suiker Industrie op Java*.
13. Prinsen Geerlings, 'De Suikercultuur'.
14. Prinsen Geerlings, *De rietsuiker industrie in de verschillende landen van productie*, 104.
15. As Locher-Scholten has concluded, all nineteenth-century colonial documentation assumed male work to be the economic factor of native welfare. Locher-Scholten, 'Door een gekleurde bril: Koloniale bronnen over vrouwenarbeid op Java in de negentiende eeuw'.
16. De Clercq, 'De tegenwoordige toestand van het Inlandsch onderwijs'; Oosthoek, 'Het Onderwijs van Kinderen van Europeaanen en met dezen Gelijkgesteld in Nederlandsch-Indië'.
17. Much criticism of government practice in the journal focussed on its failure to consider the broader educative value of government legislation and of imperial policy for its ignorance of local needs and conditions. See for instance C. van Kesteren's extensive reports on policy on animal husbandry (Van Kesteren, 'De veestapel op Java') and colonial government response to the famine in Bantan (Van Kesteren, 'De nood van Bantam'). The latter he suggested belied 'what has in fact always been tendentious, the assertion that even the worst European government is better than the best native one.' (704). This article concluded with a prescient warning of the possibility of events which were, in fact, to take place in the region eight years later, the so-called 'Bantam revolt' about which Pieter Brooshooft wrote what Elsbeth Locher Scholten considers the article which marks the turning point in Brooshooft's thinking. See Locher Scholten, 'Mr P. Brooshooft: Een biographische schets in koloniaal-ethisch perspektief'.
18. *De Indische Gids*, 1879, No. 1, 3–5.
19. Van Kesteren, 'Een subsidy voor het uitgeven van statistische overzichten betreffende Ned. Indië'. In this article Van Kesteren argued the need for a special fund to allow the development of an accurate statistical survey of colonial life as the basis of reformed government. The importance of statistics was central to the modernisation of the European state and was then becoming the key to an emerging welfarist orientation advocated by progressive liberals in metropolitan Europe. P. Corrigan and D. Sayer, argue that the 'statistical idea'

involved both the identification of the subjects of the state as well as the definition of their social identity. Corrigan and Sayer, *The Great Arch: English State Formation as Cultural Revolution*, 131 ff.

20. Van Kesteren, 'Een en Ander over de Welvaart der Inlandsche Bevolking en de Toekomst der Europeesche Landbouw-Nijverheid'.

21. It preceded by three years a similar statement by Pieter Brooshooft in *De Locomotief* and coincided with a lengthy and influential statement by N.P. van den Berg, director of the colonial bank, entitled *Debit en Crediet* which Van Kesteren had favourably reviewed

22. As Corrigan and Sayer express it, 'Not the State, but the *idea* of the state' is radically changed in this solution to the crisis of liberalism in the evolution of the capitalist state. (*The Great Arch*, 173). Political rights were raised in this kind of argument, although not in this article. Van Kesteren had earlier in 1879 written on a 'Minahassan demand for political recognition' while in the same year, Henry Van Kol in *De Soerabaiasche Handelsblad* (9 December, 1879) raised the question of political representation generally. When raised by Brooshooft in 1888 in a proposal for a Colonial party in the Netherlands, the issue of political representation had become generalised to a question of the representation of Indies interests in the Netherlands parliament.

23. Van Kesteren, 'Een en Ander over de Welvaart der Inlandsche Bevolking', 579.

24. As note 23, above, 558.

25. As note 23, above, 553.

26. As note 23, above, 616.

27. As note 23, above, 616.

28. Brooshooft, *De Ethische Koers in de Indische Politiek*.

29. See for instance Locher Scholten, *Ethiek in Fragmenten. Vijf studies over koloniaal denken en doen*.

30. Brooshooft, *Memorie over de Toestand in Indie ter begeleiding van den Open Brief op 7 Maart 1888 gezonden aan 12 Nederlandsche Heeren*, 76.

31. Brooshooft, 'Tjiomas Balans', *De Locomotief*, 30 June – 10 August 1887 (Brooshooft Archive, KITLV, H 896:64).

32. Van Kesteren, 'Een en Ander over de Welvaart der Inlandsche Bevolking', 603.

33. As note 32, above, 614.

34. Conrad van Deventer was later to write the influential article 'A Debt of Honour' in 1899 that called on the Netherlands to return some of the wealth taken from the colony in order to rebuild its economy. This is generally regarded as having initiated the 'ethical policy' and its principal themes of education, irrigation and welfare. It, however, failed to address actual issues, concentrating instead on estimating the extent of the 'debt' (7.5 million guilders) and emphasised the need for infrastructure investment, and like Van Kesteren, emphasised the threat that neglect might lead to loss of the colony: 'It is not too late: the majority of natives are still content, at least not malcontent, under Dutch overlordship, know no better than that it is their natural situation.' Colenbrander and Stokvis, *Leven en Arbeid van Mr. C.Th. Van Deventer*, vol. 2, 42.

35. Van Deventer, 23 November 1884, Colenbrander and Stokvis, *Leven en Arbeid van Mr. C.Th. van Deventer*, vol. 1, 144–45.

36. He once described in a letter an official reception he was required to attend as a colonial official in Semarang ridiculing the 'artificialness of colour and form [of the decorations, which] would have better suited a circus than a quasi-chic party. Where one looked, nowhere was there a trace of fresh green or live flowers. And this in a land where one only needs to go into a forest to find the palms and orchids, ferns and vines which would make European decorators gasp.' Van Deventer, 22 June 1884, Colenbrander and Stokvis, *Leven en Arbeid van Mr. C.Th. van Deventer*, vol. 1, 143.

37. Colenbrander and Stokvis, *Leven en Arbeid van Mr. C.Th. van Deventer*, vol. 1, 161.

38. Van Kesteren, 'Feiten en Cijphers uit het Koloniaal Verslag voor 1878'.

39. Daum, '*Ups*' en '*downs*' in het Indische Leven, Vol. 3 Verzamelde Romans, 671.

40. *Rapport der Pauperisme Commissie*, (1903), 5–8. The Commission estimated that 11 percent of the European population in Java, or almost 6,000 individuals, were paupers.
41. Brooshooft, *De Ethische Koers in de Indische politiek*, 76.
42. Riënzi, *Land en Volk van Java*, 13.
43. Van Kol quoted extensively from Brooshooft's 1888 calculations to show the inequitable burden of government taxes and unpaid labour but also showed that the combined operation of increased population, reduced individual landholdings and over supply of labour had significantly depressed the income of roughly 3.6 million families dependent on agriculture of the 800,000 non-agricultural families. (Riënzi, *Land en Volk van Java*, Chapter 5).
44. Ticheleman, the historian of the socialist movement, has in fact questioned Van Kol's socialist credentials. Tichelman, 'De SDAP en Indonesië'.
45. The value of imports and exports (both for Semarang and for Java as a whole) for 1900 were not again achieved until 1905 although the volume of sugar exports from Semarang continued to increase with some fluctuation between 1900 and 1910 from 138,692 tons to 243,054 tons far exceeding the value of other exports of tobacco (8,701 tons to 10,496 tons), skins (1,504 to 2,152 tons), kapok (1,508 to 4,526 tons), copra (597 to 7,458 tons), coffee (4,523 to 1,639 tons). See Sneevliet, 'De Handel van Semarang'.
46. Van Kol, *Uit Onze Koloniën*, 595.
47. As note 46, above, 660.
48. As note 46, above, 661–2.
49. Van Kol added a cautionary note here – 'despite the many problems that this entails'. It suggests he had taken note of Brooshooft's criticisms in his 1901 publication.
50. See Sneevliet, 'De Handel van Semarang'. As reference to Yogyakarta suggests, traditional Javanese rulers were no more protective of 'the little Javanese farmer' than the colonial.
51. Van Kol, *Uit Onze Koloniën*, 663.
52. *Mindere Welvaart Onderzoek*, Overzicht, VIIIb., 'Recht en de Politie', Part One, 1911, 87–8.
53. *Mindere Welvaart Onderzoek*, Overzicht, VIIIb, 1, 87.
54. *Mindere Welvaart Onderzoek*, Overzicht, VIIIb, 1, 89.
55. *Mindere Welvaart Onderzoek*, Overzicht, VIIIb, 2, 32. By far the largest number (4,453) were tried for robbery. Of the total, 2,315 were convicted, 4,781 placed in the custody of parents or guardians without conviction recorded, and 20 sent to reform homes. 304 were second-time offenders, 42 third-time and 58 fourth-time offenders. (32).
56. Van Kol's description of Grobogan is therefore reflected in annual robbery rates of over a 1,000, although aggregated robberies there were significantly less than for Semarang. The worst figures were for Bandung where annual figures were constantly over 2,000.
57. Van Kol, *Uit Onze Koloniën*.
58. *Mindere Welvaart Onderzoek*, Overzicht, Vol. VIIIb.,2, 'Recht en de Politie', Slotbeschouwingen, 9–20.
59. Figures from Tillema-Weehuizen and Tillema, *Kampongwee*, 8, 10 and Tillema, *Kromoblanda*, vol. 2, 11. While mortality rates had improved somewhat since the nineteenth century (in the 1830s there were an estimated 141 deaths per 1,000 of population (compared to 176 per 1,000 in contemporary Amsterdam) the mortality rate for Semarang in the second decade of the twentieth century still averaged around 50 to 60 per 1,000. This situation was replicated in Batavia, which recorded 68 per 1000 in 1912. In that year figures for Surabaya were 57.3:1000, 30.6:1000, with 52.3:1000 for the Indonesian, European and Chinese communities.
60. Tillema, *Van Wonen en Bewonen, van Bouwen, Huis en Erf*, 104.
61. Tillema, *Riolinana*, 22.
62. Tillema, *Van Wonen en Bewonen, van Bouwen, Huis en Erf*, 33.
63. Tillema, *Van Wonen en Bewonen, van Bouwen, Huis en Erf*, 82.
64. Sijthoff, *Verslag van de Honger en Watersnood in de Residentie Semarang*, 111.

65. Memorandum Dept A, Ministry of Colonies (The Hague) 23 January, 1902, quoted in Van Miert, *Bevlogenheid en Onvermogen*, 58.
66. *Mindere Welvaart Onderzoek*, Overzicht, VIIIb, 2, 90.
67. *Pauperisme*, p. 5.
68. The point was made however in contrasting Java with Sumatra, where Sumatrans had taken on business practices and shown signs of self-initiated modernisation. *Mindere Welvaart Onderzoek*, Vol. IXb, 2, *Overzicht Economie van de Desa, Slotbeschouwingen*, 1914, 158.
69. As note 68, above, 162.
70. The point is hammered home in *Mindere Welvaart Onderzoek*, Vol. IXb, 2, *Overzicht Economie van de Desa, Slotbeschouwingen*, 1914, 163 ff. Extensive extracts from Piepers, *Macht tegen Recht* (1884) are including as a running footnote on out-of-date colonial attitudes. Van den Doel locates the Piepers, member of the *Hooggerechtshof van Nederlands Indië*. Van den Doel, *De Stille Macht*, 110–11.
71. *Mindere Welvaart Onderzoek*, Vol. IXb, 2, *Overzicht Economie van de Desa, Slotbeschouwingen*, 1914, 165.
72. Van Hinloopen Labberton, 'Invloed van de Suikerfabriek op hare omgeving', p. 18. The article was originally published in 1908 in *Bijblad, Archief voor de Java Suikerindustrie*, vol. 16 but reproduced, according to the *Archief*'s editor, without permission in *Tijdschrift van Nijverheid en Landbouw*, vol. LXXVII, 1918, 1–119.
73. As note 72 above, 69.
74. As note 72 above, 73.
75. As note 72 above, 22 n.
76. In particular, Van Deventer, 'De Java Suiker-Industrie', (1910); Colenbrander and Stokvis, *Leven en Arbeid van Mr. C.Th. van Deventer*, vol. 2, 261–78. See also extracts from parliamentary speeches in Colenbrander and Stokvis, Ibid., vol. 3.
77. Colenbrander and Stokvis, *Leven en Arbeid van Mr. C.Th. van Deventer*, vol. 2, 27.
78. H. Sneevliet, *Correspondence*, 1916 (documents 102, 114) in Tichelman, *Socialisme in Indonesië*, 337 and 366–67.
79. H. Sneevliet to W. van Ravesteyn, 10–5–1916 (document 114) in Tichelman, *Socialisme in Indonesië*, 366.
80. Wijbrands, *Nieuws van de Dag van Nederlandsch-Indië* 15.11.1910 quoted in Breman, *Koelies, Planters en Koloniale Politiek*, 316. Breman's detailed account of the tobacco plantation culture, further removed from the eye of the colonial European public, indicates the extreme end of the mistreatment that Indonesian labour experienced on plantations.
81. This significant moment in the history of Indonesian nationalism, referred to as the Indies Weerbaar movement, focussed on the issue of representation in return for specific financial and manpower contributions for defending the Indies. It gave rise to the establishment of the Volksraad in 1918, a pseudo- parliamentary advisory council which, in a formal sense, represented the culmination of the 1880s liberal demand for the establishment of a colonial civil society.
82. *Sarekat Islam Congress, 20–27 October 1917*, Batavia 1919, 109–113, reproduced in Tichelman, *Socialisme in Indonesië*, 549–53, note 24.

8

SUGAR, SLAVERY AND BOURGEOISIE: THE EMERGENCE OF THE CUBAN SUGAR INDUSTRY

Manuel Barcia

The nexus between black African slavery and the large-scale production of cane sugar for export in nineteenth-century Cuba has long excited the interest of historians. Slavery continued to be the predominant form of labour in Cuba through into the 1880s, making the Spanish colony, along with Brazil, one of the great hold-outs for black slavery, where it persisted some decades after it had been abandoned in most sectors of the Atlantic circuit of commodity production. What was particularly striking about Cuba (although it is no longer considered 'paradoxical') was the extent to which slave labour fused in the island's sugar industry with a high level of technological innovation in the sphere of manufacture. During the middle decades of the nineteenth century, Cuba became, at one and the same time, the world's largest single industrialised producer-exporter of cane sugar and one of the world's largest exploiters of black slave labour, thanks in both cases to its well-developed colonial bourgeoisie of cane-planters and merchants. At the mid-century, Cuba had nearly half a million slaves, accounting for over 40 percent of the island's total population, working for the most part in an industry that was soon to supply nearly one-third of the world's internationally traded sugar.

The 'classic' debate about the nexus between labour and technology focused on the contention that slavery, which in Cuba remained the dominant form of the labour process until the 1880s, formed a significant (although not the sole) obstacle to technological advance within the industry. This was because of inherent contradictions between the rigidity of slave labour and the requirements of machine technology. This was a position most famously associated with the work – in its partial English version at least – of the distinguished Cuban historian Moreno Fraginals. Referring to the mid-nineteeth-century advances in production centered on the vacuum pan, he argued[1] that 'the new apparatus was too complicated for slaves ... Producers now felt the urgent need of labour, which would be cheap, but of a minimal technical level unattainable by slaves. The Industrial Revolution meant the changeover to the wage worker.' Even more succinct was the argument of Franklin W. Knight that 'slave labour was woefully incompetent to deal with the scientific advances in the industry.'[2] Transposed, this could then be re-formulated as the hypothesis that 'the conditions for industrialising the Caribbean sugar economy emerged towards the middle of the century ... the first was the creation of a rural proletariat'.[3]

In retrospect, these and similar contentions seem largely discredited by arguments from a variety of area specialists that they simply did not fit the facts. Rebecca J. Scott, in particular, demonstrated unequivocally that considerable technological advance in the industry preceded slave emancipation in Cuba in the 1880s, and, conversely, that the putative proletarian labour of indentured workers associated with this precocious degree of industrialisation was anything but 'free'.[4] Similar arguments have been advanced for much of the rest of the Caribbean production area.[5] Furthermore, in the specific case of Cuba, it has been convincingly argued not only that industrialisation rendered slavery more efficient, as evidenced by increasing slave prices just before abolition in the 1880s,[6] but also that the high point of slave-production in Cuba – that is to say, the middle decades of the nineteenth century – coincided almost exactly with a period of technological advance in manufacture that placed the Spanish colony at the very forefront of the international sugar economy in terms of the 'modernity' of its factories.

This chapter addresses aspects of the early nineteenth-century origins of this situation. On the basis of new data from the archives in Havana, it argues that the importation of black African slaves into Cuba during the early decades of the nineteenth century was significantly greater than researchers have previously realised, and goes on to point up the importance of the profits of this trade for the foundation of a colonial bourgeoisie in which the interests of Spanish *peninsulares* and Caribbean-born Creoles were fused to a greater degree than has sometimes been assumed. As we shall see, the size of the Cuban slave trade in the early nineteenth century has been underestimated. In fact, there is reason to suppose that the numbers involved were approximatly double existing estimates. Slave trade was both a source of labour for the emerging sugar economy as well as a source of capital accumulation for investments in the sugar and coffee plantations. Most important is that Cuban slave traders themselves took over from British and Americans after 1810, thus gaining a degree of economic independence on which it was possible to erect the foundations of a truly Cuban bourgeoisie.

Modern sugar production commenced with the decline of Brazil and the demise of Saint-Domingue as the world's foremost sugar producers. Prior to the sudden collapse of French colonial sugar production in Saint-Domingue in the wake of the great slave revolt there in 1792, Cuban sugar manufacture played only a lesser part part in the island's economy and had only a small role in Caribbean sugar economy as a whole. During the course of the 1790s, all this began to change. Building on the foundation of an industry that had already begun to expand beyond the environs of Havana in the mid-eighteenth century, Cuba rapidly developed into a major manufacturer, eventually supplanting Brazil as the largest single producer in the New World. By the 1840s, not only had sugar expanded considerably throughout the eastern part of the island – notably in the province of Matanzas – but it had also taken on the status of a virtual monoculture, effectively driving out other colonial commodities such as tobacco.[7] In so doing, it confirmed the status of black African slavery as the basis of Cuba's export production.

Whereas the eighteenth-century Caribbean sugar production was a crucial element in the emerging European capitalist economy,[8] its nineteenth-century successor emerged as an early adaptor of the industrial modes of steam and steel. The rising sugar giant Cuba was, for example, the seventh country to build railways.[9] But this precocious industrialisation did not lead to the emergence of proletarian wage labour. On the contrary, Cuba's ascent to the forefront of the world sugar market was dependent on a massive import of slaves from Africa. Their numbers rose to tens of thousands just after Great Britain had forced Spain to sign a treaty to eliminate the slave trade in 1817. In short, until the end of slavery in 1886, Cuba defied what was once taken for fact, namely that capitalism in its progressive stages was not commensurable with slave labour.[10] As Dale Tomich has remarked, slave relations, continually forming and reforming over time and place, 'contained within themselves conditions of modern economy and polity.'[11]

Havana and the Atlantic Trade

In 1792 the *Discurso sobre la agricultura en La Habana y medios de fomentarla* (Discourse on the agriculture in Havana and the means of promoting it) was written and published by the cleverest and most influential Cuban of his day, Francisco de Arango y Parreño.[12] The pamphlet set out to convince the Spanish King Charles IV to allow the import of large numbers of African slaves into the island. In itself, the importation of slaves was no novelty in Cuba, but, with the publication of the *Discurso* and its acceptance by the Spanish crown, the slave trade from Africa to Cuba reached unprecedented proportions. In his pamphlet, Arango petitioned the Spanish king, on behalf of the Havana City Council, to allow a significant increase in the import of slaves. Slavery had existed on the island from the very onset of Spanish colonial rule in the sixteenth century, and, more recently, British traders had been responsible for bringing in large numbers of slaves during the British occupation of Havana from 1762 to 1763. Numbers had further increased during the mid-1780s.[13] After the great slave rebellion and subsequent revolution in Saint-Domingue in the following decade, however, the trade increased exponentially.

Until 1798 British and American traders dominated this commerce, but a further outbreak of war between Spain, which was occupied by Napoleon, and England made the position of British merchants in Havana and its surrounding plantation area untenable.[14] Neutral Danish ships replaced the British for a while, but Cuba-based merchants themselves now began to enter into the profitable business, and established a company to facilitate their operations. Inspired by Liverpudlian companies (the English port was one of the Atlantic world's greatest centres for slaving voyages), a trading society was formed in Havana in 1803. A petition to King Carlos IV outlined their strategy. They proposed establishing a commercial house in London or Liverpool in order to supply the departing ships with all sorts of commodities, including food and trading merchandise. In Africa, two or three locations would be chosen as the base for their operations, which, it was envisaged would remain sea-borne. No land-based establishments were envisaged. The aim of the voyages was depicted as laudable as well as profitable: 'These floating factories will be the practical school where our youth will acquire a detailed knowledge of the trade ...'[15]

The principal sponsors of the new company were the cousins Pedro and Francisco María de la Cuesta y Manzanal and Tomás de la Cruz Muñoz, joined by the Royal Consulate of Commerce and Agriculture of Havana. Some of the most renowned noblemen and businessmen of the city were among the first to join the company, among them Francisco de Arango y Parreño, the Counts of Jaruco, and Casa Bayona and Bernabé Martínez de Pinillos, all sugar plantation owners who saw a profitable new field of operation in the slave trade.[16] The company took the leading place in this commerce in the short term. Subsequently, many of its members became involved in the slave trade on an individual basis. Ten years after the establishment of the company in 1803, almost 100 percent of the slave ships arriving in Havana were the property of the city's inhabitants, or chartered by them. Simultaneously, the same group of men took an active role in the production and export of sugar, and sugar plantations became the main economic-administrative unit throughout the Cuban countryside. Slave imports and sugar exports grew simultaneously and complemented each other. By the first decade of the nineteenth century this relationship was already deeply rooted and sugar and slaves were conceptually and factually interconnected.

The Origins of the Bourgeoisie: *Peninsulares* and Creoles

One of the main upshots of these devlopements was to locate Havana in the commercial networks of the Alantic zone as one of the main centres of the slave and sugar trades. By the end of the eighteenth century, the city had become a truly international place. The British occupation of 1762, the different migratory waves from Louisiana and Florida – and subsequently from Saint-Domingue – and the escalating commerce with the United States of America had transformed the already cosmopolitan Cuban capital into a place of destination and transit for thousands of foreigners every year.[17] But who, more precisely, were the people responsible for the island's transformation into the foremost cane-sugar-producing area in the world?

During the first half of the eighteenth century some well-known Creole families, most of them of Spanish descent, already owned a significant proportion of the sugar plantations established on the western side of the island.[18] The names of Herrera, Montalvo, Peñalver, Santa Cruz and Calvo de la Puerta became symbols of wealth as well as of power. After the British occupation from 1762 to 1763, their business wealth and personal fortunes increased considerably.[19] Simultaneously, in Havana, Matanzas and other important ports, a significant group of Spanish-born men (i.e. *peninsulares*) took control of trading and shipping. In this way two factions became clearly distinguishable hereafter. Even in the Havana City Council, their names appeared followed by their sphere of influence, which also denoted their origin. They were planters (Creoles) and merchants (*peninsulares*). On many of the everyday aspects of running the colony, the opinions of the Creoles and *peninsulars* diverged. Although these divergences were always present, they reached extremes during periods of crisis. They were apparent during the Napoleonic invasion of the Iberian peninsula in 1808 and again during the three-year Spanish Constitutional period that followed the rebellion headed by General Riego in 1820.

However, with respect to the importance of giving slavery a leading role in the development of the island, they were definitely united. When Arango and the Count of Casa Montalvo travelled in the mid-1790s to Haiti, Jamaica and England to learn about sugar manufacturing and trading, they had been sent as representatives of both the Creoles and *peninsulares*. Although their personal fortunes were derived from two main – and different – sources, namely production and trade of sugar and imports of African slaves, their interest in the promotion and improvement of the colony as the first international sugar producer in the market kept them united as never before. The moral and religious issues caused by slavery may have given some of them qualms on a personal level, but they entered the slaving business nonetheless. Even in the face of international agreements and treaties designed to curb or abolish the trade, they persisted relentlessly with their activities well into the second half of the nineteenth-century, and whatever differences arose in their political positions in the colony in the growing conflict with metropolitan Spain, they remained at one with respect to the crucial role of slaves and the slave trade in promoting Cuba's prosperity. Planters and traders had common interests that overrode any notional dichotomy between Creole sugar producer and *peninsular* trader.[20]

Problems with the British Anti-Slavery Policy

The most immediate problem facing the emergent bourgeoise in Havana and other centres of sugar production in early nineteenth-century Cuba was how best to deal with attempts by the British – the most formidable naval power in the Atlantic zone – to curtail the trans-Atlantic trade in slaves from 'black' Africa. In fact, as Tomich has argued, the same process that contributed to the abolition of the slave trade, and subsequently of slavery itself, within the British empire, contributed mightily to 'the intensification of slave production elsewhere in the hemisphere' as other colonial producers sought to combat British commercial hegemony. The restructed international sugar economy of the first half of the nineteenth century was one in which 'slave production no longer monopolized the production of particular commodities', one consequence of which was an increased exploitation and expansion of slavery as slave production found itself in competition with other forms.[21]

The legal ending of the slave trade was perhaps the most important event of this period. First for Britain and then for the rest of the European powers, the international transatlantic slave trade was formally abolished between 1807 and 1820. For merchants, planters and authorities in Cuba these were difficult times. Since the abolitionist campaign overflowed Britain's frontiers, spreading to the rest of the Western Hemisphere, the economy of the island was in grave danger. Therefore, both institutional bodies and private individuals and enterprises began to fight British Abolitionism, a fight that only ended when slavery was finally abolished in 1886. Without slaves there would be not sugar to export, hence, Cuban-born or based merchants and planters defended themselves against any measure intended to affect this crucial commerce. Several battles took place within the Spanish *Cortes* between 1811 and 1823. British representatives in Spain, supported by some Spanish abolitionists, began pressuring the Regency Council from 1811 onwards. In that year the Cuban deputy Andrés de Jáuregui fought back against the ideas introduced to the debate by Miguel Guridi y Alcocer and Agustín de Argüelles. The debate closed on a satisfactory note for the Cuban slave traders and planters, but the long-term situation remained threatening. They had to face another tremendous onslaught during the Congress of Vienna in 1814 when Britain literally obliged all the European nations, including Spain, France, and Portugal, to sign a formal agreement condemning the slave trade. Legally this agreement meant nothing, but for Ferdinand VII of Spain, it was the first solid step forward for the acceptance of the 'necessity' of eliminating the slave trade.

Based on this agreement and taking advantage of the Spanish King's debts towards Britain, Charles Vaughan, the British minister in Madrid, continued to put pressure upon Ferdinand to sign a legal treaty enforcing abolition. This time, despite all the complaints of Cuban supportets of the slave trade, an official decree was issued and signed by the Spanish King on 20 September on 1817,[22] according to which the slave trade north of the equator was declared illegal immediately, while the slave trade south of the equator would be legal only until April of 1820.

Such news had a traumatic effect in Cuba. Many warnings and objections appeared in the newspapers of the island. The treaty was the chief topic of conversation in the streets, docks and halls of Havana. Slave dealers and the Spanish authorities in Havana, however, decided to ignore the royal command and continued trading in slaves. After the three-year republican period in Spain and the restoration of Ferdinand VII to the monarchy in 1823, more slaves than ever before entered Cuba, always with the acquiesence of both the civil and military authorities of the island, including governors and finance administrators.[23] For example, when, in 1842, Captain-General Jerónimo Valdés decided to promulgate a new slave code for the colony, he first took care to consult some of the wealthiest and influential planters of the time, some of them well-known for their heavy involvement, either directly or indirectly, in the slave trade itself.[24] In short, Cuba's rising bourgeoisie was able to collude with the Spanish authorities on the island to evade the threat to their wealth posed by the British attempts to bring the slave trade to an end. That wealth, in turn, was grounded not only in the production of sugar but also in the slave trade that made that production possibe. Hence it is important to arrive at a reasonably accurate figure of the number of slaves actually imported into Cuba during the period in which the bourgeoisie were accumulating their wealth. As we are about to see, that number was very substantially greater than existing estimates would lead us to suppose.

Havana: Centre of the Atlantic Slave Trade

To date, by far the best account of the slave trade to Cuba has been that found in Eltis, Behrendt, Richardson and Klein's remarkable compilation of slave imports to the New World. Eltis and his collaborators tracked some 27,233 trans-Atlantic slave ship voyages between 1595 and 1866, and arranged them in a historical and regional sequence.[25] In the case of Cuba, however, the present argument, based on evidence from the Port of Havana, is that their figures regularly under-represent the actual ones. Indeed, according to data from the port of Havana, the imports of slaves were much higher – probably twice as high – than those calculated by Eltis. According to the latter, the number of slaves imported in Havana for the years with available comparable data – 14 years between 1794 and 1811 – was 36,746, whereas my own research has established that the real figure is likely to have been nearly double this – in the region of 64,777 and possibly more (see below). The difference (allowing for gaps in the Havana records) is demonstrated by the following table:[26]

Table 8.1: Slave imports in Havana

Year	Eltis et al.	Havana Port Books	Difference
1790	1,923	–	–
1791	1,564	–	–
1792	3,592	–	–
1793	686	–	–
1794	1,180	3,500	2,320
1795	1,603	3,686	2,083
1796	1,592	–	–
1797	1,569	–	–
1798	349	1,427	1,078
1799	2,680	4,054	1,374
1800	1,368	3,993	2,625
1801	283	1,523	1,240
1802	5,563	13,832	8,269
1803	5,300	9,671	4,371
1804	2,895	–	–
1805	3,178	4,240	1,062
1806	1,937	3,899	1,962
1807	689	2,248	1,559
1808	250	–	–
1809	841	1,052	211
1810	6,377	6,672	295
1811	5,398	4,980	418
1812	3,010	–	–
1813	2,820	–	–
1814	1,765	–	–
1815	6,779	–	–
1816	17,066	–	–
1817	23,922	–	–
1818	14,457	–	–
1819	1,835	–	–
1820	1,070	–	–

Even these figures, moreover, probably underestimate – possibly by a significant margin – the number of slaves actually landed in Cuba in any given year. The sources for the study of the slave trade to Havana pose a lot of problems for the historian. First, many slave traders preferred to disembark their human cargoes far from the port, both to avoid taxes and inspections and to expedite the sale of the slaves. Planters were aware of this situation and many of them acquired slaves in this way. It is not rare, then, to see in the books of the customhouse of Havana many ships arriving from Africa without any cargo. For example the Spanish sloop 'Mercurio' arrived on 17 August 1811 from the Coast of Africa after 88 days at sea, and the American schooner *Campee* arrived on 8 November 1811 after a 37 days at sea from Sierra Leone. Both arrived suspiciously empty from their trans-Atlantic trips.[27]

Other cases serve to illustrate the various types of irregularities that took place in relation to the disembarkation of African slaves. In 1805 John Teenwood, master of the American sailing vessel 'Nancy', was forced to land the 84 slaves he was carrying from Africa due to the imminent threat of corsairs.[28] Shipwrecks in Cuban shores were also frequent events. In October 1805 the Spanish brigantine 'Santa Bárbara' 'shipwrecked' a few miles away from Havana, landed her 43 slaves there rather than in the port.[29] Another case took place during the first week of November 1810: the Spanish frigate 'La Criolla', was also shipwrecked near Havana, in Marianao, where her 461 slaves were disembarked.[30] The point was that such 'irregular' arrivals only rarely made their way into the official records of the Port of Havana, thereby creating an impression that fewer slaves were landed in Cuba than was actually the case. Although it is impossible (given the nature of the 'evidence') to arrive at any hard figure, it can reasonably be assumed that landings like this, either forced or expeditious, account for a significant ingress of slaves, over and above those recorded in the Havana Port books.

Apart from the clandestine imports, there were facts never known and other mistakenly registered. Episodes such as that the Spanish brigantine *Santa Ana* assaulted by 'pirates from the liberated Saint-Domingue' in May of 1811 can offer a clue towards what is missing. According to the captain José Peoli, the '... Negroes from Santo Domingo released his cargo of 205 bozales' before allowing him to continue.[31] Other ships collapsed in the sea, losing part – or the entire – 'cargo'. Two known cases are the Danish brigantines *Hengis* and *General Lindermann*. Both suffered this fate in front of the port of Havana on 22 November and 2 December 1800. The only thing we know is that they were able to save just 90 and 50 slaves each before going down into the deep waters of the mouth of the harbour.[32] It is worth noting that both shipwrecks were recorded because of the exceptional circumstance of having sunk right in front of the Cuban capital.

Whatever the precise numbers – and they unlikely ever to be known – the sheer scale of the trade in black African slaves to Cuba, far greater than was previously realised, clearly confirms the importance of the port of Havana in the trans-Atlantic slave trade during these post-abolition years.[33] They also confirm the role played by the slave trade in the formation of a Cuban bourgeoisie in which economic interest ultimately over-rode the differences between Creoles and *peninsulares.* In Havana, regardless of the period, merchants were always ready to receive these 'cargoes'. Most of them were Cubans and Spaniards who lived in Cuba. Many of them made huge fortunes from this trade and some were even able to obtain titles of nobility. This group of Havana merchants still awaits a serious and detailed study to reveal their real importance to the island's economy and public opinion of these years.[34] Some of them received between 500 and 1,200 slaves each year in the period studied here.[35] Some also invested in sugar estates around Matanzas and Havana.

Conclusion

When, at the end of the eighteenth century, Arango y Parreño wrote his most famous line: 'From now I speak for the future', he was well acquainted with the meaning of his words. From a meagre colony with a limited number of slaves, Cuba – and especially its western region – became the site of one of the most formidable and wealthiest sugar plantation societies of the modern world. Between 1790 and the mid-1820s, sugar production on the island quadrupled, in tandem with the importation of slaves. Slave trade, slavery and sugar marked every sphere of Cuban society. Agricultural research, economic discussions at all levels, medical treatises, novels and poetry, political decisions and wealth were all influenced and sometimes determined by the duo of slavery and sugar. Slave rebellions and plots were a constant threat in the minds of the inhabitants of the island, both powerful and powerless.[36] Slaves, however, were necessary to produce sugar, and sugar was the backbone of the Cuban economy. Consequently, they arrived to stay, despite the constant danger they represented for the wealthy planters, and for the 'stability' of the island.[37]

By the second and third decades of the nineteenth-century the slave trade was a reality that involved every single colonial governor of the island as well as the rest of the administrative and military authorities. By then it was inconceivable to think of prosperity without slaves. In 1834, in the western part of the island alone there were 551 sugar mills hosting an astounding number of 57,387 slaves.[38] Slavery remained until the late years of the century, and the slave trade survived despite all the obstacles in its way. The British Consul in Havana, Joseph T. Crawford, was not entirely correct in stating, early in 1848, that 'None of the Sugar of this island is produced by free labourers, working for wages or other ways.'[39] As has been clearly demonstrated by recent research, the workforce engaged in sugar production in mid-nineteenth-century Cuba was more heterogenous that has sometimes been imagined, and after the mid-century, it became increasingly so until slavery itself was abolished in the 1880s.[40] Nonetheless, it is indeed the case that slavery was the predominent labour form throughout the colony in the mid-century decades and that barrack-slavery, in particular, often in its harshest form, was absolutely central to the successful transformation of the industry into both the world's single largest producer-exporter of cane sugar and its most technologically advanced. Sugar, in turn, made the Cuban bourgeosie and slavery made them both.

Notes

1. Moreno Fraginals, *The Sugar Mill*, 112.
2. Quoted in Scott, *Slave Emancipation in Cuba*, 5.
3. Schnakenbourg, 'From Sugar Estate to Central Factory', 85. An elaborated and deeply nuanced re-interpretation of the limitations imposed by slave relations of production appeared in Dale W. Tomich's monograph on the nineteenth-century sugar industry in Martinique: Tomich, *Slavery in the Circuit of Sugar*, 124–38.
4. Scott, *Slave Emancipation in Cuba*; Scott, 'Labour Control in Cuba after Emancipation'.
5. Boomgaard and Oostindie, 'Changing Sugar Technology and the Labour Nexus: The Caribbean, 1750–1900'; Craton, 'Commentary: The Search for a Unified Field Theory'; Tomich, 'Sugar Technology and Slave Labour in Martinique 1830–1848'; Baud, 'Sugar and Unfree Labour: Reflections on Labour Control in the Dominican Republic, 1870–1935'.
6. Bergad, 'The Economic Viability of Sugar Production based on Slave Labour in Cuba, 1859–1878'; Bergad et al., *The Cuban Slave Market: 1790–1880*; Scott, *Slave Emancipation in Cuba*.
7. For a detailed discussion in relation to Cuba's key nineteenth-century sugar province, see Bergad, *Cuban Rural Society in the Nineteenth Century*, 1–66.
8. See James, *The Black Jacobins: Toussaint L'Overture and the San Domingo Revolution*; and Mintz, *Sweetness and Power: The Place of Sugar in Modern History*.
9. The best work to date on the establishment and development of the Cuban railway is Zanetti and García, *Caminos para el Azúcar*.
10. For a succinct re-appraisal of the relationship between technological change and slave labour, see Tomich, *Through the Prism of Slavery. Labour, Capital and the World Economy*, 88–93.
11. Tomich, *Through the Prism of Slavery*, 77. For an extended discussion of the nexus between slavery and modernity, see Blackburn, *The Making of New World Slavery. From the Baroque to the Modern, 1492–1800*.
12. Arango y Parreño, 'Discurso sobre la agricultura en La Habana y los medios de fomentarla' (1792).
13. The Council of Havana used the service of the British house of Baker and Dawson, from the mid-1780s to 1793. See Arango y Parreño, 'Discurso sobre la agricultura en La Habana', 34–35.
14. The already mentioned British house of Baker and Dawson absolutely dominated this trade from the mid-1780s to early 1790s. See Kuethe, 'Los Llorones Cubanos: The Socio-Mili-

tary Basis of Commercial Privilege'; and Kuethe, *Cuba, 1753–1815: Crown, Military and Society.*

15. Landowners and Merchants of Havana to King Charles IV. Havana, 12 January 1803. Archivo Nacional de Cuba (Hereafter ANC). Asuntos Politicos, 106/9. Since Cuba-based slave traders did not own any factory in Africa, it seems that they decided to use ships, rather than castles, as slave factories.

16. As in note 15, above.

17. See Kuethe, 'Havana in the Eighteenth Century'; and Johnson, *The Social Transformation of Eighteenth-Century Cuba*, 14–16, and 111–15.

18. See Bergad, *Cuban Rural Society in the Nineteenth Century.*

19. Johnson, *The Social Transformation of Eighteenth-Century Cuba*, 178–80. See also Johnson, 'Casualties of Peace: Tracing the Historic Roots of the Florida Cuba Diaspora, 1763–1800'.

20. See Lampros, 'Merchant-Planter Cooperation and Conflict', and Tornero Tinajero, *Crecimiento económico y transformaciones sociales.*

21. Tomich, *Through the Prism of Slavery*, 79–87.

22. Murray, *Odious Commerce: Britain, Spain and the Abolition of the Cuban Slave Trade.*

23. Pérez de la Riva, *La correspondencia personal del Capitán General Don Miguel Tacón y Rosique*, Introduction.

24. Some of the questioned planters were notoriously involved in the slave trade, among them Joaquín Gómez, Jacinto González Larrinaga and Domingo Aldama. Others, although probably not involved themselves, owed their fortunes to the same source, among them the Marquis of Arcos, the Count of Fernandina, Ignacio Herrera, and Rafael O'Farrill. See 'Expediente instruido por orden superior para reformar el sistema moral, higiénico y alimentario de los siervos que se emplean en la agricultura, 1842'. ANC: GSC 941/33186 and GSC 940/33158.

25. Eltis, Behrendt, Richardson and Klein, *The Trans-Atlantic Slave Trade: A Database on CD-ROM.*

26. For 1809 and 1811 the information is not complete in the books of data of the port of Havana. The values offered for these years are valid just for May–December (1809) and for March–December (1811). Archivo Nacional de Cuba: Miscelánea de Expedientes. Books 1115, 1950, 1986, 2516, 2519, 2524, 2787, and 6797. For the years 1802 and 1803 the information has been recovered from the Manifest written to the King by the Landowners and Merchants of Havana. Havana, 12 January 1803. ANC: Asuntos Políticos, 106/9. The slave imports steadily increased throughout the next decades. See Eltis at al., *The Trans-Atlantic Slave Trade.*

27. ANC: Miscelánea de Expedientes. Book 2524.

28. ANC: Miscelánea de Expedientes. Book 1986.

29. ANC: Miscelánea de Expedientes. Book 1986.

30. ANC: Miscelánea de Expedientes. Book 1115.

31. ANC: Miscelánea de Expedientes. Book 2524.

32. ANC: Miscelánea de Expedientes. Book 2519.

33. For slave import figures to other ports of the Americas see Eltis et al., *The Trans-Atlantic Slave Trade.*

34. Some of the most notorious Havana-settled slave merchants who later bought sugar or coffee estates were: Clemente de Ichazo, Pedro de la Cuesta y Manzanal and his brother Francisco María, Antonio de Frías, Enrique Disdier and Santiago Drake, among others. There are very few studies on the merchants responsible for the slave-trade boom to Havana. These works lack depth and are insufficient to provide understanding the significance of the role within the late eighteenth-century and early nineteenth-century Cuban society. See, for example Moreno Fraginals, *El Ingenio*, vol. I; and Ely, *Cuando reinaba Su Magestad el azúcar.*

35. Pedro de la Cuesta y Manzanal, Salvador Martiartu, Francisco Antonio Comas, Clemente de Ichazo, Francisco Hernandez, Cristobal Madan, were some of them. Other foreigners were able to profit as much as them, these are the cases of Santiago Drake and David Nagle, two of the leading slave merchants in the city from the 1790s until the 1820s.

36. Slave revolts were a constant concern for Cuban authorities, planters and merchants. Some of the most relevant works on this issue are: Franco, *La conspiración de Aponte*; Franco, *Las minas de Santiago del Prado y la rebelión de los cobreros, 1530–1800*; Franco, *La gesta heróica del Triunvirato*; Paquette, *Sugar is Made with Blood*; Barcia Paz, *La resistencia esclava en las plantaciones cubanas*; Matt Childs, 'The Aponte Rebellion of 1812 and the Transformation of Cuban Society'; and more recently, García, *Conspiraciones y revueltas*.

37. On this topic see Barcia Paz, 'Herencia y Racionalidad'.

38. ANC: Miscelánea de Expedientes, 3772/Añ.

39. Joseph T. Crawford to Viscount Palmerston. Havana, 28 January 1848. Public Record Office, London: Foreign Office, 72/748.

40. See, for example, Bergad, *Cuban Rural Society in the Nineteenth Century*, 245–59.

9

THE SPANISH IMMIGRANTS IN CUBA AND PUERTO RICO: THEIR ROLE IN THE PROCESS OF NATIONAL FORMATION IN THE TWENTIETH CENTURY, 1898 TO 1930

Jorge Ibarra

After the sinking of the *Maine* in 1898, the United States of America annexed Puerto Rico and the Philippines and granted semi-independence to Cuba under the Platt Amendment. The year 1898 definitely marked a rupture in the national histories of these former Spanish colonies, not only because the Spanish immigrant elites became foreigners, but also because 1898 marked the beginning of mass production of sugar. This article will deal with the question how this rupture impinged upon the emergence of new loyalties and identities among the Spanish economic and political elites of Puerto Rico and Cuba, and will emphasise differences over similarities. At the same time, our analysis problematises the meanings of 'Spanish', 'Cuban', 'Puerto Rican', and 'Creole'. This allows us to remain closer to the historical social relations in both Antilles, and to the transformations that both societies experienced in the tumultuous period immediately before and after 1898.

Significant differences existed between the Puerto Rican Spanish immigrant bourgeois, many of whom shared the island's local loyalties and Cuba, whose Spanish immigrants were deeply suspicious of Cuban nationalism. In both cases, the Catholic and Hispanic identities were interwoven. In Puerto Rico, this occurred especially after 1898 as part of the quest for nationhood and in opposition to Protestant inroads, while in Cuba, Catholic-Hispanic identities stood in opposition to the national project.

This comparison suggests the complex position of these local bourgeoisies. On the one hand, they accepted the political hegemony of the United States in order to protect their social privileges. On the other, they resisted the expanding American dominance of the islands' economy in order to protect their considerable economic interests. The rupture of 1898 changed the matrix of what could be considered national and foreign, and the parameters of what constituted local bourgeoisies and foreign capital.

One major reason for the divergent patterns of Cuba and Puerto Rico is the different demographic position of the Spanish immigrants: in absolute and relative terms, Puerto Rico simply had a much smaller Spanish population than Cuba. 'There are few regions of the Western Hemisphere in which the proportion of natives is so high and that of persons from abroad so low', according to the 1899 American Census of Puerto Rico. In 1899, Puerto Rico's Spanish immigrant population was only 7,690: only 0.8 percent of the total population. Compared to the 129,240 Spanish immigrants living in Cuba in that same year (8.2 percent of the total population) the Spanish immigrants in Puerto Rico constituted an extraordinarily small minority. After 1898, demographic trends in Cuba and Puerto Rico diverged even further.

By 1920, the Spanish population decreased to 4,975 persons, constituting only 0.4 percent of the total population. In contrast to that, the Cuban Census of 1919 reported that the Spanish immigrant population had more than tripled, to 404,074 persons (14 percent of the total population, compared to 8.2 percent in 1899. In 1919, there were 45,090 Spanish immigrants in Havana above twenty-one years of age, making up 39 percent of the male population in that age group.[1] However, demographic differences between Cuba and Puerto Rico are only part of the explanation for the contrasts between the two islands.

Reactions of the Spanish Immigrant Press to 1898

Our point of departure for testing these contrasts is the editorial stance of the Havana newspapers *La Lucha* and *Diario de la Marina* and San Juan's *El Heraldo Español*. These newspapers reflect substantial differences in perspective between the Spanish immigrants in Cuba and in Puerto Rico. In 1899, the *Diario de la Marina*, the voice of Spanish commercial capital and large plantation owners, began to favour American intervention in their conflicts with the Creole Cubans. The military defeat of Spain in 1898 uncovered deep historical resentment against the Cuban patriots. From the Spaniards' point of view, the Cubans had dared to rebel against their Mother Country and they deserved to pay for their crime under a more powerful and less merciful master. Of course, pro-American annexationism in Cuba had its own roots (certainly deeper than in Puerto Rico) and the annexationist stance of the 'Spanish' interests there cannot simply be reduced to vindictiveness. No doubt, this attitude was also bolstered by fears that once Cubans obtained control of their country, they would take revenge on the Spanish community. The financial interests of the Spanish wealthy classes played another important role. The establishment of a truly independent Cuban republic could lead, it was feared, to measures against the illegal practices of the local Spanish bourgeoisie such as tax evasion, contraband, and bribery of officials. The Spanish Cuban press therefore favoured annexation to protect their commercial interests against a state controlled by their erstwhile foes.

The *Diario de la Marina* initially took a neutral stance towards the U.S. occupation. However, the *Diario* soon acknowledged that '… we are neither supporters nor enemies of a protectorate, but there are many Cuban, and also many Spanish immigrant, proprietors who have become convinced that the idealised Cuban sovereignty will never be more than a dream …'.[2]

The *Diario de la Marina* increasingly called for U.S. annexation, the sooner the better. Some of its articles pointed out that the North Americans wanted to ensure order on the island before annexing it, but the editors took the view that annexation by the United States would only expedite the imposition of order. At the same time, they insisted that Cuba would be less independent as a republic under the Platt Amendment than as a part of the United States. Annexation was viewed by this newspaper as not only desirable but indeed inevitable.

Published reports of meetings held at the Casino Español in Havana stressed that the majority of the assembled Spaniards favoured annexation.[3] In congruence with its editorial line, the *Diario* admonished Spaniards to abstain from Cuban political struggles. Non-participation in electoral politics was commended by the *Diario de la Marina,* under the premise that while Spaniards tended to concentrate work and family, the Cubans wasted their energies on political and personal conflicts.[4] Therefore this newspaper considered the Platt Amendment as a healthy deterrent against political skirmishing and, even more importantly, against Cuban insurrectionism.[5]

La Lucha, the newspaper of the small Spanish shop keepers of Cuba, also shifted from an apparently equidistant position to acceptance of American interventionist orientations. It criticised the Cuban supporters of independence for their rejection U.S. Military Governor Leonard Wood's formula for a civil government, as they believed that this scheme entailed the indefinite prolongation of the intervention and an eventual annexation. According to *La Lucha*:

> at the same moment in which foreign capital is preparing to enter the country, in which U.S. Secretary of State Elihu Root was going to bring the project for a Civil

Government, the agitators at times attack the merchants and at others, the planters, affirming that their interests should be postponed and sacrificed if necessary to the ideal of absolute independence of the Island, launching on other occasions poisonous accusations against the Cubans who sympathise with annexation or the protectorate.[6]

La Lucha displayed a similar outlook towards the American intervention when Juan Gualberto Gómez called upon the Cuban Constitutional Convention (1901) to contest the U.S. military governor's decree incorporating the Platt Amendment into the Cuban Constitution. According to *La Lucha's* director Antonio San Miguel, 'The Governor's message is not a message that can be debated, but it is rather the source that makes possible and limits the constitutional action of the delegate's Convention'.[7] San Miguel did not even recognise the right of the convention delegates to protest against the imposition of the Platt Amendment.[8] The *Diario de la Marina* and *La Lucha* clearly viewed Cuban nationalism as a danger and the political forces supporting independence as rivals who aspired to exercise undisputed hegemony over the Spanish community.

In Puerto Rico, the newspaper *El Heraldo Español*, with a substantial audience among the island's Spanish residents, took a position that was quite different from *El Diario de la Marina* and *La lucha*. Going beyond his newspaper's Spanish identity, the editor of *El Heraldo Español* proposed the creation of a national historical bloc to oppose the penetration of American capital. The *Heraldo* announced an extraordinary rallying cry: 'The U.S. Trusts: There is the Enemy!'[9] To some extent, the editorial position of *El Heraldo Español* reflected the rapprochement between the autonomists and Spanish integrationists that had taken place in the nineteenth century. That rapprochement was made possible by the defeat of separatism in 1868, the repression of radical autonomism from the 1880s, and extraordinary prosperity of coffee and other exports in the 1880s to 1890s. Supporters of Puerto Rican independence were unable to attain political and moral leadership over the different social strata of the island.

In Cuba, the War of Independence, with its inevitable sequels of blood and destruction, had opened a rift between Cuban and Spanish immigrant families. In Puerto Rico the political conflicts between Puerto Ricans and Spaniards were not insignificant: these conflicts included the *Grito de Lares* uprising (1868), the imprisonment and emigration of hundreds of political dissidents in the wake of that failed uprising, a campaign of torture and repression in 1887 (the *compontes*) at a time when Cuba was quiescent, urban boycotts and riots in 1894 to 1895, and widespread attacks on Spanish merchants in 1898 during the early months of the American invasion (the *partidas sediciosas*). However, these conflicts provoked relatively few lasting political tensions. Eventually, the disputes between autonomists and pro-Spanish integrationists (or *incondicionales*) were resolved in a largely institutional and legal manner within the large plantation-owning and commercial class. This process culminated in universal male suffrage and an autonomist charter in 1897. The integrationists were primarily wealthy merchants who had invested their capital in sugar plantations and, to a lesser degree, in coffee plantations. Their leaders were, for the most part, Spanish immigrants of the first and second generation.

The director of *El Heraldo Español*, Vicente Balbás Capó (1864–1926), was one of the leaders of the integrationist pro-Spanish party in the colonial epoch. Before *El Heraldo Español*, Balbás directed the integrationist newspaper *La Integridad Nacional* (which his father owned) and served as a deputy to the Spanish Cortes. There, he called for the cultural and spiritual fusion of Puerto Ricans and Spaniards. Balbás, of Spanish parents, was born and raised in Ponce, Puerto Rico, Puerto Rico's Creole 'second city' and economic capital in the late nineteenth century. Hardly a provincial, knee-jerk integrationist, Balbás studied at high school in Paris and engineering in Vallalodid (Spain). His Puerto Rican birth left him without Spanish citizenship under the Treaty of Paris; this was one of his main quarrels with the new regime. Balbás was also an active member of the executive board of the Casino Español, the most important Spanish immigrant association in the island.

For Balbás, the concepts of Puerto Rican homeland and Spanish nation were commensurable. Balbás had strong credentials and a family history as an *Incondicional*; this both constrained his political trajectory and afforded him space for radical political transformation. Although there is every reason to believe that Balbás did not speak for most of the Spanish immigrant population of Puerto Rico, *El Heraldo Español* functioned as the Spanish community's official newspaper in the early years of the twentieth century and Balbás's editorial line represented significant currents in the Hispanic community.

Balbás was also sensitive to agrarian issues in Puerto Rico, and directed the journal *Tierra*. *El Heraldo Español* aimed to represent not only the small Spanish producers, merchants and domestic industry, but also island agrarian interests generally. The newspaper repeatedly urged coffee-growers to better organise themselves politically. In response to a legislative bill that promoted the establishment of agrarian syndicates in order to detain the invasion of American capital, Balbás went a step further and advocated consumer and production co-operatives, which would cover the entire economy of the island. Balbás made an almost utopian call for a fraternal union of all producers to confront the ruinous competition of American production.

In Balbás's view, American capital would exhaust Puerto Rico's economy. His list of the different trusts that were taking over the Puerto Rican economy included the sugar refineries of the American Atlantic coast, the tobacco trust that monopolized the purchase of leaf tobacco from Puerto Rican growers, the electric-power trust, the maritime-transportation trust, and the railroad-transportation trust. Balbás sharply denounced the activities and objectives of the trusts, the powers of which were such that even 'in Congress itself, the trusts govern'. According to Balbás, Puerto Ricans should not expect any law or provision acting against the interests of these corporations.[10]

Moreover, Balbás proposed the creation of a nationalist bloc to oppose the penetration of U.S. capital. However, the Spanish immigrants could not become a nucleus of resistance to the cultural, political and economic hegemony of the United States. Spaniards in Puerto Rico were foreigners under their new colonisers. They were disenfranchised and any political activity could lead to their deportation. Under these circumstances, Balbás's discourse expressed a broad opposition to the American presence in Puerto Rico ... a stance whose success depended on mobilisation of the Puerto Rican people as a whole.

Balbás made an acute analysis of the hegemonic and global character of U.S. imperialism, calling it by name. He warned of the consequences that financial domination by the trusts would inevitably have for the Latin American countries; he called for a Latin American union against imperialist penetration.[11] The *Heraldo Español* became *El Heraldo de las Antillas*, and joined Puerto Rican patriot José de Diego in calling for the *Unión Antillana*: a union of the three Spanish-speaking Antilles in face of U.S. imperialism. Balbás, very much the activist, was jailed in federal prison in Atlanta by American authorities in 1917 on charges of sedition because he denounced conscription into the American military. Remarkably, Balbás the 'Spaniard' was the only public figure in Puerto Rico who dared criticise conscription and served prison time for it.

The political leaders of the nineteenth-century planter class, the Puerto Rican Creole politicians of the Autonomist Party, played a leading role in the Partido Unión after 1898. Coterminous with Balbás's political stance, the Unionist newspaper *La Democracia*, criticised the American trusts and praised the Spanish institutions of the colonial times, which it had censured in the past. It also defended the position of the Catholic Church against the inroads of the North American Protestant sects in the island's community.[12] Balbás's project for a national bloc was actually broader than the (timidly) pro-independence Partido Unión. Balbás saw Unionist pro-independence leanings around 1910 as a transient urge that actually held back other, more immediate, forms of economic and political self-organization.[13]

El Heraldo Español and *El Heraldo de las Antillas* converged not only with the discourse of the *Partido Unión* but also with outspoken advocates of Puerto Rican independence such as Rosendo Matienzo Cintrón and de Diego in the early 1900s and Pedro Albizu Campos in the 1930s. Albeit in different contexts and with different meanings, the proclamations of Balbás, Matienzo Cintrón, de Diego and Albizu Campos present a comparable mix: patriarchal values and Hispanic catholicism as well as anti-imperialism and a defense of the *unión antillana*.[14]

Measures favouring the role of women in society were criticised by Balbás in 1907 with expressions similar to those employed by Albizu Campos's *Par-*

tido Nacionalista in 1930. In his view, co-education in the same classroom 'feminised' males and 'masculinized' females. For Albizu and his followers, the confluence of the sexes in public schools tended to 'the corruption of our customs and the dissolution of the Puerto Rican home'.[15] Pervasive Puerto Rican patriarchal values resented the mixing of the sexes in public. Some Cuban intellectuals at the time were for co-education, others believed that the two sexes should be separated in schools. Outside marriage and the family, relations between the sexes should be ascetically compartmentalised. Balbás's Catholicism and Hispanism was echoed by de Diego and in Albizu. Balbás viewed with consternation the propagation of Protestant sects in Puerto Rico inasmuch as they were an expression of Anglo-Saxon values, the antithesis of Latin civilisation. And he never ceased to praise the norms and customs of Hispanic culture vis-à-vis those of the United States. Likewise, de Diego repudiated the presence of Protestant churches on the island as tending to subvert the values of Hispanic Catholicism, bulwarks of the island's cultural autonomy against the United States.[16]

The importance of Catholicism and *hispanidad* for Puerto Rican nationhood was expressed by Albizu as follows: 'Puerto Rico is the most perfect nationality of the New World. It is a true social unit. Although it is almost 70 percent of Spanish blood, Catholicism has erased all deep racial divisions.' These assertions suggest how traditional values helped to legitimate a developing national discourse. In this way, the cultural and political penetration of U.S. imperialism was confronted by effective appeals to the original Hispanic matrix of the nation. In the more ornate expressions of this nationalist discourse, the glorious Spanish accomplishment of the discovery of America by the Catholic monarchs was comparable only to the 1868 *Grito de Lares* uprising.

Balbás's writings in *El Heraldo Español* demonstrate that at least one segment of Spanish opinion in Puerto Rico framed its resistance to American economic competition and domination in terms that went beyond specific Spanish interests; instead, a broader, national opposition was proposed.

Spanish Sugar Barons as a National Class in Early-Twentieth-Century Puerto Rico?

In the nineteenth century, an important segment of the coffee-planter class in Puerto Rico consisted of Spanish immigrant and Corsican merchants. Friendships and marriages of immigrants into local landowning families and length of residence in Puerto Rico moderated unconditional loyalties to Spain. Many foreign planters were seen as members of Puerto Rican society and as part of the island's elite. Spaniards and Corsicans were well represented among the autonomist and nationalist movements. On the other hand, there were also leading Spanish planters who fiercely opposed any nationalist claims. That is not surprising as many immigrants, including planters, returned to Spain after having made their fortune and never considered Puerto Rico as their home-land. In any event, in the long run planters were reliant upon metropolitan force (whether Spanish, or, later, American) to maintain social supremacy over their labourers, as Fernando Picó has pointed out:

> These Catalonians, Ballerinas, Basques, Asturians, Galitians, Canary Islanders and Andalusians arriving in Puerto Rico do not necessarily sympathise with the government in Madrid, nor do they necessarily foment in their offspring and dependents the loyalty that is too easily attributed to them. But it is clear that those who acquired economic power were going to depend on the political power, whether Spanish or of the United States, to maintain their plantations and businesses.[17]

After 1898, Spanish merchants and sugar planters in Puerto Rico (as in Cuba) evolved a complex relationship with their American overlords. It would be hard to believe that these sectors entirely withdrew from agricultural enterprise in the twentieth century. Many Spanish immigrant merchants and coffee planters shifted to sugar production, although the Spanish presence in coffee continued to be strong. Whereas the total acreage of the coffee plantations remained fairly stable in the twentieth century – 197,000 *cuerdas*[18] in 1899, compared to 191,000 in 1929 – coffee production became concentrated in larger estates. As Laird Bergad has pointed out, more research should be done to determine the level of continuity in the ownership of coffee estates.[19] The same is true of sugar. Juan Giusti-Cordero and Angel Quintero Rivera have underscored the notable presence of resident Spanish sugar barons in Puerto Rican political circles in the first decades of the century.[20]

The Spanish sugar barons in Puerto Rico, while seemingly overshadowed by American investors, had a considerable share in the island's sugar production. In the first two decades of the twentieth century, the 'Spanish group' controlled at least 19 (out of 44) factories, producing one-third of Puerto Rico's sugar in 1913.[21] The rise of the new class of domestic sugar planters was linked to the high prices of sugar in the world market and the abrupt fall of coffee prices.

A Spanish newspaperman and writer, Luís de Araquistaín, wrote in his traveller's chronicles of the Hispanic Antilles about the close relations between Spaniards and Puerto Ricans and their common opposition to American hegemony,

> One of the dikes that offers a major resistance to Puerto Rico's Americanisation is the Spanish community in the island. They almost monopolized the country's commerce and have a great influence in banking and in some industries. They own a large bank and various sugar mills. They enjoy public credit and a high reputation. The Spanish community lives mixed with the Puerto Rican population. U.S. control of the island has contributed to tie the links between Spaniards and Puerto Ricans.[22]

A similar view was expressed by Luis Lloréns Torres, writer, leader of the Partido Unión, and spokesman for the Creole and Spanish coffee planters. According to him, the Spanish domestic bourgeoisie, built 'a wall of contention that gradually changed the conditions of the new regime and its absorption by big American capital'.

Against the Protestant religion and the Anglo-Saxon culture of the North American hegemony, Catholic religion and Hispanic culture were defended as dimensions of a Latin culture endowed with antiquity and sophistication. The Puerto Rican nationalists appealed to every legitimate argument in order to wage the battle of their gravely compromised historical destiny. Hence they identified Catholicism and Hispanic characteristics as an essential part of their own discourse and the foundation of their national culture.

According to Quintero Rivera and Giusti-Cordero, by the 1920s the growing conservatism of the local sugar barons brought them within the orbit of the pro-American *Partido Republicano*. The increasing pressure of the working classes undermined the planters' anti-American stance. Nationalist leader Albizu Campos took notice of this *volte face* and criticised it as immoral. By that time, however, the integration of the Spanish immigrants in the Puerto Rican nation was well on its way; and there was no dearth of Puerto Rican planters who shared their anti-labour, anti-nationalist views.

The Post-1898 Spanish Economic Presence in Cuba

Cuba was different. As the moderate Cuban intellectual, Jorge Mañach, wrote in the 1920s:

> Like the Negro, although more ostensibly for more obvious reasons, the Spaniard constitutes a world apart, with his separate section in the newspapers. Our celebrations are not his, nor are his enthusiasms ours.[23]

This process of social compartmentalization (à la 'plural society') was also asserted by Cuban writers and thinkers such as Fernando Ortiz, José Antonio Ramos, Miguel de Carrión, Luis de Sola, Enrique Jose Varona and Carlos de Velasco. The historian Emilio Roig de Leuchsenring and the Spanish writer Luís de Araquistaín argued that Spaniards were isolated from Cuban society by the regional mutual aid societies, headed by important Spanish merchants and industrialists.[24] '*La España Invertebrada*', as referred to by the Spanish philosopher, Ortega y Gasset, revealed itself in the division among the Spaniards residing in Cuba, who were separately grouped in mutual aid associations representing Galicians, Asturians, Catalonians, Basques, and Andalusians. These cultural and institutional patterns of regional allegiances of Spanish immigrants, as well as cleavages within the Cuban black and mulatto population and finally, of white Cubans, hindered Cuban national integration.

The large export and import merchants, the domestic industrialists and the sugar mill owners constituted the hegemonic class among the Spanish in Cuba (and perhaps in Cuba generally). These groups were opposed to the increasing economic influence of the United States, but they endorsed the 'Platt republic's'only partial sovereignty

Investment in Tobacco Manufactures, by Nationality (1927)

Spanish immigrants	%	Cubans	%	Americans	%
$13,809,154	33.6	$23,829,091	58	$3,425,278	8,3

In the sugar mills, a similar shift took place,

Owners of Sugar Mills by Nationality[25]

Years	Cubans	Spanish Immigrants	Americans	Other Foreigners
1915	67	42	43	18
1920	103	27	55	13

A major characteristic of the Cuban economy under American neo-colonial rule was that most of the island's industries continued to belong to Spanish immigrant financiers. The Banco Español de la Isla de Cuba, owned by Jose Marimón, controlled seventeen industries. Another important Spanish immigrant financier, Jose López Rodríguez, owned five domestic industries and three sugar mills. Ramón Crusellas Faure merged six soap factories and shared the Cuban soap market with Sabates and Co., also a Spanish firm.

After the First World War, Spanish and Cuban sugar-mill owners and large cane contract growers (*colonos*) joined forces with the Spanish financier-industrialists, headed by Marimón, in order to block the American sugar refineries' growing control of Cuba's sugar economy. The Spanish immigrant bourgeoisie aimed to reverse the trend and to control the final refining of Cuban sugar, in order to increase their profit margins. The climax of this struggle was the crisis provoked in 1920 by the domestic mill owners and Spanish financiers when they withheld the sale of the Cuban sugar harvest, with the immediate objective of raising the price so that the refineries would have to pay for Cuban semi-refined sugar, in order to loosen the refineries' grip over Cuban sugar production.

From the *Diario de la Marina*, the Spanish bourgeoisie launched a 'buy-Cuban' campaign against the North American refineries and associated American interests. While *El Diario de la Marina* had favoured American political intervention in Cuba whenever there was any threat of insurrection, now it called upon patriotic Cuban feelings in its campaign for economic nationalism. As a result of the economic crash provoked by countermeasures taken by the North Americans, the Spanish financiers and sugar mill owners involved in the retention of the Cuban harvest went bankrupt. In 1921, Jose López Rodríguez committed suicide. Marimón fled from Cuba to escape from his creditors. Falla Gutierrez could scarcely survive as an entrepreneur. Crusellas and Sabates, on the other hand, were forced to sell their stocks to North Americans. Many Cuban and Spanish sugar mills were sold to North American creditors.

As happens in every immigrant community, Cuba's Spaniards became more and more Cuban over time. Thus the Cuban sector of the domestic bourgeoisie increased, while the share of Spanish newcomers declined. In any event, the domestic bourgeoisie, refrained from mobilising the lower classes of society against the domination of American financial capital; this was in line with their class interests. By 1926, they would strongly support Gerardo Machado's government, urging changes in the Reciprocity Treaty and the imposition of new tariffs on the American products imported into the country. Meanwhile, the *Diario de la Marina* insisted that the Platt Amendment was a necessary brake on the unruly middle and lower classes of Cuba.

In Puerto Rico, similarly, the Spanish and Creole propertied classes became increasingly conservative when social unrest loomed large over the island. It is not this parallel, as important as it might be, which interests us here, but the divergent modes in which Spain, *hispanidad*, and Catholicism were invoked in Puerto Rico and Cuba. This contrast may have been especially notable in the domain of culture.

Post-1898 Spanish Culture in Cuba: from Catholicism to *Zarzuelas*

In contrast to their counterparts in Puerto Rico, *el grupo español* in Cuba rejected Cuban cultural miscegenation, *mestizaje*, as vehemently as it rejected the North American cultural presence. At the Casino Español and other Spanish societies, Spanish cultural manifestations reigned. The Catholic Church also struck similar, and different, registers in Cuba and in Puerto Rico. Whereas Catholicism became an important element in forging a sense of Puerto Rican nationhood (despite strong North American control of the upper Church hierarchy for decades after 1898), in Cuba the Catholic Church was a constant source of tension and an obstacle to Spanish-Cuban fusion. The Catholic Church's alignment with the Spanish colonial power during Cuba's wars of liberation excluded that institution, in great measure, from an active participation in the process of national formation. Only a

minority of native-born priests collaborated with the independence movement. Since the mid-nineteenth century, the majority of the island's clergy
had been Spanish, and these were naturally inclined in the course of Cuba's
wars of independence to make common cause with the Church hierarchy and
with Spanish colonial rule.

In the aftermath of the Spanish domination of Cuba, the allegiances of the
Catholic Church became deeply problematic; for Catholicism actually underwent a renaissance in the island after 1898. The Constitutional Convention of
1901 adopted the principle of separation of church and state and of the
responsibility of the latter for secondary and university education, but the
Catholic Church recovered lost ground by gaining control of elite schools.
The clergy, still predominantly Spanish-born, was closely linked to the bourgeoisie and middle classes of the Spanish immigrant population. The census
of 1899 showed that 190 of a total of 283 clergymen were foreigners, and
173 of these were Spanish. Subsequently, the ecclesiastical hierarchy underwent a drastic reorganisation. Bishop Sbarretti created two new dioceses, one
in Pinar del Río and one in Cienfuegos, to accommodate the national feelings
of the believers, but the Church leadership continued to be in the hands of
Spanish priests. During the first twenty years of the Republic, eight religious
associations and fraternities for poor relief were founded. Several religious
schools for the privileged were built in Santiago de Cuba, Cienfuegos and
Sagua.

Financed by the local Spanish bourgeoisie, the renaissance of the Catholic
Church in Cuba was stimulated by the torrent of 800,000 Spanish immigrants.
These immigrants arrived on the island in the first decades of the republic, typically to work in the sugar industry. The growing influence of the Catholic
Church seriously troubled advocates of Cuban nationhood. They agreed on the
fact that the Cuban people were indifferent to Catholic proselytes, but they perceived a dangerous trend: '… the foreign clergy, that is the Spanish priests, were
constantly acquiring more wealth and more power, in the absence of adequate
laws to restrict the undesirable immigration of members of religious orders
…'[26] At the same time, the Cuban House of Representatives was concerned
about the immigration of numerous Spanish priests and requested a report on
this question from the Department of Immigration. According to this report,
from 1912 to 1915, 627 priests and 835 nuns entered the country (compared
with a total of 190 foreign clergymen in 1899).

The argument against leaving education in the hands of the clergy, particularly foreigners, was that they 'feel no love for our great men or for our
country, nor do they know our history'. This was especially perilous because
the clergy's students generally belonged to the ruling classes and would
become, according to influential Cuban thinkers like Enrique José Varona,
'the men destined to govern Cuba'.[27] The widely read journal *Cuba Contemporánea*, led by outstanding Cuban intellectuals like Carlos de Velasco,

Miguel de Carrión, José Sixto Sola, and Julio de Villoldo, waged an unabated campaign against the Catholic Church and Catholic education.

The 1919 Census registered the presence of 880 members of religious orders of both sexes, of whom 129 were Cuban, 653 were Spanish immigrants, and 27 of other nationalities (there was apparently an undercount, in comparison with the earlier study conducted by the Cuban House of Representatives). During this period, the ecclesiastical hierarchy had kept aloof from political controversies in order not to jeopardise its rapid gains in the field of education. In the 1920 to 1921 academic year, 314,000 children were registered in the country's public schools. It was estimated that some 80,000 children, primarily of the upper and middle class, studied in private schools. According to statistics obtained from information provided by more than 100 private schools attended by some 25,000 children, 44 percent of the teachers were priests or nuns and 44 percent were foreign – the majority, of course, Spanish. And Spanish regional cultural centres financed twenty-five private schools, which enrolled 3,000 children.[28]

At the same time, Cuban attitudes towards Spanish artistic and literary manifestations revealed the survival of a taste and sensibility that was not completely severed from the cultural Spanish matrices of the colonial past. Although a taste for Creole cultural manifestations prevailed among the Cuban people, in the last half of the nineteenth century and the first decades of the twentieth, the fondness for diverse genres of Spanish cultural expression persisted among broad sectors of the population. Residents of Havana and Santiago enthusiastically welcomed operetta and theatre companies from Spain. The audiences drawn to these spectacles outnumbered those attending the performances of local companies. Statistics for the period 1909 to 1915[29] document the predominance among the Santiago public of Spanish *zarzuelas* and operettas over Cuban folkloric theatrical offerings: performances of Cuban theatrical works did not reach 30 percent of the total. The comedies and dramas that were presented by Spanish theatre companies, with Spanish actors, were also written by peninsular authors. Operas and operettas were also performed by Italian and Spanish companies.[30]

In Havana, the Spanish and Cuban upper and middle-class public flocked to the urban cultural spectacles. According to Primelles, Havana's theatre companies were predominantly Spanish. Creole vernacular theatre was only on stage in three of Havana's fifteen theatres; Spanish comedies, dramas, and *zarzuelas* predominated, as well as Italian operas.[31] Even in the years from 1915 to 1922, when Cuban literature was more widely read, it suffered from competition with Spanish authors published in Madrid, Barcelona or Havana. A Spanish-Cuban narrator, Alfonso Hernández Catá wrote novels set in Madrid whose plots turned on the adventures and infidelities of married Spanish women. Hernández Catá's racy novels delighted Cuban female readers and were the best sellers of the epoch (significantly, no post-1898 Puerto Rican author of note wrote in such a *madrileño* genre).

The eminent philologist and critic of Cuban and Spanish folklore and literature, Carolina Poncet de Cárdenas, noted that white, mulatto, and black children playing in Cuba's public squares and tenement patios sang centuries-old rhymes that embodied 'the form, the characters, and the plots of the Castilian romances'. In Cuba as in Spain, the oral tradition of the old romances was kept alive by women whose lullabies followed Castilian, Catalonian, or Galician tradition. These lullabies formed an inseparable part of Cuban culture and remained so into the second half of the twentieth century. In them, you could feel the 'beat', as Poncet de Cárdenas liked to say, of 'the soul of the (Spanish) race'.[32]

During the first three decades of the twentieth century, Havana continued to be a good market for Spanish novels. In the literary gatherings at the Café Alhambra, the most outstanding Cuban writers often met in animated discussion with members of Spain's 'Generation of '98', itself critical of the Spanish social and political regime that the Cubans had rebelled against in 1895. Jacinto Benavente, Blasco Ibáñez, Luis de Zulueta, Fernando de los Ríos, Miguel de Unamuno, Rafael Alberti, Federico García Lorca, Zamacois, Zuloaga, Juan Ramón Jiménez, Valle Inclán, Marañón and other Spanish thinkers and writers visited Havana occasionally to give lectures, present expositions, on pleasure trips, or were simply at the invitation of Cuban institutions or friends. Their presence unquestionably inspired the young Cuban intelligentsia, including the protagonists of the *Protesta de los Trece* (Protest of the Thirteen) in 1923 (in fact, one of the original fifteen participants in the protest was a young Spaniard, who did not sign their manifesto for fear of being deported). This protest sparked what became the powerful national movement of the 1930s. It was thus that the dialogue between Spanish and Cuban culture reached its highest point in history. Never before had the values of progressive Hispanic culture played such a re-animating and vivifying role in the country's thought and national life.

Concluding Observations

Although many of our observations require further research and conceptualisation, we can draw a few important conclusions. Balbás's *El Heraldo Español*, which tried to reach out to a comprehensive Puerto Rican nationalism after 1898, did not cover the entire Spanish range of opinion in Puerto Rico. Yet it was a prominent voice that was virtually absent in Cuba. The attitudes towards Catholicism and *hispanismo* of the most prominent nationalist leaders in Puerto Rico on the one hand, and in the Cuban Congress and of Cuban intellectuals, on the other, were significantly different. The transculturation process that took place between Spanish immigrants and the Creole/mulatto Puerto Rican society deserves more scholarly attention, and might help to detect and conceptualise comparable processes in Cuba.

In Cuba, the Spanish immigrants were present in larger numbers, and the Spanish elites had a more prominent position in Cuba's economy. Thus the Spanish immigrants maintained a stronger distinctiveness and cultural influence in Cuba than their counterparts in Puerto Rico. Likewise, the Spanish bourgeoisie in Puerto Rico did not play such a leading role in the economic confrontation with the United States as their counterparts in Cuba. The fact that the Spanish immigrant community in Puerto Rico was marginal compared to the one in Cuba, was partly offset by the fact that 'Hispanism' and 'Catholicism' were not the monopoly of the Spanish immigrant community and had their own roots and complex trajectory in Puerto Rico's four-centuries social history. The old nineteenth-century rapprochement between autonomists and Spanish integrationists to acquiesce in the colonial status quo was decisive in this respect. The Creole and/or mulatto elite in Santo Domingo also invoked a Catholic and Hispanic legacy in their opposition to Haitian labour invasions and North American economic and political interventions.

In Cuba, however, the hegemonic national discourse was less rooted in that Catholic and Hispanic legacy than in Puerto Rico; in Cuba, that legacy was to some degree overshadowed by a nationalist secular ideology of opposition against Spain. Cubans had fought against Spanish colonialism and the Catholic Church. The Cuban nationalists felt that a Spanish bourgeoisie that aligned itself with Gerardo Machado's government and with North American interventionism endangered the country's independence. The national popular bloc that was established in the 1930s revolution confronted both the corporatist bourgeoisie, and North American neo-colonialism.

In Puerto Rico, *El Heraldo Español* advocated the formation of a national front against American policies. The Partido Unión (with many links to resident Spanish bourgeoisie) dominated the Puerto Rican Legislature, and many *unionistas* sympathised with the early Nationalist Party. In Cuba, *El Diario de la Marina* instructed its readers to abstain from politics and favoured the Platt Amendment's encroachment upon Cuban sovereignty. A closer look at the Spanish immigrants' attitudes in the Antilles could however reveal important deviations from the directives issued by their elites, press and institutions. In fact, many immigrants adopted a different stance from the one advocated by their patrons. According to some testimonies, the *Casino Español* and other Spanish societies in Cuba tried to keep Spanish workers away from labour struggles. However, other evidence shows that anarchist leaders from the Peninsula mobilised Spanish and native workers in the Hispanic Antilles.

The most relevant lesson of this comparative inquiry is that culture and tradition can sometimes mobilise public opinion as effectively as actual social institutions. The Spanish bourgeoisie and its community in Puerto Rico were weak from an economic and demographic point of view, compared to their homologues in Cuba. However, its past cultural traditions, customs and way of life were alive in the minds of twentieth-century Puerto Ricans; and autonomist and separatist intellectuals and political leaders invoked them effectively to oppose American presence in Puerto Rico.

A closer – not necessarily microhistoric – look at the Spanish immigrants in Cuba and Puerto Rico could reveal a variety of responses towards the exhortations made by their press, patrons and institutions. As a matter of fact, many immigrants did not isolate themselves from the Puerto Rican population, despite their superiors' advice. A great many joined their interests and aspirations with the Puerto Rican people. Others married Puerto Rican women and established Puerto Rican families. Detailed studies on the relations of Spanish immigrants and their institutions with the population of the Hispanic Antilles should disclose further contrasts and similarities.

Notes

1. U.S. Bureau of Census. Informe sobre el Censo de Cuba de 1899; Informe sobre el Censo de Puerto Rico de 1899.
2. *Diario de la Marina*, July 1, l901, 1.
3. Fernández, 'La presencia española en Cuba después de 1898', 515.
4. *Diario de la Marina*, September 1, 1901, 'Justificaciones'; October 13, 1899, 'Nuestras clases conservadoras'.
5. Rivero Muñiz, *Actualidades, 1903–1919*.
6. *La Lucha*, Octobre 12, 1899, 'Agitación ficticia, pero artificial'.
7. *La Lucha*, Octobre 30, 1899, 'Nuestras clases conservadoras'.
8. *La Lucha*, Novembre 15, 1899, 'Una moción deliciosa'.
9. Balbas Capó, *Puerto Rico a los diez años de su americanización*, 447.
10. As note 9 above, 239–43.
11. As note 9 above, 438.
12. As note 9 above., ix.
13. As note 9 above, xvi, 39–42, 235–38, 383–86.
14. De Diego, *Obras completas*, Vol. 2, 85–89; Albizu Campos, *Obras escogidas*, Vol. 4 (1997).
15. Albizu Campos, *Obras escogidas*, Vol. 4 (1997), 50. See also Negrón Portillo, *El autonomismo puertorriqueño: su transformación ideológica (1895–1914)*. See also in Díaz Soler, *Rosendo Matienzo Cintrón, orientador y guardián de una cultura*, Vol. 1.
16. Díaz Quiñones, 'Isla de Quimeras, Pedreira, Palés y Albizu'. See the Nationalist Party programme in Bothwell González, *Puerto Rico: Cien años de lucha política*, 461–66.
17. Fernando, 'La religiosidad popular es religiosa'. In order to see the role of Spanish and European immigrants from St. Thomas in the foundation of the Puerto Rican plantations, see Marazzi, 'El impacto de la inmigración a Puerto Rico de 1800 a 1830: análisis estadístico'; Cifre de Loubriel, 'Los inmigrantes del siglo XIX. Su contribución a la formación del pueblo puertorriqueño'; Scarano, *Sugar and Slavery in Puerto Rico*; Scarano, *Inmigración y clases sociales en el Puerto Rico del siglo XIX*; Bergard, *Coffee and the Growth of Agrarian Capitalism in Nineteenth-Century Puerto Rico*; Cubano, 'La emigración mallorquina a Puerto Rico en el siglo XIX'. And: *Historia y sociedad*, No. 7, 1992. Universidad de Puerto Rico, Recinto de Río Piedras.

18. 1 *cuerda* = 0.393 hectare or 0.971 acre.
19. Bergad, *Coffee and the Growth of Agrarian Capitalism.*
20. Quintero Rivera, *Conflictos de clase y política en Puerto Rico,* and Quintero Rivera, *Patricios y plebeyos: burgueses, hacendados, artesanos y obreros.* See also Giusti-Cordero, 'En búsqueda de la nación concreta'; for a fuller analysis, see Giusti-Cordero, 'Hacia otro 98: el 'grupo español' en Puerto Rico, 1890–1930'.
21. Giusti-Cordero, 'En búsqueda de la nación concreta'.
22. de Araquistaín, *La agonía antillana.*
23. Mañach, *Pasado vigente.*
24. Ibarra, 'Herencia española, influencia estadounidense'; Ibarra, *Nuestra común historia Cuba-España.*
25. Ibarra, *Cuba: 1898–1921: Partidos políticos y clases sociales,* 77–78, 81–82 and 436–39.
26. Sola y Bobadilla, *Pensando en Cuba,* 194 and 197. See also De Velasco y Pérez, *Aspectos nacionales,* 113–23, 89–112, and Villoldo, 'Necesidad de colegios cubanos'.
27. Varona, 'Con motivo de las fiestas de Belén'; Ramos, *Manual del perfecto fulanista,* 172–192; Carrión, 'El desenvolvimiento social de Cuba en los últimos veinte años'; Ortiz, *Orbita de Fernando Ortiz,* 101.
28. Ibarra, *Nuestra común historia Cuba-España.*
29. The statistics were reproduced in the study made by Lomba Milán , 'Los espectáculos culturales en Santiago de Cuba'.
30. As note 29, above.
31. Primelles, *Crónicas cubanas,* I & II. Data from Primelles, Volume I, on pages 94–95, 98–99, 211–12, 402–04, 516–17, 519–21; and from Volume II, on pages 112–13, 115–17, 274–75, 277–79, 427–28, 430–32, 573–74, and 576–77.
32. Poncet de Cárdenas, *Investigaciones y apuntes literarios,* 62–63, 64–65.

10

COMPRADORS OR COMPADRES? 'SUGAR BARONS' IN NEGROS (THE PHILIPPINES) AND PUERTO RICO UNDER AMERICAN RULE

Juan Giusti-Cordero

A Filipino 'Indigenous Planter Class'?

In the early twentieth century, it has been contended, 'the Philippines, unique among the lands that gird the world's tropical latitudes, had produced an indigenous planter class under colonial rule ... nowhere else in colonial Asia did an indigenous elite develop and then dominate a modern plantation industry'.[1] However, the Philippines' sugar planters were not unique; for one, a similar grouping existed in another colony of the U.S.A., Puerto Rico. Like the Philippines, Puerto Rico was also a former Spanish colony. In both colonies, the foundations for the *central* era were in place before 1898. Yet the massive development of locally-owned sugar plantations occurred within the American colonial framework ... and in the sector that was ostensibly the American economic enclave par excellence.

Sugar planters in the Philippines and Puerto Rico played a complex role as both subalterns and rulers in the context of U.S. colonialism. Sugar planters looked out for their interests vis-à-vis the American and Spanish colonists as well as local labourers. Diffuse economic, ethnic, and cultural boundaries existed between native and metropolitan sectors and within native sectors.

Social relations and cultural patterns from the Spanish era were continued under U.S. colonialism in the Philippines and Puerto Rico. Most strikingly, in some ways the Spanish economic and cultural presence was reinforced in the sugar-planter milieu after 1898. The imbrication of pre-1898 social relations in the U.S. colonial era in the Philippines and Puerto Rico, and their significance for that era, cannot be overstated.

In both the Philippines and Puerto Rico, sugar planters were themselves diverse, even in the economic terrain. Most planters were landholding sugar growers under contract with sugar mills (*colonos* in Puerto Rico, *hacenderos* in the Philippines). A tiny portion of 'sugar planters' were also sugar-factory owners (*centralistas*); this is the group that was usually considered as the 'sugar barons'. The activities and social relations of the 'sugar planters' often ranged far beyond sugar, and extended from cattle-raising to retail trade to import-export commerce, urban professions, railways, and banking. Beyond the 'material' diversity of economic roles, how the planters identified themselves (e.g. as *hacenderos* or as merchants, or as hybrid permutations of the two) is of utmost importance. The 'sugar planters' had heterogeneous, and evolving, ethnocultural profiles. In this context, calling them a planter class is doubly heuristic.

Most research on the Filipino and Puerto Rican colonial experience views planter elites as mere intermediaries. The multiple social identities of the sugar planters are usually left unexamined; and their ethnocultural profiles are registered only fragmentarily. One major consequence is that 1898 is misperceived as a mere shift from 'Spain' to the 'United States', construed as different colonial metropoles ruling passive colonial formations. This approach implies little awareness of the ways in which sugar planters and other social groups in the Philippines and Puerto Rico were active and resilient in shaping the relationship between the pre- and post-1898 colonial eras. Even the peculiar position of pre-1898 Spanish colonial elites under conditions of 'colonial succession' is brushed aside.

While the Filipino and Puerto Rican planter elites may not have had the strength and self-assurance of other peripheral bourgeoisies, like other such bourgeoisies they may be usefully analysed in terms of negotiation and self-interest rather than strict subjugation and intermediary roles. At the same time, the ostensible independence of other peripheral bourgeoisies has been seriously challenged. When the history of those peripheral bourgeoisies is traced back to their colonial eras, their supposed self-assurance vanishes into a maze of largely assimilationist and autonomist currents that later nationalist mythmaking largely obscures. In particular, our inquiry compares Puerto Rico and the Philippines' Negros island, historically the centre of the Filipino sugar industry and the original 'Sugarlandia'.

The Philippines and Puerto Rico

On the whole, comparing the Philippines and Puerto Rico may seem inapposite. Just one of the 7,000 Philippine islands, Luzón, is twelve times the size of Puerto Rico, and the Philippine archipelago is larger than all the Caribbean islands. Puerto Rico would rank only eighth in size among the Philippine islands. Their precolonial and colonial history also imply remarkable differences. The Spanish legacy is more visible in Puerto Rico than in the Philippines, where the aboriginal Filipino-Malay population was not decimated and pre-Conquest languages are widely spoken. The U.S.A. annexed the Philippines after a brutal three-years war of occupation that began in the context of the Cuban-Spanish-American War; in Puerto Rico the American invasion was largely welcomed as a way of liquidating Spanish rule. The Philippines began a transition towards independence in 1935 but was occupied by Japan in the Second World War. Subsequently, the Philippines attained independence while Puerto Rico remained a U.S. territory with broadened self-government. The differences between the Philippines and Puerto Rico are integral to their respective regions: beyond sharing tropical islands and a history of colonialism, Southeast Asia and the Caribbean are so contrasting that they seem to lie on opposite sides of the world ... as they do.

Yet similarities between Puerto Rico and the Philippines do exist. Both were Spanish colonies from the sixteenth century onwards to 1898, both received the impact of Spanish political institutions, the Spanish language, and Roman Catholicism, and both remained colonies (as did Cuba) long after the Latin American wars of independence had shattered the Spanish colonial empire. Both territories thus became 'exceptional' in their regions. Both Puerto Rico and the Philippines were 're-colonised' by the U.S.A. and were ruled directly as 'unincorporated territories'.[2] Indeed, this is where the Philippines and Puerto Rico parted ways with Cuba, as the Philippines and Puerto Rico ostensibly became exceptions in the history of American global hegemony ... although the independence of the Cuban 'Platt Republic' must not be overestimated.[3] Both Puerto Rico and the Philippines were subject to kindred colonial policies and, while the differences between the two territories were recognised,[4] Congress often discussed both possessions at the same time, from 1898 until Filipino independence. At times, the Philippines 'wagged' Puerto Rico almost as Cuba had under Spain.

Differences and similarities between Puerto Rico and the Philippines are also notable with respect to their sugar industries. The timing of sugar –industry development in the two territories, for one, was different. Sugar cane was a major product in Puerto Rico long before 1898. *Central* production began in Puerto Rico the 1870s, and the production of centrifugal (96°) sugar was common by 1898; under American rule, *central* production grew by leaps and bounds and was preponderant by 1912. In the Philippines, there were no *centrals* in 1898 and muscovado (semi-refined) sugar was the universal norm until 1912, when the first *central* was established. Thus when *central* production attained predominance in Puerto Rico it was barely beginning in the Philippines. However, *centrals* developed rapidly in the Philippines during and after the First World War, and after 1920 comparisons between Puerto Rico and the Philippines are more in line.

One reason for the different timing of the Philippine and Puerto Rican sugar industries is their contrasting access to the American market: Puerto Rico had duty-free entry to the U.S.A. from 1900 onwards, while the Philippines entered later (1909) and remained more vulnerable to Washington political cross-winds. There were also important differences between the Philippines and Puerto Rico in the relationship between American investment and *central* landholding. In Puerto Rico, four American corporations operated *centrals* and controlled immense estates, in the Philippines the role of American sugar corporations was almost negligible. Moreover, in Puerto Rico, sugares (whether American or local) owned and operated extensive canefields, while in the Philippines independent landholders (*hacenderos*) produced nearly all the sugar cane. Less than 5 percent of the sugar cane was grown on *central*-owned land by the *centrals* themselves; even in Cuba, where *colono* production was stronger than in Puerto Rico, the percentage of *central*-owned land was higher (20 percent). 'Philippine sugar mill companies do not play as important a role in the local industry as do the mill companies of Hawai'i, Puerto Rico and Cuba'.[5] 'The ownership of agricultural land in the Philippines is widely diffused and characterised by relatively small holdings'.[6]

Hence in the Philippines the combination of sugar grower and manufacturer was rare, while in Puerto Rico all *central* owners were also sugar growers (and only a minute portion of the sugar growers were also *centralistas* in Puerto Rico).[7] On the whole, however, in Puerto Rico and Negros the *colonos* and the *hacenderos* remained a major force in the sugar industry, and the growers shaped in both islands a major dimension of the social relations of sugar production, and of sugar politics.[8]

While the differences between the sugar industries of Puerto Rico and the Philippines are as wide as their contrasting contexts, in both territories sugar became the premier export under American rule. In both, the formation of large-scale, mechanised *centrals* occurred essentially after 1898; and in both territories local sugar planter classes attained a strategic position under American rule. American colonialism was the condition for the formation (Philippines) or the consolidation (Puerto Rico) of a local planter class that thrived behind U.S. tariff protection but was also in significant tension with the metropolis concerning issues of commerce, tax policy, municipal government, language and cultural identity ... and the timing and degree of territorial self-government or independence.

The relationship between the sugar planters of the Philippines and Puerto Rico and their U.S. metropolis was deeply ambivalent: and it is on this terrain that the comparison between the two planter classes becomes especially textured. Philippines sugar planters played 'a Janus-faced role as both subjects and beneficiaries of imperial rule',[9] as part of a Filipino elite that, as a whole, even 'manipulated American colonialists to serve their own interests, while the Americans formulated their colonial policy in response to the needs of the colonised'.[10] After the Second World War, the U.S.A. often favoured the same wealthy Filipino sugar planters who had been at the summit of the Japanese occupation regime. '[M]any of the same families and companies that controlled plants in the 1930s [...] retained their domination following 1946.'[11] The sugar bloc was pre-eminent in the Marcos regime roughly until the 1972 declaration of martial law,[12] when Ferdinand Marcos clashed with the 'Old Society oligarchs'.[13]

While sugar plantation elites elsewhere often had antagonistic relations with nationalist movements, in the case of the Philippines and Puerto Rico the role of the sugar planters was more complex.[14] In Puerto Rico, non-*central* sugar growers (*colonos*) owning thousands of acres were conspicuous in the ranks of pro-autonomy forces identified with the Popular Democratic Party. Even local *central* owners had discreet links with the Nationalists before the 1930s, when the colonial government (now with sugar-planter support) began open persecution of the movement. José Coll Cuchí, a conservative attorney, academic and legislator who was first president of the Nationalist Party, wrote: 'it is not that the Puerto Rican sugar producer [*el azucarero puertorriqueño*] lacks dignity and patriotism, but that he responds to the system that has educated him'.[15] In the Philippines, despite harsh labour conditions in the sugar *haciendas* 'the simple fact of Filipino ownership exempted the plantations from critical examination'[16,] and the *centrals* were 'elite nationalist symbols'.[17]

In Puerto Rico, many economists and historians have emphasised the extent of post-1898 American control over Puerto Rican sugar production.[18] Subsequently, however, the complexity of the American colonial era has been recognised. Gervasio García pointed out that the American occupation strengthened Creole sugar producers through the duty-free access to the immense American market and that U.S. capital did not penetrate most of the regions where *centrals* existed before 1898, except late and only partially.[19] Quintero Rivera noted the significance of the locally-owned *centrals* and traced its political implications.[21] James Dietz highlighted American corporate control of the post-1898 sugar industry but also found that the extent of local control was worthy of closer analysis.[22] In one of his last studies on Puerto Rican economic history, Dietz expressed puzzlement at the non-U.S. sector of the Puerto Rico sugar industry and called for closer research on the matter.[22]

Negros and Puerto Rico

For a closer comparison between Puerto Rico and the vast Philippines archipelago, one might well focus on Negros island. Negros is one of the Visayas, the sub-archipelago that bridges the islands of Luzón and Mindanao. Negros, like Puerto Rico, was a site of a major sugar industry after 1898.[23] Negros was one of the two major sugar-producing areas of the Philippines' 'sugarlandia': the other was the Pampanga valley in Luzón. While much smaller than Luzón, Negros became the Philippines 'sugar island' par excellence,[24] and the original 'Sugarlandia'.[25]

The inner histories of Negros and Puerto Rico sugar production, while quite different, both suggest how exclusive emphasis on the post-1898 American colonial presence and investments leaves too much unaccounted for. Alfred McCoy locates the origins of Negros's sugar industry in the hand-textile industry of nearby Panay island.[26] Chinese *mestizos* were the core of Panay's hand-textile entrepreneurs.[27] This industry had extensive overseas markets, principally in China, but declined steeply in the second half of the nineteenth century. Chinese *mestizo* entrepreneurs from Panay moved into Negros, purchased land and began to produce sugar cane. Local networks formed through the textile industry were important in this process, as many of the early labourers recruited by the *mestizo* entrepreneurs to clear land and establish cane cultivation originated in the 'textile' villages, while and relatives and foremen of the entrepreneurs who came from those same villages supervised the plantations. Settlers from other areas also came to Negros and tended to intermarry, often complicating and blurring distinctions of origin. 'For example, many of the descendants of the great Iloilo merchant Basilio Lopez (circa 1810 to circa1875), many of whom became great Negrense planters, within two generations had intermarried into numerous other Ilongo families, but also with Cebuanos, Spaniards, Spanish *mestizos*, and Americans'.[28]

When large-scale commercial production of sugar in the Philippines began in the 1870s, Negros (in particular Negros Occidental) quickly became the main producing area in the archipelago.[29] Rapid increases in Negros's population in the late nineth century ensued from a large inflow of migrant labourers (called *indocumentados*, i.e. 'without legal authorisation'; and more recently *sacadas*, i.e. 'those removed') Panay, Cebu, and other Visayas. Many of the migrants remained.

In Puerto Rico, slave-based sugar production boomed between the 1820s and the 1850s; slavery was abolished in 1873. While immigrant Spanish planters and merchants were the single most important group (Scarano 1984), there was a significant presence of foreign planters and merchants in Mayagüez, Guayama and Ponce. Many of these planters and merchants had migrated from the nearby British, French, and Danish islands in the first half of the nineteenth century, in the midst of emancipation and declining production in those islands.

At the same time, Mayagüez, Guayama, and Ponce descended from earlier economic centres such as San Germán in the southwest and Coamo in the southeast. These two regions were deeply involved in the cattle-and-contraband economy of the eighteenth century linked to Saint-Domingue, the Lesser Antilles, and Curaçao.[30] In the nineteenth century San Juan was economically important but remained above all the centre of Spanish colonial power. The fusion of immigrant and more native planters in the nineteenth century shaped the pre-1898 Puerto Rican planter class. In Puerto Rico, the first *centrals* were established in the 1870s just after slave emancipation, with the proceeds from compensations to slaveholders by the Spanish Crown.

A process of concentration within the Puerto Rican sugar industry was well under way before 1898.[31] The number of ox-driven and steam-powered sugar mills (*trapiches*) declined 30 percent before 1898, from 446 in 1870 to 345.[32] The number of sugar mills declined further to 146 by 1910. The *centrals*, like many *trapiches*, were powered by steam engines (and firewood), but produced on a larger scale and included innovations such as larger and stronger cane crushers, vacuum pans (rather than open boilers), and centrifugals. Puerto Rico's twenty-two *centrals* in 1898 were more than half of the highest number of *centrals* reached in the twentieth century (42); about half of them continued after 1910.[33]

The Post-1898 Sugar Industry: Negros

After 1898 there was some expansion of Negros sugar production, though initially at a slow pace (unlike Puerto Rico, where sugar production grew rapidly). Until the First World War the same hacienda system prevailed in Negros: relatively small-scale steam-powered sugar mills, grinding cane grown by networks of sharecroppers. Negros mainly produced muscovado (semi-refined or brown sugar), in animal-driven mills.[34] Muscovado had a sizeable local market, and a regional market in Southeast Asia; but it rarely went further. The Philippines 'remained the last major world producer without a sugar central'.[35] Negros planters had substantial difficulties in securing a labour supply; the planters often had to give, and lost, advances to the labourers or their recruiters. Partly for this reason, large-scale sugar production was slower to develop in Negros, in a pattern broadly shared by the rest of the Philippines (Puerto Rico was itself slower than Cuba and Java). 'Filipino planters continued far longer as the primary producers of both cane and sugar.'[36] Negros eventually shifted to *centrals* and 96° sugar, and to consequent production for the U.S. and world sugar market, but did so several decades after Puerto Rico.

It took changes in the U.S. tariff system (1909, 1913)[38] and a tenfold price increase in the First World War and postwar period to pull Philippines sugar into the American and world markets, while its production underwent radical technical and social transformation. From 1914 to 1927, 820 Negros plantation steam mills were replaced by 17 *central* factories ... about half the Philippines total (33).[38] These *centrals* accounted for more than half of the Philippines' total sugar production. The total production of the eleven largest Negros *centrals* increased six-fold from 1922 to 1934 (144,077 to 714,702 tons).[39]

The Negros sugar mills were fewer in number than Puerto Rico's, but had a larger individual capacity. Eight *centrals* in Negros produced above 55,000 tons of semi-refined sugar from 1933 to 1934, while only one *central* in Puerto Rico, Guánica Centrale (of the American-owned South Puerto Rico Sugar Company) consistently topped 50,000 tons (the largest Cuban sugar mills produced over 100,000 tons annually). Significantly, in Negros only one North American *central* operated, and it was not directly owned by mainland American capital but by Hawaiian-born planters of North American descent. Indeed, the strongest U.S. corporate presence in the Philippines sugar industry was the Hawaiian-American Company, which operated *centrals* in Negros.

Filipino capital was strongly predominant in Negros, both in landowning and in *central* ownership; in fact, American interests were no more important than the Spanish. Contrary to scenarios of American domination of sugar production, Filomeno Aguilar notes, in the Philippines 'sugar – the most heavily capitalised industry – presented the paradox that, because of the contradictions of American colonialism, American capital had no hegemonic position in the Philippine colonial economy, particularly in Negros. Mestizo Power had reason to be exultant over sugar'. The logic behind the 'paradox', of course, involved other factors; not simply the characteristics of American colonial rule, or 'the strategic participation of Filipino interests in the colonial state', or limitations on land acquired from the public domain (maximum 16 hectares or 39.5 acres for individuals, 1,024 hectares or 2,530 acres for corporations.[40] However, the thrust of Aguilar's argument is indisputable.

In 1922, Negros produced 144,000 tons of semi-refined sugar, a large increase from the previous decade but still substantially less than Puerto Rico's 405,000 tons. By the 1930s the difference between the two islands, which expanded production considerably in the 1920s, had narrowed. In 1934, just before the Jones-Costigan tariffs were established, Negros produced 715,000 tons, compared to Puerto Rico's 1.1 million tons.

By 1935, although the largest American investments had been made in sugar [...] American capital accounted for a small 10.5 percent and Spanish capital only 9 percent of total investments in the sugar industry. Filipino capital controlled 79 percent of all sugar investments. Filipinos held most of the sugar lands. Except for some inconspicuous *haciendas* owned by a few former U.S. Army soldiers in the remote southern part of Negros, American capital owned hardly any sugar lands. In sugar manufacturing, Filipino investments reached a 47 percent plurality, while American capital accounted for 27 percent and Spansh capital 24 percent.[41]

By the end of the 1930s, there were 47 *centrals* in the Philippines as a whole; and eighteen of those were in Negros, whose sugar industry thus appears as more concentrated than Puerto Rico's. By this time, the U.S. corporate presence was actually weaker than in the 1910s.

The Second World War and the Japanese occupation left the much-expanded sugar mills of Negros in ruins. Favourable U.S. trade policy and rehabilitation funds allowed the Negros sugar production to regain prewar levels by the late 1950s, in some cases with sugar-mill machinery imported from Puerto Rico (see below). The history of Negros demonstrates the importance of scrutinising pre-1898 history on a local level, while underscoring the significance of overseas trade even for areas far from Manila. The connections between textile and sugar production in Negros and in adjacent Panay island also challenge linear views that would preclude a transition from a manufacturing industry, a sort of thatched-roof Manchester, to ... sugar plantation production.

The Post-1898 Sugar Industry: Puerto Rico

Puerto Rico after 1898 became a 'latter-day Sugar Island', an almost perfect example of plantation economy' based on wage labour ...' and this in the Caribbean, 'the locus classicus of plantation societies'.[42] In the 1890s, sugar made up 21 percent of Puerto Rico's exports; by 1920, the proportion reached 65.6 percent (Gayer et al. 1938: 27). From 1898 to 1926 the 'big three' sugar corporations owned by North American interests operated five (and later seven) *centrals*, of a total of over forty *centrals*. They owned or leased 100,000 acres (1920), and controlled the majority of the island's sugar production for a few years, from the late 1920s to the early 1930s. After 1926, there were four U.S. sugar corporations, with ten *centrals*. Even though Puerto Rico underwent far greater penetration of American capital and direct landowning in comparison with Negros or the Philippines, and had more land under sugar cane cultivation in proportion to its size,[43] the Puerto Rican sugar economy was also Janus-faced. Of the 40 to 44 sugar corporations in Puerto Rico in the early twentieth century, the vast majority were not North American-owned. Puerto Rico's twenty-two *centrals* in 1898 were half of the highest number of *centrals* reached in this century (42).

A regional optic, attention to *central-colono* and grower-labourer relations, and awareness of the continuities/discontinuities that 1898 entailed is essential to apprehending the complex social relations of twentieth century sugar production in Puerto Rico. Arguments for discontinuity will find much evidence in their favour,[44] but may miss the two-sided 'Janus face' of the Puerto Rican sugar industry. Through the sugar boom of the early twentieth century, several regions in Puerto Rico remained almost untouched by direct American investments. Indeed, in most areas where sugar production had been important in the late nineteenth century, direct American investment and landownership did not develop. The local planter class was especially strong in the north coast. In the east and west coasts, the American sugar corporations' operations intertwined with diverse agrarian relations with a history of their own.[45] Even in the south coast, where the North American corporate *centrals* predominated, a large portion of the ground cane was supplied by *colonos*. In the case of the very largest central, Guánica, *colono*-grown cane was always the majority.

Until its decline in the 1950s, Puerto Rico's sugar industry was the leading economic sector in Puerto Rico. Negros, which had become a large-scale producer somewhat later than Puerto Rico, has remained a 'Sugarlandia' several decades longer (with a highly exploitative and reviled sugar industry). In the 1950s, several of Puerto Rico's declining and closed-down *centrals* were shipped lock, stock, and barrel to Negros.

A Sugarlandia Planter Visits Puerto Rico

The 1956 visit to Puerto Rico of Filipino sugar planter Oscar Ledesma may be emblematic. Ledesma, the scion of a powerful Negros *centralista* dynasty, was then the Philippines' ambassador to the U.S.A.[46] In the 1950s Ledesma acquired three Puerto Rican *centrals* and shipped them to Negros, where they were reconstructed.[47] Perhaps part of the machinery from Puerto Rico was installed at San Carlos, Ledesma's flagship *sentral*, the Philippines' oldest continuously-operating sugar mill.[48]

The San Juan newspaper *El Mundo* profiled Ledesma as *un rico terrateniente y azucarero* ('a wealthy landowner and sugar man').[49] Ledesma also held various positions of importance in Negros, including mayor and provincial governor; at the national level he had been a senator and a secretary of commerce, and presided over the National Federation of Sugar Planters, officially named in Spanish as the *Confederación de Asociaciones y Plantadores de Caña Dulce* ('Confederation of Associations and Sugar Cane Planters', so named because the confederation included *hacendero* associations in sugar-mill districts). Ledesma was 'on a visit to Puerto Rico, but not to buy *centrals*', according to the news report. While Ledesma was received at the San Juan airport by an official delegation and had several meetings with high government officials, he described his relaxed five-days stay in Puerto Rico as that of 'almost a tourist'. Indeed, his visit had no stated official purpose. Ledesma was also to visit the Serrallés family in Ponce, who owned the largest Puerto Rican *central* as well as a leading rum distilling company.

According to *El Mundo*, Ledesma was 'one of the leaders of the resistance during the occupation in the past war'. Indeed, a Filipino historian has described Ledesma as being active in the resistance underground and as one of the 'eyes and ears' of the guerrilla movement.[50] Larkin, however, states unequivocally that Ledesma was a leading collaborationist.[51] More probably, Ambassador Ledesma worked both for and against the Japanese, a long-standing skill of the Filipino economic and political elites in various contexts, including that of the American colonial regime after 1898.

Indeed, American colonialism may rarely have been a burning issue for *centralistas* like Ledesma, who were part of a 'sugar bloc' whose main antagonists were the *hacenderos*. In an interview with historian Violeta López-Gonzaga, Ledesma denied the existence of a Filipino 'sugar bloc'. From Ledesma's angle, there was only a 'consortium of boys in the sugar industry'; although he recognised that in presidential elections in the new Philippines republic in the 1950s, '... we came out, we (came) all out as in a military exercise'.[52] López-Gonzaga asserts that the main institutional expression of the 'sugar bloc' was indeed the sugar planters' federation that Ledesma himself founded and over which he presided. When Puerto Rican sugar production went into a tailspin in the 1950s, Filipino *centralistas* like Oscar Ledesma were among the major purchasers of Puerto Rican sugar-mill machinery. Some Puerto Rican *centrals*, perhaps with some of their machine components dating back to the early twentieth century, may still be in operation in Negros to this day.

Compradors and *Compadres*

Writing of the sugar-planter elite of Negros and others of the Western Visayas, McCoy observed:

> The sugar planters of the Western Visayas, for example, became citizens of the world market in the 1860s but did not become citizens of the Philippine Republic until 1946 – a difference of nearly a century that left them with strong anti-national economic interests[53] and close political ties to their premier sugar customer, the United States.[54]

This may be true, but the sugar planters of the Negros and the others were also energetic local actors in the Philippines' colonial regime, before or after 1898; the Filipino elites 'included as one of their more formidable segments the ascendant sugar capitalist class of Negros'.[55] After 1898, American hegemony to some extent assisted those elites in consolidating their presence in the national formation and in the configuration of the dependent state. This process took on a larger scale in the Philippine archipelago but was also in evidence in Puerto Rico. In a strikingly different register from his *Imagined Communities* (1983), Benedict Anderson wrote:

> It was above all the political innovations of the Americans that created a solid, visible 'national oligarchy'. Congress [the Filipino legislature], which thus offered

them guaranteed access to national-level political power, also brought them together in the capital on a regular basis. There, more than at any previous time, they got to know one another well in a civilised 'ring' sternly referred by the Americans [...] They were for the first time forming a self-conscious ruling class.[56]

Ongoing, provocative historical discussions in the Philippines revolve around the concepts of 'compadre colonialism',[57] 'colonial democracy',[58] and Anderson's own considerations on 'cacique democracy'.[59] Aguilar, too, notes that the U.S.A. relied 'upon indigenous elites who were provided with ample room to participate in colonial governance'.[60] Several caveats are in order, however.

First, from the Spanish colonial *cabildos* to the colonial assemblies of the Thirteen Colonies to British 'indirect rule' to French *départementalisation*, the history of colonialism presents many instances of flexibility and complexity in colonial policy, of course in pursuit of broader metropolitan objectives ... even if American colonialism may have gone somewhat further in that direction. Two salient dimensions of American colonialism: its federalist constitutional framework, which emerged from a republican, anticolonial revolution, and its gargantuan economy.

Second, the Filipino and Puerto Rican elites, like plantation elites elsewhere, are usually bundled into a category of colonial 'intermediary' classes that has attained its widest currency in the concept of *comprador*. *Comprador* usefully bridges colonial and non-colonial situations but, like colonialism itself, tends to be oversimplified. Mao Tzedong 'canonised' the concept in his 'Analysis of the Classes in Chinese Society' (1926), where he placed *compradors* (alongside landlords) at the top both of Chinese society and of the list of right-wing enemies.[61] Twentieth century anti-colonial Marxism presupposed the essential political inconsequence of *compradors*, except as 'lackeys' of imperialism.

Thirdly, recent studies of colonial rule have analysed with greater subtlety the relationship between colonial hegemonic and subaltern classes, and have focused on the endogenous dimensions of colonial social relations and cultural constructions. The historical agency of all groups is explored, and the historical substance and responsibility of all colonial social groupings is asserted: none can be brushed aside as mere 'appendages' as the *compradors* were. Notions such as 'dominance without hegemony' attempt to grasp the internal tensions of colonial rule among and between 'native' groupings. The cultural complexity of colonial domination, the construction of cultural (particularly racial, ethnic, gender, national) categories, and the role of other unstated contexts have been foregrounded in the study of colonial social formations.

However, these 'postcolonial' studies have not fully met the challenge of analysing colonialism and ostensibly intermediary groupings like planter elites and *comprador* classes in their historical and conceptual fullness. It would seem useful to extend notions of ambiguity, interaction, and complexity to the relationship between metropolitan and colonial elites, exploring the complex meanings of 'dominance' and 'hegemony' within that relationship.

The comparative history of the Philippines and Puerto Rico in the early twentieth century, which I have addressed here through a discussion of the Philippines 'sugar island', Negros, adds an interesting twist to ongoing thinking on colonial and postcolonial realities: two countries where the elites fashion a 'national', if not 'postcolonial' culture under colonial rule. The next section explores various ethnic and cultural dimensions of the local planter classes in the Philippines and Puerto Rico in the twentieth century. I then inquire as to what are the implications of these questions for the question of continuity and discontinuity after 1898.

Sugar Planters: 'Planter', Ethnic and Cultural Dimensions

Up to this point, I have used the term 'local planter class' in tacit or express opposition to American capital and/or sugar corporations, without further ado. In fact, 'local planter class' teems with questions that need to be addressed, and which are in fact useful clues to the two-sided historical trajectories of the Filipino and Puerto Rican planter classes. In this context, 'local' is a useful, if provisional term akin to 'resident'.[62] It presupposes a dimension that 'resident' makes explicit: that the planter is not an absentee, a trait too often seen as inherent to plantation ownership (and historically accurate in many cases in the British and French sugar islands in the seventeenth and eighteenth centuries; not so in the Spanish Antilles).

Even by itself, 'planter' (equated with 'sugar planter') is itself a conceptual minefield of sorts. In Puerto Rico as in the Philippines and elsewhere, 'planters' were landholders and sugar cane growers. In itself this indicates several possibilities: the 'planter' might be an individual owning a single estate, or several; or a family group; or the 'planter' might be a corporation (often but an alter ego of individual families, or family networks). The planter-cum-landholder could also be a sugar-factory owner, or indeed only a (non-land-holding) sugar-factory owner, known in Puerto Rico as a *centralista*. Whatever the combination between land and factory, 'planters' could also be commercial farmers producing other crops, cattle ranchers, merchants (from retail to wholesale to import-export), urban professionals, and bankers. At the same time, landholdings as well as sugar mills were of widely different scales and social import.

The economic complexity of planters is interwoven with – and inseparable from – their ethnic and cultural complexity (with inherent discussions of *mestizaje*). The ethno-cultural profile of the 'planter' groups that owned sugar factories and sugar-growing estates in the Philippines and Puerto Rico is quite remarkable. In 1935, 43 percent of the total capital invested in Philippines *centrals* was Filipino, 33 percent American and 23 percent Spanish.[63] The

'Filipino' portion was largely mestizo. Several of the leading *central* families in Negros traced their origins to the Panay Chinese mestizo textile manufacturers of the nineteenth century. The *hacenderos* were ethnically closer to the *central* owners, as largely mestizo, but proportions varied between the two sectors: up to 91 percent of *hacenderos* were Filipinos, but only 50 percent of the *centralistas*. The rest of the *centralistas* were largely Spanish, other European, and North Americans.[64] Categories such as 'Filipino', 'American' and 'Spanish' raise a number of problems. 'Filipino' and 'Spanish' are of special interest here.

The Philippines and Puerto Rico were criss-crossed by local, strongly historical ethnic-cultural relations. In the Philippines, these relations imbricated native Malay Filipinos (called *indios* by the Spanish), Spaniards and Filipinos of Spanish descent, and Chinese *mestizo*. Filipino was employed for Philippines-born descendants of Europeans, mestizo for similarly-born children of Chinese. In the twilight years of Spanish colonialism in the Philippines, *mestizos* began to call themselves 'Filipinos'.[65] 'Native *principales* and *mestizos* [of Spanish and/or Chinese descent] amalgamated through intermarriage and participation in a common culture.'[66] Negros is probably the most arresting case of ethnic and cultural amalgamation among the sugar planters, as Benedict Anderson has observed: 'nothing better illustrates [the] interplay between Anglo-Saxons, *mestizos*, and Chinese than the modern history of the island of Negros'.[67]

In Puerto Rico, comparable interactions existed between native Puerto Ricans (mulattoes and *blancos del país* in the nineteenth century), immigrant Spaniards and Creoles from Venezuela or the eastern Caribbean, and other immigrants. Important constraints were imposed by the legal racial-purity standards of *limpieza de sangre* ('cleanness of blood') with respect to African genealogies (crucial for holding government posts, and for suffrage). These racist bars resembled Spanish legal exclusions of *indios* and Chinese in the Philippines. Questions concerning the on-going Spanish presence in Puerto Rico and the Philippines after 1898 pose acute issues of economic and ethno-cultural complexity. Several themes calling for research are set out below.

The Spanish Presence in the Filipino and Puerto Rican Sugar Industries

In the Negros sugar industry, Spaniards overshadowed North Americans long after 1898. Through the period of sharp expansion during and after the First World War, the Spanish presence held its own, and in some ways even grew in importance.[68] The largest and oldest *central* in Negros was the huge La Carlota *central*, of the Elizalde-Ynchausti group. Its owners retained their Spanish citizenship until the Second World War. La Carlota was also the largest *central* in the Philippines as a whole into the 1930s. Joaquín J. Elizalde

(1891–1937) was described in his *New York Times* obituary as the 'foremost Spanish business man in the Philippines'. At the time, Elizalde & Co. had 10,000 employees, and was engaged in sugar and hemp export and inter-island shipping.[69]

In Puerto Rico, where local sugar corporations accounted for the majority of sugar production until the late 1920s, several of the major sugar corporations were also controlled by Spanish citizens. The closer the company's interests were to the actual process of cultivation, the more limited the North American role became. As a group, the Spanish *central* owners in Negros were far more important than the North American or the *haole* Hawaiian *central* corporations. This is perhaps the most striking difference between the sugar industries of Puerto Rico and the Negros.

In Puerto Rico, the Spanish vernacular, greater proximity to Spain, continued Spanish immigration after 1898, and a broader European component in the population, among other reasons, fostered a stronger Spanish economic presence. In *The Sugar Economy of Puerto Rico* (1938), Arthur Gayer identified an important component of the local *centralistas* that had significant regional dimensions: the 'Spanish group'[70] (actually more a 'Spanish-Creole group'). Gayer distinguished the 'Spanish group' *centrals* from other locally-owned mills in terms of their specific family and ownership networks. While the inability of the 'Spanish group' (and of local *centralistas* generally) to form an encompassing, operationally-unified corporate structures surely contributed to its early demise, there may be yet other factors which require analysis.

One solution to the problems of lack of capital for improvement would have been the mergers of Puerto Rican *centrals* and sale of the equipment of the less efficient to raise money for modernising and enlarging the remaining mills. Yet there is no record of voluntary mergers of two or more mills to form a consolidated company, as distinct from occasional purchases of smaller mills by larger ones. The barrier to mergers, a process that seemed so inevitable in the United States, appears to have been the same kind of unyielding individualism and family pride that had prevented combination among importers. Not only did the sugar producers fail to coalesce into five or six big companies, they did little to promote joint action on industry-wide problems. The Association of Sugar Producers of Puerto Rico had carried on practically no collective activities on a permanent basis.[71]

The 'Spanish group' *centrals* were 'rather intimately associated, through interlocking stock ownership and directorates'.[72] The 'group' was connected by stock ownership, interlocking directorates, *compadrazgo* and marriage, a pattern that also existed among the larger ensemble of Creole-Spanish *centrals*. Quintero Rivera largely agrees:

> In many of the *centrales* established in the nineteenth century and which continued to be among the most important in the twentieth, Spanish immigrants who continued to reside in [Puerto Rico], or their descendants, occupied prominent

positions in their board of directors: *los* Ruberts, Fabian, Arsuaga, Gonzalez, Caubet, Oliver, Serrallés, among many others.[73]

Around the time of the First World War, Puerto Rico's 'Spanish group' owned or controlled ten of 44 *centrals* in the island. In general, the north coast was the stronghold of the 'Spanish group' and local sugar production generally, while on the south coast the American sugar corporations (mainly Guánica and Aguirre) were dominant. Thomas Cochran in his study *The Puerto Rican Businessman* (1959) concluded that in Puerto Rico, '[u]ndoubtedly families held together better than in the United States, and family groups that would have split apart there with the coming of a new generation remained intact in Puerto Rico'.[74]

The 'Spanish group' *centrals*, like the locally-owned concerns generally, benefited from such family networks as well as from other conditions not usually recognised. Gayer went so far as to say that he saw 'no clear relation between size and efficiency; larger mills may have more technical efficiency, but many smaller ones do well with more compact area of cane supply and lower overhead charges; anyway there are many local variables'.[75]

Spanish Identities

But *who* is or is not 'Spanish'? The question applies equally to *mestizos*, Filipinos, or Puerto Ricans, and others, especially since to be 'Spanish' was often to be not 'Filipino', or 'Puerto Rican', in terms of self-definition as well as definition by others. Life histories and identities could vary considerably. Many of the 'Spanish' in the Philippines and Puerto Rico after 1898 were born and raised in Spain of Spanish parents, and remained Spanish citizens. They self-identified as 'Spanish' no matter their length of residence in the Philippines or Puerto Rico. However, a Spaniard who migrated to the Philippines or Puerto Rico as a child, married a *mestiza*, and returned to Spain infrequently or never, could have rather different identities (all the while retaining his Spanish citizenship); all the more so his offspring, even if defined and self-defined as 'Spanish'. And what happens when those second-generation 'Spaniards' act within a close-knit family economic network governed by older Spanish kin, as was often the case? Clearly, in post-1898 Philippines and Puerto Rico, there were different paths towards, and away from, 'Spanishness'.

Moreover, the Philippines and Puerto Rico are both 'twice-colonial' societies. Both were under the domination first of Spain and then of the U.S.A.[76] Important questions exist regarding the trajectory of indigenous/metropolitan elites who were shaped in the earlier colonial regime, and who met new colonial conditions. These colonial elites played a significant (and heterogeneous) role under American hegemony, and for them the Spanish cultural presence remained important. Decades after 1898, *mestizos* in Negros favoured intermarriage with

Spanish families[77] and actively furthered a complex Spanish-Filipino identity. This reality may qualify Larkin's reservations about the post-1898 Spanish presence in Negros and elsewhere in the Philippines:

> Spaniards had to settle for a share of the plantations, but not a dominant one, and in no place, save in La Carlota and Kabankalan, did they become a major economic force. Indeed, like their predecessors Agustin Montilla and Eusebio de Luzuriaga, they tended to intermarry with the mestizo population, and their descendants were absorbed into the group broadly defined as the Negrense planter elite. Not all Spaniards made it to the top of the social hierarchy, for they held no privileged economic position in Sugarlandia simply because of their nationality.[78]

Yet even if the Spanish were not 'dominant', as they were not, what was the scope and manner of their presence? Clearly they had major positions in several *centrals*, as well in financial circuits that connected with sugar production (e.g. Banco Filipino Español). Perhaps Larkin's perspective is more relevant to Pampangas, where the Spanish presence was less substantial than in Negros, before and especially after 1898.

In any case mestizo-Spanish intermarriage did not, of course, necessarily entail 'absorption' of the Spanish spouse. More subtle interactions seem to have been at work. In some ways, intermarriage could actually have expanded the scope of the cultural resonance of the Spaniards in such important areas as family intimacy, religious life, and leisure time. Note, for instance, the wide audience appeal of Spanish *zarzuelas* in Puerto Rico and the Philippines through the early decades of the twentieth century; the *zarzuela*, an often picaresque operetta genre, did not otherwise travel well outside Spain. Moreover, beyond more 'objective' patterns, *hispanismo* may, as a matter of choice, have been a major social marker among the planter elite.[79]

Even in 1925, a Baptist missionary in Bacolod wrote: 'people in Negros seem to possess an anti-American attitude and clung to the old Spanish Catholic culture'.[80] At the same time – and perhaps as part of the same process – 'old Filipino-Spanish culture and values gave way to the manners and norms of the new conqueror, and the sugar industry provided means and motives for the change'.[81] Larkin probably overstates Negros's and the Philippines' uniqueness on this score, even in Southeast Asia, but his general point is well taken:

> On Negros there existed a situation virtually unknown elsewhere in Southeast Asia [...] In no other area outside Manila did such an easy relationship between Europeans and the native elite spring up as in the sugar provinces. With Americans it took longer for such an interaction to develop, in part because of racial prejudices and stereotyping the new rulers brought with them and also because of the language barrier ... [82]

For Puerto Rico and the Philippines, one might ask why an ostensibly modernising elite such as the sugar planters defined themselves so largely in the early decades of this century – and virtually throughout the American colonial period – with such strong recourse to the culture of the defeated, 'backward' Spanish metropole ... rather than opting overwhelmingly for the culture of the American colonial authorities, supposedly more easily accessible and, in principle, politically and ideologically hegemonic?[83] In Cuba, despite the anti-Spanish legacy of the War of Independence, Spanish culture (e.g. literature, *zarzuelas*) was much in vogue in the early twentieth century (Ibarra, this volume)

The question may be premised on distorted images of Spanish colonialism and of the meaning of its displacement by the American colonial regime: for instance, it is often assumed that there was little or no capitalist development in Puerto Rico or the Philippines prior to 1898; that wealthy Spanish residents in the colonies were all merchants more intent on blocking socio-historical transformation than in profiting from it; that capitalism crashed down in full force after 1898 in the Philippines and Puerto Rico; that Spanish residents and their families returned to Spain en masse after 1898 and in any case remained largely irrelevant under American colonial rule.

The perspective that is suggested here is rather different. There was indeed significant capitalist development prior to 1898 in the Philippines and Puerto Rico, both of which had long-standing connections with regional and world markets. In both territories there was a segment of merchant capitalist and landholders, partly Spanish and partly Creole in various degrees, that included a major Chinese presence in the Philippines and a non-Spanish European presence in Puerto Rico. These groups frequently intermarried with native groups (*indios* in the Philippines, *criollos* of greater generational depth in Puerto Rico). The trajectory of the hybrid ruling classes of Puerto Rico and the Philippines was hardly settled by the limited emigration of Spanish military and officialdom that took place immediately after 1898.

Thus 1898 was not the cataclysmic event that radically different political perspectives often make it out to be. Long-term American interests in the Philippines and Puerto Rico lay in not overturning – and indeed in strengthening – the land and sugar-mill configurations that had developed under Spain. Other economic sectors were more accessible (e.g. the consumer market) and American interests aggressively pursued those. In the case of sugar, there were other forms of subtle control such as credit and pricing mechanisms, brokerage and overseas export that were safer for North Americans and more lucrative. Landownership and sugar production generally was one area where too narrowly-defined American objectives could produce a social explosion. In the pursuit of its colonial policy, American political and economic interests did not need to, or indeed could not, control all fields of social relations.

We also need to take a closer look at the interactions between ethno-cultural patterns and social relations, in order to dispel easy generalisations about given identities being 'backward' or 'progressive'; it is hard to argue for a backward Spanish identity in social settings where the local 'captains of industry' were Spaniards and their children. Spanish identities were closely linked with Roman Catholicism; religious dimensions of cultural identity are of course especially resilient and transferable. On the other hand, Spanish identities were, and long had been, fluid and permeable to local history, such that the lines between 'Spanish' and 'Filipino', or between 'Spanish' and 'Puerto Rican' were hardly distinct; intermarriage was a crucial avenue for, of course, cultural hybridity.

Because of their long association with landed and political power, 'Spanish' identities remained useful markers of class differentiation, power and privilege. *Hispanidad* was an avenue to identification with Europeanasition, more accessible and familiar (indeed literally so) to *mestizos* and Filipinos generally than North American identities, and was indeed one way of facing the American presence with greater assurance. The social relations of the sugar industry, especially in years of rapid expansion were fluid enough to facilitate intermarriage between ethnic and racial groups that crossed paths in the evolving sugar social structure: 'In Sugarlandia, moreover, familiarity with Occidental ideas and tastes became ever more pronounced because of interaction with Spaniards and Americans through the industry and through intermarriage, especially with the former group [i.e. the Spaniards]'.[84]

Conclusion

In most accounts of the colonial history of the Philippines and Puerto Rico, whether apologetic or critical of American rule, the U.S.A. appear as the irresistible force, and the territories as quite moveable objects. Whether the U.S.A. is seen to have brought technological development, massive capital inflows, and democracy, or rather exploitation, impoverishment, and oppression, local social groups are seen as passive actors in a story not theirs. In Puerto Rico and in the Philippines the U.S.A. was evidently a commanding presence, politically and economically, after 1898. In terms of the sugar industry, the U.S.A. offered sugar-mill technology, mill machinery, and financing and marketing[85]; not coincidentially, large-scale, central-based sugar cane production became fundamental under American colonial rule.

Yet this is not the whole story. In both the Philippines and Puerto Rico, the onset of American rule in 1898 was not a radical rupture, but the beginning of another period in a long historical process of evolving local social groups with substantial autonomy and initiative. These groups had already been following their own trajectories in the context of regional and global social relations. Larkin has proposed a long historical period (from 1820 to

1920) wherein the Philippines were unevenly transformed as part of a full incorporation into the world market, linked to a massive process of internal colonisation.[87] McCoy similarly proposes a 'long nineteenth century', starting in 1780 and ending in 1920.

American colonialism in Puerto Rico and the Philippines needs to be studied more historically and with a greater sense of complexity and historical agency. In particular, the relationship between metropolitan and colonial elites is intricate, and needs to be viewed with reference to socioeconomic processes as well as in its ethnocultural dimensions. Spanish and American colonialism, which are supposed to be profoundly different, on reconsideration seem closer, and more entwined, in their relationship with local social groups.

In the Philippines and Puerto Rico under American colonial rule, an ethnically and culturally complex class of sugar planters fashioned after 1898 a 'national' if uneven and subaltern hegemony under colonial (or 'twice-colonial') rule. This subaltern hegemony marshaled Spanish nationals of the former metropolis, other foreigners and their first-generation descendants alongside evolving 'Filipinos' and 'Puerto Ricans' in the control over capital and labour. In this perspective all social groups, colonised as well as coloniser, are similarly complex and important; and they have far more historical agency and materiality than is usually recognised. These considerations suggest the need for further inquiry into the role of colonial elites under Spanish and American rule in Puerto Rico and the Philippines, and more broadly into the specificities of all the social groupings imbricated in their sugar industries.

Acknowledgements

Earlier versions of this paper were presented at the seminar 'Legacies of 1898: Sovereignty and Colonialism in Puerto Rico, Cuba, Guam, the Philippines, and Hawaii, and their Impact on the United States', 1998 Faculty Research Seminar, Obermann Center for Advanced Studies, the University of Iowa, Iowa City, June 15 to July 2, 1998; and at the Caribbean Resource Center conference, 'From Colonial Plantations to Global Peripheries: A Century of Transformations in the Caribbean and Tropical Asia', October 8–9, 1998. Katharine Bjork Guneratne made valuable comments on both the initial and final drafts of the paper.

Notes

1. McCoy, 'Sugar Barons', 107; see also Aguilar, 'Sugar Planter-State Relations', Aguilar, 'Masonic Myths', and Aguilar, *Clash of Spirits*; Nagano 'The Oligopolistic Structure of the Philippine Sugar Industry', and Nagano, 'The Agricultural Bank of the Philippine Government'. McCoy's generalisation is too sweeping even for Asia; in Ceylon, for instance, an indigenous planter class was dominant in the coconut and rubber industries. See Jayawardena, *Nobodies to Somebodies: The Rise of the Colonial Bourgeoisie in Sri Lanka*, a wide-ranging, well-documented study that critiques the concept of *comprador* bourgeoisie.
2. Rivera Ramos, *The Legal Construction of Identity*.
3. Go, 'The Chains of Empire'.
4. Thompson, 'The Imperial Republic'.
5. Lynsky, *Sugar Economics*, 67.
6. U.S. Tariff Commission, *U.S. Philippine Trade* (1937), 8.
7. The contracts signed by the Filipino growers and the *centrals* were also remarkable: *central* owners and growers subscribed to lengthy 30-year contracts, in a sense establishing a long-term partnership. The 30-year contract actually dated from the early twentieth century. The 30-year contract, a major legal and social innovation originated in Negros in the *Central San Carlos*, in 1912. Under its terms, the *central* obtained 40 percent of the sugar produced, a lower proportion than the 50 percent that was the average in Puerto Rico (Apacible, 'The Sugar Industry of the Philippines', 88; Larkin, *Sugar and the Origins of Modern Philippine Society*, 58). An important dimension of the milling contracts, only briefly noted by Aguilar, is that individual *hacenderos* were bound to specific milling districts, each under the control of a single *central*: eighteen such districts existed in Negros before the Second World War, twelve afterwards (Aguilar, *Clash of Spirits*, 201).
8. In general, grower contracts in the Philippines, as in Puerto Rico and in Cuba, established proportions of 50/50 or 60/40, with the larger portion going to the grower. The growers agreed to plant a certain area of their farms with sugar cane, while the *central* transported the cut cane to the mill. In a practice that reinforced the partnership quality of the relationship, the *centrals* did not buy the cane from the grower, but rather milled it and turned over the larger part of the sugar to the grower, retaining the rest for its grinding service.
9. Nagano, 'The Oligopolistic Structure', 109.
10. Nagano, 'The Agricultural Bank of the Philippine Government', 301. Elsewhere, Nagano states matters somewhat differently: the U.S. colonial administration 'had to convince the local elites that their interests would be served under American rule, while at the same time trying to strike a balance between elite demands and other social needs'. (Ibidem, 320).
11. Larkin, *Sugar and the Origins of Modern Philippine Society*, 240.
12. A major political episode of the Marcos regime was a confrontation between Marcos and Vice-President Fernando Lopez, of the Lopez Negros-Panay sugar (and now media) empire (see Larkin, *Sugar and the Origins of Modern Philippine Society*, 243–44; Hawes, *The Philippine State and the Marcos Regime*).
13. De Jesus, 'An Agenda for Philippine Studies', 449; Seagrave, *The Marcos Dynasty*, 284–87.
14. 'The "native" sugar planters of the Philippines shifted remarkably well from Spanish to American rule (and indeed through Japanese rule to independence), while they assured both the continuation of the colonial relationship and a growing social, political and cultural space for themselves': Larkin, *Sugar and the Origins of Modern Philippine Society*, 8. Filomeno Aguilar draws a sharp distinction between the Spanish era, when the Negros planters vied among themselves in the plantation frontier (often seizing land and labour illegally), and the American colonial period. 'Eager to pacify their new colonial subjects, the Americans who were imperialist neophytes relied upon local elites whom they provided with ample room to participate and intervene in colonial governance, resulting in the part indigenous complexion of the colonial state'. (Aguilar, 'Sugar Planter-State Relations', 68).

Similarly, Renato Constantino writes in *A History of the Philippines*: 'The Americans had a two-fold interest in strengthening the Filipino landed elite. Economically, it was the land-holdings of the elite that provided the raw materials which the Americans required (…) [t]he hacienda system that had been born as a result of capitalist linkage during the Span-ish occupation was strengthened under American rule. The tenancy problem worsened during the same period. Politically, the landed elite constituted the most stable allies of American colonialism and many of them were recruited into office. Their prosperity gave them a definite stake in the colonial set-up' (300).

15. Coll Cuchí, *Un problema en América*, 112.

16. Constantino, *A History of the* Philippines, 300.

17. Aguilar, *Clash of Spirits*, 201.

18. See, for example, Diffie & Diffie, *Porto Rico, a broken pledge*; Bird, *The sugar industry*; Her-rero, *La mitología del azúcar*; Quintero Rivera, 'El capitalismo y el proletariado rural', and Quintero Rivera, *Conflictos de clase y política Puerto Rico*; Dietz, *Economic History of Puerto Rico*. Indeed, three (later four) American landholding sugar corporations charged into the Puerto Rican sugar industry. These corporations consistently led in sugar production and landholding. Each produced 90 to 120 thousand tons of sugar and owned or rented some 60,000 acres. German-American capital was conspicuous in at least one of the sugar cor-porations, Guánica, as García-Muñiz has noted ('The South Puerto Rico Sugar Co', 88). The European dimensions of 'North American' sugar capital raise important questions that connect with the non-American dimensions of colonial capital in the Philippines and Puerto Rico.

19. García, *Armar la historia*.

20. Quintero Rivera, *Patricios y plebeyos*, 165–79. Also, '[I]n many of the *centrales* established in the nineteenth century, and which continued to be the most important in the twentieth, Spanish immigrants, who continued to reside in the country, or their descendants, occupied prominent positions in their boards of directors: los Ruberts, Fabián, Arsuaga, González, Caubet, Oliver, Serrallés, among many others'. (316).

21. Dietz, *Economic History of Puerto Rico*, 108–9.

22. Dietz, 'Reviewing and Renewing Puerto Rican and Caribbean Studies'.

23. Sugar production was also important in Luzón, the archipelago's largest island, although on a smaller scale than Negros; and sugar production also had less relative importance within Luzón.

24. Anderson, *Imagined Communities*, 8.

25. At 4,907 square miles, Negros is fairly similar in size to Puerto Rico (3,435 square miles). Negros is 135 miles by 25 to 50 miles; Puerto Rico is 100 miles by 35 miles. Despite its smaller size, Puerto Rico has historically been more densely populated than Negros. In 1898, Negros's population was 330,000 (Walker, *The Sugar Industry in the Island of Negros*, 16) while Puerto Rico's was over 1,450,000 – three times higher. By 1940, after rapid population growth in Negros, the difference narrowed but was still important: Negros reached about 950,000, while Puerto Rico doubled Negros' population at 1.9 million. Negros (10° latitude) is closer to the Equator than Puerto Rico (18°).

26. Panay's capital, Iloilo, the 'Queen City of the South', was the Philippines' second city in terms of population and economic strength. Unlike Manila, whose size and importance was partly due to its government functions and entrepot commerce, Iloilo was built essentially on its own production and commerce. In the 1850s, the population of Iloilo (71,000) sur-passed Sydney's (52,000) and approached Chicago's (84,000) (McCoy, 'A Queen Dies Slowly', 301). The one other city that competed with Iloilo was, significantly, also in the central Visayas: Cebu City, on Cebu island just east of Negros. Iloilo's production was inserted in trade circuits linking ports elsewhere in the Philippines and on the South China Sea.

27. On the Philippines' resilient and powerful Chinese *mestizos*, see Anderson, 'Cacique Democracy in the Philippines'.

28. Larkin, *Sugar and the Origins of Modern Philippine Society*, 66.
29. The transformation of coastal Western Negros from a thickly forested plain to something of a sugar bowl in those decades attests to the resiliency of late Spanish colonialism vis-à-vis endogenous social transformations. A transformation that is graphically described by a Spanish government official and planter with a long residence in Negros, Robustiano Echaúz, in his *Apuntes sobre la isla de Negros* (his account centres on 1850–1898). Negros Island, which had no sugar industry to speak of before 1850, was by 1898 a significant producer in the world market. Negros sugar was then muscovado, rather than the 96° centrifugal sugar then commonly produced in the *centrals* of Cuba and Java, which was then gaining ground in Puerto Rico.
30. Ponce has interesting affinities with Iloilo. In the late-nineteenth century, Ponce surpassed the capital city of San Juan in trade volumes on account of the coffee and sugar production of the surrounding littoral and the central highlands, and attained an outstanding cultural development (the *danza* was to Ponce somewhat as the *zarzuela* was to Iloilo). Ponce is still called *La Ciudad Señorial* and *La Perla del Sur* ('The Pearl of the South', as Iloilo was the 'Queen City of the South'). British merchants of Virgin Islands and Leeward Island backgrounds were of strategic importance in Ponce.
31. Dietz, *Economic History of Puerto Rico*, 108; see García, *Armar la historia* .
32. U.S. War Department, *Census of Porto Rico, 1899*; Bagué, *Del ingenio azucarero patriarcal*, 9.
33. Giusti-Cordero, *Labor, ecology and history,* 96.
34. The *central* was known as *sentral* or *centrale* in the Philippines (Aguilar, *Clash of Spirits*, 199). Some of the corporate names in the Philippines that employed the terminology of *la centrale* were Central Azucarera de Bais, Central Azucarera de Calatagan, Central Azucarera de Tarlac, etc.; or, in English, Asturias Sugar Central (Apacible, *The Sugar Industry of the Philippines*, 88). *Centralista* was used in Puerto Rico, *sentralista* in the Philippines. In the Philippines, the term *colono* is not used, but rather *hacendero* and, to a lesser extent, *plantadores* (Larkin, *Sugar and the Origins of Modern Philippine Society*, 161). Hacenderos establishes a greater continuity with a past where the cane grower also operated a steam or ox-driven sugar mill. In Puerto Rico, neither *hacendado* nor *plantador* was used commonly to refer to *colonos*. In Cuba, *hacendado* remained common into the twentieth century not only as a synonym for *colono* (also widely used) but also meaning *central* owner, even when only a mechanised sugar mill and no land was owned. Other terms that are shared by the Filipino and Puerto Rican sugar/rural lexicon are *kapatas* (in Puerto Rico, *capataz*, foreman), *cabo* (also foreman), *encargado* (overseer), *braceros* (day- labourers), *kabisilya* (*cabecilla*, labour-gang leader), *aparcero* (sharecropper), and *antecipo* (*anticipo*, payment in advance).
35. The first attempt to establish a *central* was made by the Spreckels interests, from the U.S. West Coast, in the island of Mindoro just south of Luzón. A large *central* was built, but the project soon collapsed. Larkin, *Sugar and the Origins of Modern Philippine Society*, 54. The next *centrals* to be built were rather small: in San Carlos (by *haoles* (=non-Polynesian residents from Hawaii) and Calamba (Laguna), which began operating in 1912 (Larkin, *Sugar and the Origins of Modern Philippine Society*, 58).
36. Larkin, *Sugar and the Origins of Modern Philippine Society*, 100.
37. The initial Congressional enactments on American-Philippines trade were the Spooner Bill (1901) and the Philippine Tariff Act (1902). These laws opened the American market to Philippine sugar production only slightly: only a 25 percent reduction on the general tariff on sugar was allowed (as on any other import). The Payne-Aldrich Bill (1909) allowed 300,000 duty-free tons from the Philippines into the American market, and finally in 1913 the Underwood-Simmons Bill lifted all restrictions on Philippines sugar imports. Puerto Rico had enjoyed such free-market conditions for its sugar exports since 1902.
38. McCoy, 'A Queen Dies Slowly', 326. Constantino claimed that only one of the 33 *centrals* in the Philippines in 1922 was Filipino-owned, the Bago Central; the rest were 'American

and Spanish-controlled'. (Constantino, *A History of the Philippines*, 301). Yet Larkin notes: 'Laws inhibited the foreign ownership of land, and Americans became most numerous at top levels of finance and management and in the construction and technical operation of *centrals*'. (Larkin, *Sugar and the Origins of Modern Philippine Society*, 158).

39. In 1922, Negros produced 144,077 tons of semi-refined sugar, a large increase from a decade before but still substantially less than Puerto Rico (404,927 tons). Both islands considerably expanded production in the 1920s, but Negros grew more quickly. By the 1930s the difference between the two islands narrowed. In 1934, just before the Jones-Costigan tariffs were established, Negros produced 714,702 tons, compared to Puerto Rico's 1,112,352 tons.

40. Aguilar, *Clash of Spirits*, 198, 107, 208. The landholding limitation was enacted by Congress in 1902 in the Philippines' Organic Act. Aguilar states incorrectly that such a limitation was exclusive to the Philippines. In Puerto Rico, a 500-acre limit was imposed on agricultural corporations by the Congress, also in the island's Organic Act (1900). Like the Philippine limitation, Puerto Rico's '500-acre law' remained largely unenforced; in the 1930s, the 500-acre act was applied vigorously (1 acre = 0.4047 hectare).

41. Aguilar, *Clash of Spirits*, 208–20.

42. A phrase used by Perloff, *Puerto Rico's Economic Future*, 67; Thompson, *The Plantation*, 30; and Mintz, 'The Caribbean as a Socio-Cultural area', 96. Similarly, Gordon Lewis called the sugar industry 'the locus classicus of economic change', in Lewis, *Puerto Rico: Freedom and Power*, 89.

43. Ayala, *American Sugar Kingdom*, 195–200.

44. Ayala, *American Sugar Kingdom*.

45. The heterogeneous regional distribution of *central* ownership in Puerto Rico has not received sufficient attention, as most research has focused on the south coast and on the American sugar corporations. See Mintz, 'Cañamelar: the sub-culture', and Mintz, *Worker in the Cane*; Ramos Mattei, 'The Influence of Mechanization'; Ramos Mattei, *La sociedad del azúcar*; Quintero Rivera, 'El capitalismo y el proletariado rural'. For a well-documented study of the North American-owned Guánica Centrale Corporation, the largest in Puerto Rico, see García Muñiz, 'The South Puerto Rico Sugar Company'.

46. Quirino, *History of the Philippine Sugar Industry*, 53–55.

47. Ledesma purchased and shipped three *centrals* (Plazuela, Guamaní, Juanita) and part of a fourth one, Constancia. Central Plazuela's journey to the Philippines – probably to Negros – is especially ironic as it was the flagship Creole central in the early twentieth century, and the pride of the most powerful *centralista*, Eduardo Georgetti.

48. Billig, *Barons, Brokers and Buyers*, 132.

49. 'Embajador de Islas Filipinas ha comprado tres centrales en Puerto Rico', *El Mundo*, March 8, 1965, 3.

50. Quirino, *History of the Philippine Sugar Industry*, 82.

51. Ledesma was local director in Negros of the collaborationist Kalibapi political organization. Larkin, *Sugar and the Origins of Modern Philippine Society*, 238.

52. López-Gonzaga, *Land of Hope, Land of Want*, 234–35.

53. For Puerto Rico, Quintero Rivera has similarly written of a *burguesía antinacional*.

54. McCoy, 'Introduction', 12.

55. Aguilar, *Clash of Spirits*, 189.

56. Anderson, *Imagined Communities*, 11, emphasis added; Anderson also calls them a 'national oligarchy'.

57. Owen, *Compadre Colonialism*.

58. Paredes, *Philippine Colonial Democracy*.

59. Anderson, *Imagined Communities*.

60. Aguilar, *Clash of Spirits*, 189.

61. 'In economically backward and semi-colonial [n.b.] China, the landlord class and the *comprador* class are wholly appendages of the international bourgeoisie, depending upon impe-

rialism for their survival and growth. These classes represent the most backward and most reactionary relations of production in China and hinder the development of her productive forces.' (Mao Zdedong, *Analysis of the Classes in Chinese Society*, 11). On the comparable *collaborateurs* in Indochina, see Osborne, *The French Presence in Cochinchina and Cambodia*.

62. Quintero Rivera, *Patricios y plebeyos*, 316.

63. Constantino, *A History of the Philippines*, 301.

64. Larkin, *Sugar and the Origins of Modern Philippine Society*, 170.

65. Anderson, *Imagined Communities*, 9.

66. Anderson, *Imagined Communities*, 8; Larkin, 'Philippine History Reconsidered', 617.

67. 'Some Spaniards and Spanish *mestizos* entered the sugar industry as large landowners, perhaps because they could not compete very well in the middleman and export trade with other Europeans and the Chinese, who returned to the Philippines in 1850; however, some of the most successful exporters, bankers, and agricultural processors [i.e. *centralistas*] came from Spanish families, foreign- and Philippine-born'. (Larkin, 'Philippine History Reconsidered', 618).

68. 'At the top of the revised socio-economic pyramid stood the *centralistas*, Filipino, Spanish, and American owners and executives managing either corporate or family interests. Americans included [George] Fairchild, Renton Hind, and Horace Pond, all pillars of the expatriate community. Miguel Ossorio, the Elizaldes, and officials of Ynchausti and Company and Tabacalera represented the Iberians, while Jose de Leon, Augusto Gonzalez, and the Montillas, Aranetas, and Lizareses were the leading Filipino capitalists. Lines of nationality tended to blur, however, for Ossorio became an American citizen and Angel Elizalde married Mary Huntington Spreckels, thus forging bonds between Spanish-owned La Carlota and the Pasumil-Calamba U.S. combine [in Pampanga, Luzon]'. (Larkin, *Sugar and the Origins of Modern Philippine Society*, 167).

69. *New York Times*, October 1, 1937, 21.

70. Gayer counted six *centrals* on the north coast (probably Cambalache, San Vicente, Plata, Constancia, Vannina, San José, and Victoria). Gayer may have been keen to stress these *centrals'* foreignness. The research for *The Sugar Economy of Puerto Rico* was subsidised and facilitated by two of the 'Big Three' U.S. sugar corporations that operated in Puerto Rico since the early 1900s. Gayer's approach converged with that of the American sugar corporations, who wished to insist that they were not the only large landholders and *central* corporations in the island. See Gayer et al., *The Sugar Economy of Puerto Rico*, 62.

71. Gayer *et al.*, *The Sugar Economy of Puerto Rico*, 108 (emphasis added).

72. Gayer *et al.*, *The Sugar Economy of Puerto Rico*, 62.

73. Quintero Rivera, *Patricios y plebeyos*, 316.

74. Cochran, *The Puerto Rican Businessman*, 103.

75. Gayer *et al.*, *The Sugar Economy of Puerto Rico*, 60.

76. Or 'thrice-colonial' in the case of the Philippines themselves, if we consider the Second World War Japanese occupation as the Philippines' last colonial period.

77. Larkin, *Sugar and the Origins of Modern Philippine Society*, 167.

78. Larkin, *Sugar and the Origins of Modern Philippine Society*, 65.

79. On 'Hispanophilia' and *hispanidad* in the Philippines, see Rodao, 'Spanish Falange in the Philippines' and Rodao, 'Spanish Language in the Philippines'; García Abásolo, 'The Private Environment of the Spaniards in the Philippines'.

80. *Ibid.* Bacolod is the capital of Negros Occidental and was the 'sugar capital' of the archipelago.

81. Larkin, *Sugar and the Origins of Modern Philippine Society*, 182. In the 1930s the Spanish Falange was active in the Philippines (as it was in Puerto Rico). After Francisco Franco overthrew the Republican government in Spain, the Dominican University of Santo Tomas (Manila) bestowed on the Generalísimo the title 'Rector Magnificus'. Franco reciprocated

by knighting the Rector of the University. (Rodao, 'Spanish Falange in the Philippines').
Such loyalties may be linked to later collaboration with the Japanese.

82. Larkin, *Sugar and the Origins of Modern Philippine Society*, 115.

83. For studies on 'Hispanophilia' in early twentieth-century Puerto Rico, with 1920s 'Spanish Revival' architecture as a focus, see Vivoni Farage and Alvarez Curbelo, *Hispanofilia/Hispanophilia*. In his chapter in *Hispanophilia*, Vivoni Farage proposes two simultaneous readings of the 'Spanish Revival': on the one hand, as an institutional expression of now 'friendly' and expansive U.S. colonialism, manifest in the architecture of government buildings; and on the other hand as an expression of a stronger Puerto Rican identity that moved away from French neoclassical architecture for a more Hispanic reaffirmation. 'The Hispanic elements which had been co-opted by the Americanisation process were taken on by those Puerto Ricans who were educated in schools of architecture in the United States'. Vivoni Farage in *Hispanophilia*, 130. In a joint contribution to *Hispanophilia*, Vivoni Farage and Alvarez Curbelo offer a third reading that emphasises the 'compulsion for prestige' of the besieged Puerto Rican sugar bourgeoisie, with lavish residential architecture as one among several (ultimately failed) strategies. Jorge Rigau broaches a fourth possibility: that the 'Spanishness' is only a disguise for future-centred élan. Rigau in *Hispanophilia*, 112–13. In *Puerto Rico 1900*, Rigau similarly notes: 'What did it mean when, only twenty years after the end of Spain's extended and aborted domination, a return to all things Spanish was embraced? In spite of its Old World disguise, the Spanish Revival was acknowledged in Puerto Rico not as a remembrance of things past but as a truly contemporary expression: it was the embodiment of what lay ahead, of future possibilities.' (Rigau, *Puerto Rico 1900*, 182–83). Finally, a fifth reading in *Hispanophilia*, by Eliseo Colón Zayas, interrogates the meanings of 'Spanishness' itself in Puerto Rico, even where it is not defined as 'Spanish'. 'To study the appropriation by sectors of Puerto Rican society of certain cultural objects representative of a kind of 'Spanishness' leads to earlier forms of articulation and scenarios (…) To talk, then, about 'Spanishness' means first thinking out the boundaries of the elements that constituted such a thing as *lo español* in Puerto Rico.' Colón Zayas in *Hispanophilia*, 332–3. Less persuasively, Colón Zayas singles out melodrama as the trope of 'Puerto Rican 'Spanishness''. In light of this array of possibilities, Puerto Rican 'Spanishness' evidently presents a wide field of discussion where close study of social and economic history is pertinent. Both Spanish and 'Spanish' actors were singularly active, and quite materially so, in Puerto Rican society and politics during the early decades of the twentieth century. An ample literature exists on literary *hispanismo* in Puerto Rico's cultural-nationalist *Generación del Treinta* (see Alvarez Curbelo and Rodríguez Castro, *Del nacionalismo al populismo*). On the 'Hispanic Elites' of the American Southwest and their complex trajectories in the early decades of the U.S.A. – an important topic with many connections with the argument in this paper – see Gonzales, *The Hispanic elite of the Southwest*.

84. Larkin, *Sugar and the Origins of Modern Philippine Society*, 182.

85. Here too, one must guard against oversimplification. Until the First World War, British sugar-machinery manufacturers such as Mirlees-Watson enjoyed a major share of the market, and the London-based Czarnikow firm marketed a huge share of the world's beet and sugar production.

86. Larkin, 'Philippine History Reconsidered'.

NOTES ON CONTRIBUTORS

Manuel Barcia is a Lecturer in Latin American Studies at the University of Leeds. He studied history at the universities of Havana and Essex, and taught at the universities of Essex and Nottingham before moving to Leeds. He has published articles in various journals and has two forthcoming monographs, one of them on the 1825 slave revolt of Guamacaro, Cuba (University of Alabama Press). Email: m.barcia@leeds.ac.uk

Ulbe Bosma is Senior Research Fellow at the International Institute of Social History. He has published on colonial Indonesia in Dutch, English and Portuguese and is co-author of a general history on Dutch Creole societies in Asia (forthcoming). Email: ubo@iisg.nl

Joost Coté is a Senior Lecturer at Deakin University, in Melbourne, Australia where he teaches Indonesian and Southeast Asian history. His research and publications focus on colonial discourses in Indonesia. He has edited and translated two volumes of letters by the Indonesian feminist Raden Ajeng Kartini. A third volume of translated and annotated letters by the Kartini's sisters will appear shortly. In 2005 he co-edited *Recalling the Indies: Colonial Memories & Postcolonial Identities* (Aksant) on the memories of Dutch Indonesians in Australia, which also appeared in Indonesian translation. Email: joost.cote@deakin.edu.au

Juan A. Giusti-Cordero is Professor of History at the University of Puerto Rico, Rio Piedras. He has written on Puerto Rican and Caribbean social history and is author of *Land, Community, and Resistance in Pinoñes (Loíza), 18th-19th Centuries* (forthcoming). Email: junipama@isla.net

Jorge Ibarra is affiliated to the Cuban writer's association, Asociación de Escritores de Cuba, UNEAC. He has just finished chapter 13 of UNESCO'S General History of the Caribbean. Email: jibara@cubarte.cult.cu

G. Roger Knight teaches history at the University of Adelaide. He is widely published in the field of the social and economic history of colonial Java; his book *Steam, Steel and Cane: A Global History of the Java Sugar Industry 1830–1960* is forthcoming. Email: roger.knight@adelaide .edu.au

Sri Margana is Lecturer at the Department of History at the Gadjah Mada University in Yogyakarta, Indonesia. Since 2003 he has also been a research fellow at the TANAP programme (Towards a New Age of Partnership). His thesis is on 'The Contested Frontier: Rebellion, Economy and Social Change in Java's Oosthoek, 1763-1811'. Email: margo15id @yahoo.com

Sidney Mintz is Research Professor, Department of Anthropology, Johns Hopkins University, Baltimore, MD, USA. Professor Mintz is author of *Worker in the Cane* (1960), *Caribbean Transformations* (1974), *Sweetness & Power* (1985), and *Tasting Food, Tasting Freedom* (1997). Email: mintzsw@jhu.edu

Arthur van Schaik teaches geography at the Barlaeus Gymnasium College in Amsterdam, and a freelance researcher on the social and ecological history of Indonesia. He obtained his Ph.D. from the University of Amsterdam. With G. Roger Knight he published 'State and Capital in Late Colonial Indonesia; the sugar industry, braakhuur, and the colonial bureaucracy in North Central Java' (BKI 157–4, 2001). Email: mari-anti@xs4all.nl

BIBLIOGRAPHY

Abbreviations

ANC	Archivo Nacional de Cuba (Havana)
ANRI	Arsip Nasional Republik Indonesia (Jakarta)
CASA	Centrum voor Aziëstudies Amsterdam/Centre for Asian Studies (Amsterdam)
CNRS	Centre Nationale de la Recherche Scientifique (Paris)
GB	Gouvernementsbesluit (Ruling by the Dutch Governor-General)
HTK	Handelingen der Tweede Kamer/Records of the Dutch Parliament
IGV	Indische Genealogische Vereniging (Den Haag)/Indies Genealogical Society (The Hague)
KITLV	Koninklijk Instituut voor Taal-, Land- en Volkenkunde (Leiden)/Royal Institute for Linguistics and Anthropology
M(V)K	Ministerie van Koloniën (in NA)/Ministry of Colonies
NA	Nationaal Archief (Den Haag)/National Archive (The Hague)
NFB	Notulen/Minutes Factorij Batavia (in NA)
NHM	Nederlandsche Handel-Maatschappij (1824–1964) (in NA)/Dutch Trading Company
NI	Nederlands(ch) Indië/Dutch (East) Indies
NWIG	*New West Indies Guide*
PA	Pakualaman Archief/Archive of Pakualaman
PRIS	Programma Indonesische Studiën/Dutch-Indonesian Collaborative Research Programme
TNI	*Tijdschrift voor Nederlandsch Indië*

Archives

Archive of Pakualaman/PA, Yogyakarta
Archivo Nacional de Cuba/ANC
  – Asuntos Políticos
  – Miscelánea de Expedientes
Ardtornish Papers, Gillian Maclaine to Angus Maclaine, 19–12–1837 Gregorson of
  Ardtornish (Greenfield Papers), in private possession, U.K.
Arsip Nasional Republik Indonesia/ANRI
  – Archief Cultures
  – Politieke verslagen Residenties
Diary and Copybook (kept by Robert Hill Edwards in the mid-1830s) in private
  possession
Koninklijk Instituut voor Taal-, Land- en Volkenkunde/KITLV
  – HISDOC, Collectie Westerse handschriften
Nationaal Archief/National Archive/NA
  – Archief Ministerie van Justitie/Ministry of Justice
  – Archief Ministerie van Koloniën/Ministry of Colonies
  – Nederlandsche Handel-Maatschappij/Dutch Trading Company/NHM
Public Record Office, London
  – Foreign Office Records

Newspapers

Bataviasche Courant, Batavia 1816–1828 (Royal Library, The Hague).
De Locomotief, Semarangsch Handels- en Advertentieblad, Semarang 1863–1942
  (Royal Library, The Hague).
De Vorstenlanden, Nieuws- en Advertentieblad, Surakarta 1870–1879 (Royal
  Library, The Hague).
Diario de la Marina, La Habana 1832–1960 (Archivo Nacional de la Republica de
  Cuba, La Habana).
Javasche Courant, Batavia (Landsdrukkerij) 1828–1949 (Royal Library, The
  Hague).
La Lucha, La Habana around 1900–1910.
Mataram. Officieel orgaan van de Djokdjasche landhuurders vereeniging, Yogyakarta
  1903–[1942] (Royal Library, The Hague).
Soerabaiasch Handelsblad, Surabaya 1865–1942 (Royal Library, The Hague).
Soerakarta's Nieuws- en Advertentieblad, Surakarta 1879–1883 (Royal Library, The
  Hague).

Literature/Bibliography

Aguilar, Filomeno. *The Making of Cane Sugar: Poverty, Crisis, and Change in Negros Occidental.* Bacolod, The Philippines, La Salle Social Research Center 1984.

———. 'Sugar Planter-State Relations and Labour Processes in Colonial Philippine Haciendas', *Journal of Peasant Studies*, 22 (1994), 50–80.

———. 'Masonic Myths and Revolutionary Feats in Negros Occidental'. *Journal of Southeast Asian Studies*, 28 (1997), 285–300.

———. *Clash of Spirits: The History of Power and Sugar Planter Hegemony on a Visayan Island.* Honolulu, University of Hawai'i Press 1998.

Albert, Bill, and A.A. Graves (eds). *Crisis and Change in the International Sugar Economy, 1860–1914.* Norwich, ISC Press 1984.

———. *The World Sugar Economy in War and Depression 1914–1940.* London, Routledge 1988.

Albizu Campos, Pedro. *Obras escogidas*, 3 vol. Puerto Rico, Editorial Jelofe/Ediciones Puerto Rico, 1975–81; vol. 4, 1997.

Allahar, Anton. *Class, Politics, and Sugar in Colonial Cuba.* Lewiston, Edwin Mellon Press 1990.

Almanak en naamregister van Nederlandsch-Indië, 1826–1863 (annual). Batavia, Landsdrukkerij 1826–1863. *See also Regeeringsalmanak voor Nederlandsch-Indië, 1865–1942.*

Alvarez Curbelo, Silvia, and Maria Elena Rodríguez Castro. *Del nacionalismo al populismo. Cultura y política en Puerto Rico.* Río Piedras, Ediciones Huracán 1993.

Anderson, Benedict. *Imagined Communities. Reflections on the Origin and the Spread of Nationalism.* New York, Verso 1983.

———. 'Cacique Democracy in the Philippines: Origins and Dreams', *New Left Review*, 169 (May–June 1988), 3–31; Repr. in: Vicente Rafael (ed.), *Discrepant Histories. Translocal Essays on Filipino Culture.* Philadelphia, Temple University Press 1995.

———. 'Cacique Democracy in the Philippines: Origins and Dreams', in: V.L. Rafael, *Discrepant Histories.* (1995), 3–47; also in: B. Anderson, *The Spectre of Comparisons: Nationalism, Southeast Asia, and the World.* New York, Verso 1998.

Apacible, Alejandro. 'The Sugar Industry of the Philippines'. *The Philippine Geographical Journal*, 8, 3–4 (1964), 86–100.

Arango y Parreño, Francisco de. 'Discurso sobre la agricultura en La Habana y los medios de fomentarla (1792)', in: Francisco de Arango y Parreño, *De la Factoría a la Colonia.* La Habana, Publicaciones de la Secretaría de Educación, Dirección de Cultura [Talleres de Cultural, s.a.] 1936, 21–113.

Araquistaín, Luís de. *La agonía antillana.* Madrid, Ed. Espasa Escalpe 1928.

Attwood, Donald W. *Raising Cane. The Political Economy of Sugar in Western India.* Boulder, Westview Press 1992.

Ayala, César J. *American Sugar Kingdom. The Plantation Economy of the Spanish Caribbean 1898–1934.* Chapel Hill, University of North Carolina Press 1999.

Bagué, Jaime. *Del ingenio azucarero patriarcal a la central azucarera corporativa: glosa alrededor de las azucareras del año 1900.* Mayagüez, Taller Gráfico de la Oficina de Información y Publicaciones, Colegio de Agricultura y Artes Mecánicas 1901.

Balbas Capó, Vicente. *Puerto Rico a los diez años de su americanización*. San Juan, Tip. El Heraldo Español 1907.

Barcia Paz, Manuel. *La resistencia esclava en las plantaciones cubanas*. Havana, Pinares del Río, Vitral 1998.

———. 'Herencia y Racionalidad. La doble moral de los propietarios cubanos de esclavos', *Debates Americanos*, 9 (2000), 20–26.

Baud, Michiel. 'Sugar and Unfree Labour: Reflections on Labour Control in the Dominican Republic, 1870–1935', *The Journal of Peasant Studies*, 19, 2 (1992), 301–325.

Berg, N.P. van den. *Over de productiekosten van de Java-suiker*. Reprint from *Algemeen Dagblad van Nederlandsch-Indië*, 23 and 24 September 1886.

Bergad, Laird W. *Coffee and the Growth of Agrarian Capitalism in Nineteenth-Century Puerto Rico*. Princeton, Princeton University Press 1983.

———. 'The Economic Viability of Sugar Production based on Slave Labour in Cuba, 1859–1878', *Latin American Research Review*, 24, 1 (1989), 95–113.

———. *Cuban Rural Society in the Nineteenth Century. The Social and Economic History of Monoculture in Matanzas*. Princeton, Princeton University Press 1990.

———. et al., *The Cuban Slave Market: 1790–1880*. Cambridge: Cambridge University Press 1995.

Best, Lloyd. 'The Mechanism of Plantation Type Societies: Outlines of a Model of Pure Plantation Economy', *Social and Economic Studies* 17 (1968), 283–326.

Bevervoorde, W.F. Engelbert van, Assistant-Resident of Jogjakarta 1903. *Nota over het Rechtswezen in de Residentie Jogjakarta*. Djogja, Firma H. Buning 1903.

———. *'Eigenaardigheden en bezienswaardigheden'*, KITLV.

Billig, Michael. 'The Rationality of Growing Sugar in Negros', *Philippine Studies*, 40, 2 (1992), 153–82.

Billig, Michael S. *Barons, Brokers, and Buyers: the Institutions and Cultures of Philippines Sugar*. Honolulu, University of Hawai'i Press 2003.

Bird, Esteban. *The Sugar Industry in Relation to the Social and Economic System of Puerto Rico*. (In collaboration with Rafael Picó and Rafael de J. Cordero). San Juan, Senate Document No. 1, 15th Legislative Assembly, First Session 1941 [1937].

Blackburn, Robin. *The Making of New World Slavery. From the Baroque to the Modern, 1492–1800*. London, Verso 1997.

Bleeker, Pieter. 'Fragmenten eener Reis over Java', *Tijdschrift voor Nederlandsch-Indië*, 11, 2 (1849), 260–82.

Boomgaard, Peter, and Gert J. Oostindie. 'Changing Sugar Technology and the Labour Nexus: The Caribbean, 1750–1900', *Nieuwe West-Indische Gids*, 63, 1–2 (1989), 3–22.

Bosch, K.D. *De Nederlandse beleggingen in de Verenigde Staten*. Amsterdam, Elsevier 1948.

Bosma, Ulbe. *Karel Zaalberg, Journalist en strijder voor de Indo*. Leiden, KITLV Uitg. 1997.

———. 'Sugar and Dynasty in Yogyakarta'. Paper presented in the conference "Sugarlandia': Rethinking of Sugar Colony in the Asia and Pacific in a Global Context', Amsterdam 5–7 July 2001.

————. 'Citizens of Empire: Some Comparative Observations on the Evolution of Creole Nationalism in Colonial Indonesia', *Comparative Studies of Society and History*, 46, 4 (2004), 656–82.

Bosma, Ulbe, and G. Roger Knight. 'Global Factory and Local Field: Convergence and Divergence in the International Cane-Sugar Industry, 1850–1940', *International Review of Social History*, 49 (2004), 1–25.

Bosma, Ulbe, and Remco Raben. *De oude Indische wereld*. Amsterdam, Bert Bakker 2003. (English translation published by Singapore University Press, forthcoming in 2007).

Bothwell González, Reece (ed.). *Puerto Rico. Cien años de lucha política*. Universidad de Puerto Rico, Editorial Universitaria, 1979.

Brathwaite, Edward Kamau. *The Development of Creole Society in Jamaica, 1770–1820*. Oxford, Clarendon Press 1971.

Bree, L. de. *Gedenkboek van de Javasche Bank 1828 – 24 januari – 1928*. 2 vol. Weltevreden, Kolff 1928.

Breman, Jan. *The Shattered Image. Construction and Deconstruction of the Village in Colonial Asia*, Dordrecht, Foris 1988.

————. *Taming the Coolie Beast: Plantation Society and the Colonial Order*. Delhi, Oxford University Press 1989.

————. (ed.), *Imperial Monkey Business: Racial Supremacy in Social Darwinist Theory and Colonial Practice*. Amsterdam, VU University Press (CASA Monographs 3) 1990.

————. *Koelies, planters en koloniale politiek; Het arbeidsregime op de grootlandbouwondernemingen aan Sumatra's Oostkust in het begin van de twintigste eeuw*. Leiden, KITLV Uitg. (third revised edition) 1992.

————. 'The Village of Java and the Early Colonial State,' in: Mason Hoadley and Christer Gunnarsson (eds), *The Village Concept in the Transformation of Rural Southeast Asia*. Richmond, Curzon 1995.

Brest van Kempen, Resident van Djokjakarta. 'NOTA betrekkelijk de landverhuur in de Residentie Djokdjokarta', Bijlage IJ Verslag van het beheer en de staat der Oost-Indische bezittingen over 1860, Bijlage IJ HTK, (1861–1862).

Breton de Nijs, E. *Tempo Doeloe. Fotografische Documenten uit het Oude Indie, 1870–1914*. Amsterdam, Querido 1961.

Brooshooft, P. *Memorie over den toestand in Indië ter begeleiding van den Open Brief op 7 Maart 1888 gezonden aan 12 Nederlandsche Heeren*. Semarang, H. van Alphen 1888.

————. *De ethische koers in de Indische politiek*. Amsterdam, De Bussy 1901.

Carrión, Miguel de. 'El desenvolvimiento social de Cuba en los últimos veinte años', *Cuba Contemporánea*, Año IX, no.105, T. XXVII, Septiembre de 1921.

Castro, María de los Angeles. 'De Salvador Brau hasta la "novísima historia". Un replanteamiento y una crítica', *Boletín del Centro de Investigaciones Históricas*, 4, (1989), 9–56.

Cauna, Jacques de. *Au temps des îsles à sucre: histoire d'une plantation de Saint-Domingue au XVIIIe siècle*. Paris, Karthala 2003.

Chakrabarty, D. *Rethinking Working Class History: Bengal 1890–1840*. Princeton, Princeton University Press 1989.

Chatterjee, Partha. *The Nation and its Fragments. Colonial and Postcolonial Histories*. Princeton, Princeton University Press 1993.

Childs, Matt. 'The Aponte Rebellion of 1812 and the Transformation of Cuban Society: Race, Slavery and Freedom in the Atlantic World.' Ph.D. diss., University of Texas at Austin 2001.

Christiaans, P.A. *Het gereconstrueerde huwelijksregister van Djokjakarta 1817–1905.* 's-Gravenhage, Bronnenpublicaties van de Indische Genealogische Vereniging. Deel 3, 1994.

———. *Het rooms-katholieke doopregister van Semarang 1809–1929.* 's-Gravenhage, Bronnenpublicaties van de Indische Genealogische Vereniging. Deel 15, 2002.

Cifre de Loubriel, Estela. 'Los inmigrantes del siglo XIX. Su contribución a la formación del pueblo puertorriqueño', *Revista del Instituto de Cultura Puertorriqueña*, No 7 (1960), 32–36.

Clercq, F.S.A. de. 'De tegenwoordige toestand van het Inlandsch onderwijs', *De Indische Gids*, vol. 5 (1883), pt. 1, 335–57.

Clerkx, Lily E. and Wim F. Wertheim. *Living in Deli. Its Society as Images in Colonial Fiction.* Amsterdam, CASA series 6, VU University Press 1991.

Cochran, Thomas. *The Puerto Rican Businessman.* Philadelphia, University of Pennsylvania Press 1959.

Colenbrander, H.T. and J.E. Stokvis (eds). *Leven en Arbeid van Mr. C.Th. van Deventer.* 3 vol. Amsterdam, Kampen & Zn 1916–1917.

Coll Cuchí, José. *Un problema en América.* México D.F., Editorial Jus, 1944.

Constantino, Renato. *A History of the Philippines. From the Spanish Colonization to the Second World War.* New York, Monthly Review Press 1975.

Cooper, Frederick, and Ann L. Stoler (eds). *Tensions of Empire. Colonial Cultures in a Bourgeois World.* Berkeley, University of California Press 1997.

Corrigan, P., and D. Sayer. *The Great Arch: English State Formation as Cultural Revolution.* Oxford, Blackwell 1985.

Coté, Joost. 'The "Education" of Java: A Modern Colonial Discourse, 1865–1905'. Unpublished Ph.D. diss., Clayton Victoria, Monash University 1998.

Craton, Michael. 'Commentary: The Search for a Unified Field Theory', *Nieuwe West-Indische Gids*, 63, 1–2 (1989), 135–42.

Cubano, Astrid. 'La emigración mallorquina a Puerto Rico en el siglo XIX: el caso de los sollerenses', *Op. cit. Revista del Centro de Investigaciones Históricas*, Num. 7 (1992), 229–54.

Daum, P.A. *'Ups' en 'downs' in het Indische Leven.* Vol. 3, Verzamelde Romans, Amsterdam, Nijgh & Ditmar 1998.

De Indische Gids, 1879, no. 1, 3–5.

De Jesus, Ed. C. 'An Agenda for Philippine Studies', in: John Larkin and Ed. C. de Jesus, *Philippine Social History*, (1981), 447–53.

De Zaken van het Land Simbang nader toegelicht. Uitgegeven door de Kommissie van Liquidatie des Boedels van Wijlen de Heer J.E. Herderschee. The Hague, Nijhoff 1866.

Description of Robinson's Steam Cane Mill. London 1845.

Dessens, Nathalie. *Myths of the Plantation Society: Slavery in the American South and the West Indies.* Gainesville, University Press of Florida 2003.

Deventer, C.Th. van. 'De Java Suiker-Industrie', Overdruk uit *Vragen des Tijds* (1910, s.l.).

Dhanda, Karen S. 'Labour and Place in Barbados, Jamaica and Trinidad: A Search for a Comparative Unified Field Theory Revisited', *New West Indies Guide*, 75, 3 and 4 (2001), 229–56.

Díaz Quiñones, Arcadio. 'Isla de Quimeras, Pedreira, Palés y Albizu', *Revista de crítica literaria latinoamericana*, Año XXXIII, no. 45 (1997), Lima-Berkeley, 229–49.

Díaz Soler, Luis M. *Rosendo Matienzo Cintrón, orientador y guardián de una cultura*. Vol. 1. Río Piedras, Instituto de Literatura Puertorriqueña, Universidad de Puerto Rico, 1960.

Dick, H.W. *Surabaya, City of Work. A Socioeconomic History 1900–2000.* Athens, Ohio, Ohio University Press 2002.

Diego, José de. *Obras completas.* San Juan, Instituto de Cultura Puertorriqueña 1966, vol. 2.

Dietz, James. 'Puerto Rico's New History'. *Latin American Research Review*, 19, 1 (1984), 210–22.

———. *Economic History of Puerto Rico.* Princeton, Princeton University Press 1986.

———. 'Reviewing and Renewing Puerto Rican and Caribbean Studies: From Dependency to What?' *Caribbean Studies*, 25, 1–2 (1992), 27–48.

Diffie, Bailie W., and J.W. Diffie. *Porto Rico, a Broken Pledge.* New York, Vanguard Press 1931.

Djoko Utomo. 'Pemogokan Buruh Tani di Abad ke-19: Kasus Yogyakarta', *Prisma*, No. 8 Augustus 1983, 68–78.

Dockès, P. 'Le paradigme sucrier (XIe–XIXe siècle)', in: Fred Célimène et André Legris (eds), *L'Économie de l'esclavage colonial. Enquête et bilan du XVIIe au XIXe siècle.* Paris: CNRS Éditions 2002, 109–26.

Doel, H.W. van den. *De Stille Macht. Het Europese binnenlands bestuur op Java en Madoera, 1808–1942.* Amsterdam, Bert Bakker 1994.

Dolder, V.J. van, and H.F. Morbotter. *Verslag Omtrent hunne Bevindingen in de fabriek Poerwoedadie van A. baron Sloet van Oldruitenburgh. Betreffende de wijze van suikerbereiding daar onder de leiding en het toezight van den Heer Montclar daar gesteld*, Samarang, De Handelsvereeniging 1865.

Echaúz, Robustiano. *Apuntes sobre la isla de Negros.* Manila 1894. Translated as *Sketches of the Island of Negros.* Ohio University, Center for International Studies, Southeast Asia Series No. 50, 1978.

Elmhirst, Rebecca, and Ratna Saptari (eds). *Labour in Southeast Asia: local processes in a globalised world.* London/New York, RoutledgeCurzon 2004.

Elson, R.E. *Javanese Peasants and the Colonial Sugar Industry: Impact and Change in an East Java Residency, 1830–1940.* Singapore, Oxford University Press 1984.

———. *Village Java under the Cultuurstelsel.* Sydney, Allen & Unwin 1994.

Eltis, David, Stephen D. Behrendt, David Richardson and Herbert Klein (eds). *The Trans-Atlantic Slave Trade: A Database on CD-ROM.* Cambridge, Cambridge University Press 1999.

Ely, Roland T. *Cuando reinaba Su Majestad el azúcar.* Buenos Aires, Editorial Sudamericana, 1963.

Encyclopaedie van Nederlandsch-Indië, Tweede Druk [J. Paulus], The Hague, Martinus Nijhoff, 9 vol. 1917–1939.

Eng, P. van der. *The 'colonial drain' from Indonesia, 1823–1990*. Canberra, Australian National University 1993.

Enk, E.M.C. van. *Britse kooplieden en de cultures op Java; Harvey Thomson (1790–1837) en zijn financiers*. Amsterdam, Ph.D. diss., Free University 1999.

Errington, Frederick, and Deborah Gewertz. *Yali's Question. Sugar, Culture and History*. Chicago, University of Chicago Press 2004.

Faber, G.H. von. *Oud Soerabaia*. Surabaya, Gemeente Soerabaia 1931.

Fasseur, C. *The Politics of Colonial Exploitation*. Transl. and ed. by R.E. Elson and A. Kraal, Ithaca, Cornell University 1992.

Fernández, Áurea Matilde. 'La presencia española en Cuba después de 1898. Su reflejo en el *Diario de la Marina*', in: Consuelo Naranjo, Miguel Ángel Puig Samper, and Luis Miguel García Mora (eds), *La nación soñada: Cuba, Puerto Rico y Filipinas ante el 98*. Madrid, Ediciones Doce Calles 1996, 509–18.

Fernando, M.R. 'Peasants and Plantation: The Social Impact of the European Plantation Economy in Cirebon Residency from the Cultuurstelsel to the End of the First Decade of the Twentieth Century', Ph.D. diss., Clayton Victoria, Monash University 1982.

Franco, José Luciano. *La conspiración de Aponte*. La Habana, Publicaciones del Archivo Nacional de Cuba, no 58. 1963.

———. *Las minas de Santiago del Prado y la rebelión de los cobreros, 1530–1800*. La Habana, Editorial de Ciencias Sociales 1975.

———. *La gesta heroica del Triunvirato*. La Habana, Editorial de Ciencias Sociales, 1978.

Freyre, Gilberto. *The Masters and the Slaves [Casa-Grande y Senzala]. A Study in the Development of Brazilian Civilization*. New York, Alfred A. Knopff 1970.

Fuente, Alejandro de la. *A Nation for All: Race, Inequality, and Politics in Twentieth-Century Cuba*. Chapel Hill, University of North Carolina Press 1988.

Fuentes, C.R. *Apuntes documentados de la revolución en toda la Isla de Negros*. Iloilo, El Centinela 1919.

Furnivall, J.S. *Netherlands India. A Study of Plural Economy*. Amsterdam, Israel 1976 [Cambridge 1944].

Galloway, J.H. *The Sugar Cane Industry: an Historical Geography from its Origins to 1914*. Cambridge, Cambridge University Press 1989.

García, Gervasio. *Armar la historia*. Río Piedras, Editorial Huracán 1989.

García, Gloria. *Conspiraciones y revueltas*. Santiago de Cuba, Oriente 2003.

García-Abásolo, Antonio. 'The Private Environment of the Spaniards in the Philippines', *Philippine Studies*, 44 (1996), 349–73.

García-Muñiz, Humberto. 'The South Puerto Rico Sugar Company: The History of a U.S. Sugar Multinational Corporation in Puerto Rico and the Dominican Republic, 1900–21'. Ph.D. diss., New York, Columbia University 1997.

Gayer, Arthur, Paul T. Homan and Earle K. James. *The Sugar Economy of Puerto Rico*. New York, Columbia University Press 1938.

Geertz, Clifford. *Agricultural Involution: The Process of Ecological Change in Indonesia*. Berkeley, University of California Press 1963.

Gevers Deynoot, W.T. *Herinneringen eener Reis naar Nederlandsch Indie in 1862*. The Hague, Nijhoff 1864.

Giusti-Cordero, Juan. 'Puerto Rico and the Non-Hispanic Caribbean: un reto al exclusivismo de la historiografía puertorriqueña.' in: Juan Hernández Cruz and

María Dolores Luque de Sánchez (co-ords.), *Obra historiográfica de Arturo Morales Carrión*. San Germán, CISCLA 1993.

————. 'Labour, Ecology, and History in a Caribbean Plantation Region: Piñones (Loíza), 1770–1950'. Ph.D. diss., Binghamton University 1995.

Giusti-Cordero, Juan A. 'En búsqueda de la nación concreta: el grupo español en la industria azucarera de Puerto Rico', in: Consuelo Naranjo, Miguel Ángel Puig Samper, and Luis Miguel García Mora (eds), *La nación soñada: Cuba, Puerto Rico y Filipinas ante el 98*. Madrid, Ediciones Doce Calles 1996, 211–25.

Giusti-Cordero, Juan. 'Labour, Ecology and History in a Puerto Rican Plantation Region, 18th–20th Centuries: Rural Proletarians Revisited', in: Shahid Amin and Marcel van der Linden (eds), *'Peripheral' Labour? Studies in the History of Partial Proletarianisation*. Cambridge, Cambridge University Press 1997, 53–82.

————. 'Hacia otro 98: el 'grupo español' en Puerto Rico, 1890–1930 (azúcar, banca y política)', *Revista del Centro de Investigaciones Históricas*, 10 (1998), 75–124.

Gleeck, Lewis. *The Manila Americans (1901–1964)*. Manila, Carmelo and Bauermann 1977.

Go, Julian. 'The Chains of Empire: State Building and Political Education in Puerto Rico and the Philippines', in: Julian Go and Anne L. Foster, *The American Colonial State in the Philippines*. (2003), 182–216.

Go, Julian, and Anne L. Foster (eds). *The American Colonial State in the Philippines: Global Perspectives*. Durham, Duke University Press 2003.

Gonzales, Manuel G. *The Hispanic Elite of the Southwest*. El Paso, University of Texas at El Paso (Southwestern Studies Series No. 86), 1989.

Gortmans, J.A.Th. (ed.). *Het Landhuur-Reglement*. Jogjakarta, W.A. van der Hucht & Co. 1900.

Haan, F. de. 'De laatste der Mardijkers', *Bijdragen tot de Taal-, Land- en Volkenkunde*, 73 (1917) 219–45.

————. *Priangan: de Preanger-Regentschappen onder het Nederlandsch Bestuur tot 1811*. Batavia/'s-Gravenhage, Bataviaasch Genootschap v. Kunsten en Wetenschappen/Nijhoff 1910.

Handboek voor cultuur- en handelsondernemingen, 1888–1940. (jrg. 1–52). Amsterdam, De Bussy 1888–1940.

Haspel, C.C.H. van den. *Overwicht in Overleg: Hervormingen van Justitie, grondgebruik en bestuur op de Vorstenlanden op Java, 1880–1930*. Dordrecht-Holland, Foris Publication 1985.

Hawes, Gary. *The Philippine State and the Marcos Regime*. Ithaca, Cornell University Press 1987.

Heel, M.G. van. *Gedenkboek van de Koloniale Tentoonstelling Semarang, 20 aug–22 nov. 1914*. Batavia, Mercurius 1916.

Helg, Aline. *Our Rightful Share: The Afro-Cuban Struggle for Equality, 1886–1912*. Chapel Hill, University of North Carolina Press 1995.

Hernáez Romero, Maria Fe. *Negros Occidental Between Two Foreign Powers: 1888–1909*. Manila, Enterprise Publications 1974.

Herrero, José A. *La mitología del azúcar*. San Juan, CEREP Cuadernos No. 5, 1970.

Higman, B.W. *Montpelier, Jamaica. A Plantation Community in Slavery and Freedom, 1739–1912*. Mona Jamaica, University Press of the West Indies 1998.

Hinloopen Labberton, D. van. 'Invloed van de Suikerfabriek op hare omgeving'. [The article was originally published in 1908 in *Bijblad, Archief voor de Java Suikerindustrie*, vol. 16 but reproduced, according to the Archief's editor, without permission] in *Tijdschrift van Nijverheid en Landbouw*, vol. LXXVII, 1918, 1–119.

Historia y sociedad. Universidad de Puerto Rico, Recinto de Río Piedras, no 7, 1992.

Hobson, J.A. *Imperialism. A Study*. London, Allen & Unwin (second edition) 1905.

Hoetink, H. *Het patroon van de oude Curaçaose samenleving: een sociologische studie*. Assen, Van Gorcum 1958.

Hoëvell, W.R. van. *Reis over Java, Madura en Bali in het midden van 1847*. Amsterdam, P.N. van Kampen 1849.

Houben, Vincent J.H. 'History and Mortality: East Sumatran Incidents as Described by Jan Breman' *Itinerario*, 12, 2 (1988), 97–100.

Houben, Vincent. 'De Indo-aristocatie van Midden Java: de familie Dezentjé', in: Wim Willems (ed.), *Sporen van een Indisch verleden (1600–1942)*. Leiden, Centrum voor Onderzoek v. Maatschappelijke tegenstellingen, Rijksuniversiteit Leiden 1992, 39–50.

———. 'Private Estate in Java in the Nineteenth Century: A Reappraisal,' in: J.Th. Lindblad (ed.), *New Challenges in the Modern Economic History of Indonesia*, Leiden, PRIS 1993, 47–65.

———. *Kraton and Kumpeni; Surakarta and Yogyakarta, 1830–1870*. Leiden, KITLV Press 1994.

Houben, Vincent J.H., and Thomas Lindblad (eds). *Coolie Labour in Colonial Indonesia: A Study of Labour Relations in the Outer Islands, 1900–1940*. Wiesbaden, Harrassowitz 1999.

Howe, A. *The Cotton Masters, 1830–1860*. Oxford, Clarendon Press 1984.

Hunger, J.D. (ed.). *Javaansche wetten, verordeningen, regelingen, besluiten, bevelschriften en bepalingen op agrarische gebied geldig in Jogjakarta*. Vol. 1. Jogjakarta, H. Buning 1910.

Ibarra, Jorge. 'Herencia española, influencia estadounidense', in *Nuestra común historia. Cultura y sociedad*. La Habana, Editorial de Ciencias Sociales 1995.

———. *Partidos políticos y clases sociales. Cuba: 1898–1923*. La Habana, Editorial de Ciencias Sociales 1992.

———. *Nuestra común historia Cuba-España. Cultura y sociedad*. La Habana, Ed. de Ciencias Sociales 1995.

———. 'The Spanish Communities in Cuba and Puerto Rico: their Role in the Process of National Formation in the Twentieth Century (1898–1930)'. Unpublished paper, presented at the 'Legacies of 1898' Seminar, Obermann Center, University of Iowa, July 1998.

Ileto, Reynaldo Clemeña. *Pasyón and Revolution: Popular Movements in the Philippines, 1840–1910*. Quezon City: Ateneo de Manila University Press 1979.

Indische Navorscher, De. Orgaan van den Genealogisch-heraldischen kring. Batavia, Visser 1934–1941.

———. *Orgaan van de Indische Genealogische vereniging, New Series*. 's-Gravenhage 1988-.

Isfhani-Hammond, Alexandra. *The Masters and the Slaves: Plantation Relations and Mestizaje in American Imaginaries.* New York, Palgrave Macmillan 2004.

Jaarcijfers voor het Koninkrijk der Nederlanden (1898–1922). 's-Gravenhage, CBS/Belinfante 1899–1924.

Jagt, H.A.C. van der. *Verslag eener Reis ter Bestudeering der Suiker Industrie op Java.* Dordrecht: Stichting Industriefonds 1929.

Jain, Shobhita. 'Plantation Labour in South and South-East Asia', in: Susan Visvanathan (ed.), *Structure and Transformation: Theory and Society in India.* New Delhi/New York, Oxford University Press 2001.

James, Cyril Lionel Robert. 'French Capitalism and Caribbean Slavery', in: Cyril Lionel Robert James, *The Black Jacobins: Toussaint L'Ouverture and the San Domingo Revolution.* New York, Vintage (second edition) 1963 [1938].

Janssen, L.M. *De Burgerlijke Stand van Pekalongan. Geboorteregisters (1821)(1828–1868).* 's-Gravenhage, (Bronnenpublikaties van de) Indische Genealogische Vereniging, deel xiv 2001.

———. *Onuitgegeven materiaal van de burgerlijke stand Pekalongan,* n.p., n.d.

Jayawardena, Kumari. *Nobodies to Somebodies: The Rise of the Colonial Bourgeoisie in Sri Lanka.* London, Zed Books 2002.

Johnson, S. 'Casualties of Peace: Tracing the Historic Roots of the Florida Cuba Diaspora, 1763–1800', *Colonial Latin American Historical Review,* 10, no 1 (2001), 91–126.

Johnson, Sherry. *The Social Transformation of Eighteenth-Century Cuba,* Gainesville, University Press of Florida 2001.

Junghuhn, F. *Terugreis van Java naar Europa met de zoogenaamde Engelsche Overlandpost, in de Maanden September tot October 1848.* Zalt-Bommel, Joh. Norman & Zoon 1851.

Ka, Chih-Ming. *Japanese Colonialism in Taiwan. Land Tenure, Development and Dependency, 1895–1945.* Boulder, Westview Press 1995.

Karnow, Stanley. 'Perspectives on Philippine Historiography: A Symposium'. New Haven, Yale University Southeast Asia Studies, Monograph Series no 21, 1979.

———. *In Our Image: America's Empire in the Philippines.* New York, Random House 1989.

Kartodirdjo, Sartono. *The Peasant Revolts of Banten in 1888.* 's-Gravenhage, Nijhoff 1966.

———. *Protest Movement in Rural Java: A Study of Agrarian Unrest in the 19th and Early 20th Centuries.* Singapore, Oxford University Press 1973.

Kesteren, C.E. van. 'Feiten en Cijphers uit het Koloniaal Verslag voor 1878', *De Indische Gids,* vol. 1 (1879), 46–72.

———. 'Minahassan demand for political recognition', *Tijdschrift voor Nederlandsch Indië,* vol. 2 (1879), 81–94.

———. 'De veestapel op Java', *De Indische Gids,* vol. 2 (1880), pt. 2, 25 ff.

———. 'De nood van Bantam', *De Indische Gids,* vol. 3 (1881), pt. 1, 679–704.

———. 'Een en Ander over de Welvaart der Inlandsche Bevolking en de Toekomst der Europeesche Landbouw-Nijverheid in N. Indië', *De Indische Gids,* vol. 7 (1885), 551–619.

———. 'Een subsidy voor het uitgeven van statistische overzichten betreffende Ned. Indië', *De Indische Gids,* vol. 11 (1889), pt. 2, 2187–18.

Knight, G. Roger, 'From Plantation to Padi Field: The Origins of the Nineteenth-Century Transformation of Java's Sugar Industry', *Modern Asian Studies*, 14, 2 (1980), 177–204.

———. 'The Java Sugar Industry as a Capitalist Plantation: A Reappraisal', *Journal of Peasant Studies*, 19, 3 (1992), 68–86.

———. *Colonial Production in Provincial Java: The Sugar Industry in Pekalongan-Tegal, 1800–1942*. Amsterdam, VU Press 1993.

———. 'The Visible Hand in *Tempo Doeloe*: The Culture of Management and the Organisation of Business in Java's Colonial Sugar Industry', *Journal of Southeast Asian Studies*, 30, 1 (1999), 74–98.

———. 'The Sugar Industry of Colonial Java and its Global Trajectory', *South East Asia Research*, 8, 3 (2000), 249–74.

———. 'The Contractor as *Suikerlord* and Entrepreneur: Otto Carel Holmberg de Beckfelt (1794–1857)', in: J. Thomas Lindblad en Willem van der Molen (eds), *Macht en Majesteit. Opstellen voor Cees Fasseur*. Leiden, Opleiding Talen en Culturen van Zuidoost-Azie en Oceanië, Universiteit Leiden 2002, 190–205.

Kol, Henry van. *Uit Onze Koloniën: Uitvoerige Reisverhaal*. Leiden, A.W. Sijthoff 1903.

Kuethe, Allan J. 'Havana in the Eighteenth Century', in: Franklin W. Knight, Peggy K. Liss and James G. Cusick (eds), *Atlantic Port Cities: Economy, Culture and Society in the Atlantic World, 1650–1850*. Knoxville, University of Tenessee Press 1991, 13–39.

———. 'Los Llorones Cubanos: The Socio-Military Basis of Commercial Privilege in the American Trade under Charles IV', in: Jacques A. Barbier and Allan J. Kuethe (eds), *The North American Role in the Spanish Imperial Economy, 1760–1819*. Manchester, Manchester University Press 1984, 134–55.

———. *Cuba, 1753–1815: Crown, Military and Society*. Knoxville: University of Tenessee Press 1986.

Lach de Bère, Ph. *Genealogie van het Nederlandsch Indische geslacht Weijnschenk*. 's-Gravenhage, s.n, s.d. [1908].

Lampros, Peter J. 'Merchant-Planter Cooperation and Conflict: The Havana Consulado, 1794–1832', Ph.D. diss., New Orleans, Tulane University 1980.

Landhuur-reglement (Staatsblad 1906, No. 93): Reglement op de huur en verhuur van gronden voor den landbouw in Suracarta en Djogjacarta met intrekking der ordonanntien van 3 Februari en 11 juni 1884 (Staatsblad nos. 9 en 86) 18 December 1891 (Staatsblad no. 255), Djogjacarta, N.V. H. Buning 1906.

Larkin, J.A. *Sugar and the Origins of Modern Philippine Society*. Berkeley, University of California Press 1993.

Larkin, John. 'Philippine History Reconsidered: A Socioeconomic Perspective', *American Historical Review*, 87 (1982), 595–628.

———. and Ed. C. de Jesús. *Philippine Social History: Global Trade and Local Transformations*. Honolulu, University Press of Hawai'i 1981.

———. *Sugar and the Origins of Modern Philippine Society*. Berkeley, University of California Press 1993.

Leidelmeijer, Margaret. *Van suikermolen tot grootbedrijf. Technische vernieuwing in de Java-suikerindustrie in de negentiende eeuw*. Amsterdam, NEHA Series 1997.

Lewis, Gordon. *Puerto Rico: Freedom and Power in the Caribbean*. New York, Monthly Review Press 1963.

Lindblad, J.Th. (ed.). *New Challenges in the Modern Economic History of Indonesia.* Leiden, PRIS 1993.

Locher-Scholten, E. 'Mr P. Brooshooft: Een biographische schets in koloniaal-ethisch perspektief', in: E. Locher Scholten, *Ethiek in Fragmenten: Vijf Studies over koloniaal denken en doen van Nederlanders in de Indonesische archipel, 1877–1942.* Utrecht, HES 1981, 11–54.

———. *Ethiek in Fragmenten. Vijf Studies over koloniaal denken en doen van Nederlanders in de Indonesische archipel, 1877–1942.* Utrecht, HES 1981.

———. 'Door een gekleurde bril: Koloniale bronnen over vrouwenarbeid op Java in de negentiende eeuw', in: J. Reijs *et al* (eds), *Vrouwen in de Nederlandse Koloniën.* Nijmegen, SUN 1986, 34–51.

Lomba Milán. Enrique, 'Los espectáculos culturales en Santiago de Cuba', *Santiago*, No. 37 (1980), Santiago de Cuba, 99–118.

López-Domínguez, Violeta. *Crisis in Sugarlandia: The Planters' Differential Perceptions and Responses and Their Impact on Sugarcane Workers' Households.* Bacolod City Philippines, La Salle Social Research Center 1986.

Lopez-Gonzaga, Violeta. *The Negrense: A Social History of an Elite Class.* Bacolod, Institute for Social Research and Development, University of St. La Salle 1991.

———. *Land of Hope, Land of Want. A Socio-Economic History of Negros (1571–1985).* Quezón City, Philippine National Historical Society 1994.

Lopez-Varga, V.B. *The Socio-Politics of Sugar: Wealth, Power Formation and Change in Negros 1899–1985.* Bacolod, University of St. La Salle Press 1989.

Lynch, Owen. 'The Legal Bases of Philippine Colonial Sovereignty: An Inquiry'. *Philippine Law Journal,* 62, 3 (1987), 279–316.

Lynsky, Meyer. *Sugar Economics, Statistics, and Documents.* A publication of the United States Cane Sugar Refiners' Association 1938. New York, Research Division.

Maddison, Angus. 'Dutch income in and from Indonesia', in: Angus Maddison and Gé Prince (eds), *Economic Growth in Indonesia 1820–1940.* Leiden, KITLV 1989, 15–42.

Mañach, Jorge. *Pasado vigente.* La Habana, Ed. Trópico 1939.

Mansvelt, W.M.F. *Exportcultures van Nederlandsch-Indië 1830–1937.* Centraal Kantoor voor de Statistiek, s.l. [Batavia] 1939.

———. *Geschiedenis der Nederlandsche Handel-Maatschappij, 1824–1924.* 2 vol., Haarlem, Joh. Enschede en Zonen 1924–26.

Mao Zdedong. *Analysis of the Classes in Chinese Society.* Beijing, Foreign Languages Press 1956 [1926].

Marazzi, Rosa. 'El impacto de la inmigración a Puerto Rico de 1800 a 1830: análisis estadístico', *Revista de Ciencias Sociales,* University of Puerto Rico, XVIII, 1–2 (June 1974), 1–42.

Marc, Neri, and Pierre Cony. *Indochine française.* Paris, Editions Paris-Empire 1946.

Margana, S. 'Soerorejo versus Kartosudiro: Bekel and Bekel System in the Principalities of Central Java During the Colonial Period 1880–1912', *Lembaran Sejarah,* vol. III, no 1 (2000), 186–209.

Margana, Sri. *Kraton Surakarta dan Yogyakarta, 1796–1874.* Yogyakarta, Pustaka Pelajar 2004.

Marle, A. van. 'De groep der Europeanen in Nederlands-Indië, iets over ontstaan en groei', *Indonesië*, vol. 5 (1951–1952), 97–121, 314–41, 481–507.

Martineau, George. *Sugar*. London, s.n. fourth edition 1918.

Martinez Cuesta, Angel. *Historia de la isla de Negros, Filipinas*, 1565–1898. Madrid 1974.

———. *History of Negros*. Transl. by Alfonso Felix jr. and Sevilla Caritas, Manila, Historical Conservation Society 1980.

Marx, Karl. *Grundrisse*. New York, Vintage 1973. [*Grundrisse der Kritik der politischen Ökonomie*, 1857–1858, Moscow 1939–1941].

Mazumdar, Sucheta. *Sugar and Society in China. Peasants, Technology and the World Market*. Cambridge, Harvard University Press 1998.

McCoy, Alfred W. 'Introduction', in: Alfred W. McCoy and Ed. C. de Jesus, *Philippine Social History* (1982), 1–20.

———. 'A Queen Dies Slowly: The Rise and Decline of Iloilo City', in: A.W. McCoy and Ed. C. de Jesus, *Philippine Social History* (1982), 297–360.

———. 'Quezon's Commonwealth: Origins of Philippine Authoritaniarism', in: Ruby R. Paredes, *Philippine Colonial Democracy*, Monograph Series No. 32, Yale University Southeast Asia Studies. New Haven, Yale Center for International and Area Studies 1988, 114–60.

———. 'Sugar Barons: Formation of a Native Planter Class in the Colonial Philippines', *Journal of Peasant Studies*, 19, 3/4 (1992), 106–41.

———. and Ed. C. de Jesus, *Philippine Social History: Global Trade and Local Transformations*. Sidney, Allen & Unwin 1982.

McCusker, John J., and Russell R. Menard. 'The Sugar Industry in the Seventeenth Century: A New Perspective on the "Barbadian 'Sugar Revolution'"', in: Stuart B. Schwartz (ed.), *Tropical Babylons* (2004), 289–330.

Miert, H. van. *Bevlogenheid en Onvermogen: Mr J.H. Abendanon en de Ethische Richting in het Nederlandse kolonialisme*. Leiden, KITLV Press 1991.

Mindere Welvaart Onderzoek. See *Onderzoek naar de mindere welvaart (…)*.

Mintz, Sidney W. 'Cañamelar: The Sub-Culture of a Rural Sugar Plantation Proletariat', in: Julian Steward et al., *The People of Puerto Rico*. Urbana, University of Illinois Press 1956, 314–417.

———. 'The Plantation as a Socio-Cultural Type', in: Pan American Union, *Plantation Systems of the New World*. Washington, Pan American Union 1959, 42–49.

———. *Worker in the Cane; a Puerto Rican Life History*. New Haven, Yale University Press 1960.

———. 'Petits cultivateurs et prolétaires ruraux aux Caraïbes', in: Centre Nationale de la Recherche Scientifique (CNRS), *Problèmes agraires de l'Amérique Latine*. Paris, Editions du CNRS 1967, 93–100.

———. 'The Caribbean as a Socio-Cultural Area', in: Michael Horowitz (ed.), *Peoples and Cultures of the Caribbean*. Garden City, New Jersey, Natural History Press 1971, 17–46.

———. *Sweetness and Power: The Place of Sugar in the Modern World*. New York, Viking 1985.

———. 'Ethnic Difference, Plantation Sameness', in: Gert Oostindie, *Ethnicity in the Caribbean: Essays in Honor of Harry Hoetink*. London, MacMillan 1996, 39–52.

————. and Eric Wolf, 'Haciendas and Plantations in Middle America and the Antilles', *Social and Economic Studies*, 6 (1957), 380–412.

Moitt, Bernard (ed.). *Sugar, Slavery, and Society: Perspectives on the Caribbean, India, the Mascarenes, and the United States.* Gainesville, University Press of Florida 2005.

Montclar, A. *La 'Sucrerie' Indo-Néerlandaise et la 'Raffinerie' Néerlandaise.* Amsterdam, C.L. Langenhuysen 1866.

Morales Carrión, Arturo. *Puerto Rico and the Non-Hispanic Caribbean: A Study in the Decline of Spanish Exclusivism.* Río Piedras, University of Puerto Rico Press 1952.

Moreno Fraginals, M. *The Sugar Mill: The Socioeconomic Complex of Sugar in Cuba, 1760–1860.* New York, Monthly Review Press 1976.

Moreno Fraginals, Manuel. *El ingenio. El complejo económico social cubano del azúcar.* Barcelona, Crítica 2001.

Mrazek, R. *Engineers of Happy Land: Technology and Nationalism in a Country.* Princeton and Oxford, Princeton University Press 2000.

Murray, David. *Odious Commerce: Britain, Spain and the Abolition of the Cuban Slave Trade.* Cambridge, Cambridge University Press 1980.

Nagano, Yoshiko. 'The Oligopolistic Structure of the Philippine Sugar Industry during the Great Depression', in: Bill Albert and Adrian Graves (eds), *The World Sugar Economy in War and Depression, 1914–1940.* London, Routledge 1988, 170–81.

————. *Formation of Sugarlandia in the Late 19th Century Negros: Origin of Underdevelopment in the Philippines.* Quezon City, Third World Studies Center, University of the Philippines 1982.

————. 'The Agricultural Bank of the Philippine Government, 1908–1916', *Journal of Southeast Asian Studies*, 28, 2 (1997), 301–23.

Nagel, G.H. *Schetsen uit mijne Javaansche portefeuille.* Amsterdam, Sulpke 1828.

Nederland's Patriciaat, 1910–1997. Den Haag, Centraal Bureau voor Genealogie (en Heraldiek), 1910–1997.

Negrón Portillo, Mariano. *El autonomismo puertorriqueño: su transformación ideológica (1895–1914).* Río Piedras San Juan, Editorial Huracán 1981.

Netscher, F.J.H. *Regt en Onregt of Den Toestand der Gewestelijke Besturen in Indie tegenover de Particuliere Industrie.* 's-Gravenhage, H.C. Susan 1864.

Ngo Vinh Long. *Before the Revolution: The Vietnamese Peasants under the French.* Cambridge, MIT Press 1973.

Niel, R. van. *Java under the Cultivation System.* Leiden, KITLV Press 1992.

Onderzoek naar de mindere welvaart der inlandsche bevolking op Java en Madoera (1905–1920). Batavia, Ruygrok 1905–1920.

Ong Tae Hae. *The Chinaman Abroad: An Account of the Malayan Archipelago, particularly Java.* Transl. by W.H. Medhurst, London, John Snow 1850.

Oosthoek. 'Het Onderwijs van Kinderen van Europeaanen en met dezen Gelijkgesteld in Nederlandsch-Indië', *De Indische Gids*, vol. 1 (1879), pt. 2, 8–36.

Ortiz, Fernando. *Orbita de Fernando Ortiz*, Colección Orbita, La Habana, UNEAC 1973.

Osborne, Milton E. *The French Presence in Cochinchina and Cambodia: Rule and Response (1859–1905).* Ithaca, Cornell University Press 1969.

Ottow, S.J. 'De oorsprong der conservatieve richting. Het kolonisatierapport Van der Capellen, uitgegeven en toegelicht door S.J. Ottow'. Ph.D. diss., University Utrecht 1937.

Owen, Norman G. *Compadre Colonialism: Studies on the Philippines under American Rule*. Ann Arbor, University of Michigan Papers on South and Southeast Asia No. 3, 1971.

Padmo, Soegijanto. *The Cultivation of Vorstenlands Tobacco in Surakarta Residency and Besuki Tobacco in Besuki Residency and its Impact on the Peasant Economy and Society: 1860–1960*. Yogyakarta, Aditya Media 1994.

Paquette, Robert. *Sugar is Made with Blood: The Conspiracy of La Escalera and the Conflict between Empires over Slavery in Cuba*, Middleton Connecticut, Wesleyan University Press 1987.

Paredes, Ruby R. *Philippine Colonial Democracy*. Monograph Series No. 32. New Haven, Yale University Southeast Asian Studies 1988.

Partido Nacionalista de Puerto Rico, 'Programa político, social y económico del Partido Nacionalista de Puerto Rico' (1930), in: Reece González (ed.), *Puerto Rico: Cien años de lucha política*, vol. I, T. I,. Río Piedras, Editorial Universitaria, Universidad de Puerto Rico 1979, 461–66.

Het Pauperisme onder de Europeanen in Nederlandsch-Indië. 5 vol., Batavia, Landsdrukkerij 1901–1902.

Pérez de la Riva, Juan. *Correspondencia reservada del Capitán General Don Miguel Tacón con el gobierno de Madrid, 1834–1836: el General Tacón y su época, 1834–1838*. La Habana : Consejo Nacional de Cultura, Biblioteca Nacional José Martí, Departamento de Colección Cubana 1963.

Perloff, Harvey. *Puerto Rico's Economic Future*. Chicago, University of Chicago Press 1950.

Picó, Fernando. 'La religiosidad popular es religiosa', in: *Vírgenes, magos, y escapularios: etnicidad y religiosidad popular en Puerto Rico*. Río Piedras, Editorial Universidad de Puerto Rico 1998.

Piepers, M.C. *Macht tegen Recht: de vervolging der justitie in Nederlandsch Indië*. Batavia, Van Dorp & Co 1884.

Piqueras, José A. comp. *Azúcar y esclavitud en el final del trabajo forzado: homenaje a M. Moreno Fraginals*. Madrid, Fondo de Cultura Económica 2002.

Poerwokoesoemo, Soedarisman. *Kadipaten Pakulaman*. Yogyakarta, Gadjah Mada University Press 1985.

Poncet de Cárdenas, Carolina. *Investigaciones y apuntes literarios*. La Habana, Ed. Letras Cubanas 1986.

Post, Peter. 'The Kwik Hoo Tong Trading Society of Semarang, Java. A Chinese Business Network in Late Colonial Asia', *Journal of Southeast Asian Studies*, 33, 2 (2002) 279–96.

Primelles, León. *Crónicas cubanas*. Tomos I y II, La Habana, Ed. Lex 1957.

Prinsen Geerligs, H.C. *De rietsuiker industrie in de verschillende landen van productie: historisch, technisch, economisch en statistisch overzicht over de productie en den uitvoer van de rietsuiker*. Amsterdam, Het proefstation voor de Java Suiker Industrie, 1924. Handboek ten dienste van de suikerrietcultuur. Vol. 4.

———. 'De Suikercultuur', in: M.G. Heel, *Gedenkboek van de Koloniale Tentoonstelling, Semarang, 20 Augustus–22 November, 1914*. Mercurius, Batiavia 1916, 96–107.

Quintero Rivera, Angel. 'El capitalismo y el proletariado rural'. *Revista de Ciencias Sociales*, 19, 1 (1974), 61–103.

———. *Conflictos de clase y política en Puerto Rico*. Río Piedras, Ediciones Huracán 1976.

———. and Gervasio García, *Desafío y solidaridad*. *Breve historia del movimiento obrero puertorriqueño*. Río Piedras, Ediciones Huracán 1982.

———. *Patricios y plebeyos: burgueses, hacendados, artesanos y obreros. Las relaciones sociales en el Puerto Rico de cambio de siglo*. Río Piedras, Ediciones Huracán 1988.

Quirino, Carlos. *History of the Philippine Sugar Industry*. Manila, Kalayaan 1974.

Rafael, Vicente L. *Discrepant Histories. Translocal Essays on Filipino Culture*. Philadelphia, Temple University Press 1995.

———. *White Love and Other Events in Filipino History*. Durham, Duke University Press 2000.

Ramos, José Antonio. *Manual del perfecto fulanista: apuntes para el estudio de nuestra dinamica político-social*. La Habana, J. Montero 1916.

Ramos Mattei, Andrés. 'The influence of mechanization in the Puerto Rican system of sugar production, 1873–1890'. London, Ph.D. diss., University College 1977.

———. (ed.), *Azúcar y esclavitud*. Rio Pedras, Puerto Rico, Universidad de Puerto Rico, Recinto de Rio Piedras 1982.

———. *La sociedad del azúcar en Puerto Rico: 1870–1910*. San Juan, Editorial de la Universidad de Puerto Rico 1988.

Rapport der Pauperisme Commissie. Batavia, Landsdrukkerij 1903.

Regeeringsalmanak/Regerings-almanak voor Nederlandsch-Indië, 1865–1942 (jaarlijks). Batavia, Landsdrukkerij 1865–1942. *See also Almanak (…) Nederlandsch-Indië, 1826–1863*.

Riënzi (H.H. van Kol). *Land en Volk van Java*. Maastricht, Pieters 1896.

Rigau, Jorge. *Puerto Rico 1900. Turn-of-the-Century Architecture in the Hispanic Caribbean 1890–1930*. New York, Rizzoli International Publications 1992.

Rivera Ramos, Efrén. *The Legal Construction of Identity: The Judicial and Social Legacy of American Colonialism in Puerto Rico*. Washington DC, American Psychological Association 2001.

Rivero Muñiz, Nicolás. *Actualidades, 1903–1919*. La Habana, Cultural 1929.

Rodao, Florentino. 'Spanish Falange in the Philippines, 1936–45', *Philippine Studies*, 43 (1995) 3–26.

———. 'Spanish Language in the Philippines', *Philippine Studies*, 45 (1997), 94–107.

Rodney, Walter. *A History of the Guyanese Working People 1881–1905*. Baltimore, Johns Hopkins University Press 1981.

Rouffaer, G.P. *Vorstenlanden*. Overdruk uit *Adatrecht Bundel*, 34, 81 (1931).

Roosevelt, Theodore. 'Land Problems in Puerto Rico and the Philippine Islands', *Geographical Review*, 24, 1934, 182–204.

Ross, Robert (ed.). 'Christianity, Status and Respectability', in: *Status and Respectability in the Cape Colony, 1750–1870*. Cambridge, Cambridge University Press 1999, 94–124.

Rost van Tonningen, D.W. 'Physisch en chemisch onderzoek van der gronden der suikerfabriek Wonopringo in Pekalongan', *Tijdschrift voor Nijverheid in Nederlandsch Indie*, vol 3 (1856), 423–67.

Rush, James R. *Opium to Java: Revenue Farming and Chinese Enterprise in Colonial Indonesia 1860–1910.* Ithaca, Cornell University Press 1990.

Salamanca, Bonifacio. *The Filipino Reaction to American Rule, 1901–1913.* Quezon City, New Day Publishers 1984.

Sampson, Anthony. *The Sovereign State of ITT.* New York, Stein and Day 1973.

Scarano, Francisco (ed.). *Inmigración y clases sociales en el Puerto Rico del siglo XIX.* Río Piedras, Editorial Huracán 1985.

———. *Sugar and Slavery in Puerto Rico, The Plantation Economy of Ponce, 1800–1850.* Madison, University of Wisconsin Press 1984.

Schaik, A. van. 'Colonial Control and Peasant Resources in Java; Agricultural Involution Reconsidered'. Ph.D. diss., University of Amsterdam 1986.

———. 'Bitter and Sweet. A Hundred Years of Sugar Industry in Comal', in: H.F. Kano, F. Hüsken, D. Suryo (eds), *Beneath the Smoke of the Sugar-Mill; Javanese Coastal Communities During the Twentieth Century.* Yogyakarta, Universita Gadjah Mada. Institute of Oriental Culture 2001, 39–72.

Schnakenbourg, C. 'From Sugar Estate to Central Factory: The Industrial Revolution in the Caribbean', in: Bill Albert and Adrian Graves, *Crisis and Change in the International Sugar Economy* (1984), 83–94.

Schwartz, Stuart B. (ed.). *Tropical Babylons: Sugar and the Making of the Atlantic World.* Chapel Hill and London, University of North Carolina Press 2004.

Scott, Rebecca J. *Slave Emancipation in Cuba: The Transition to Free Labor, 1860–1899.* Princeton, New Jersey, Princeton University Press 1985.

———. 'Labour Control in Cuba after Emancipation', in: Malcolm Cross and Gad Heuman (eds), *Labour in the Caribbean. From Emancipation to Independence.* London, Macmillan 1987, 80–87.

Scott, William H. 'The Spanish Occupation of the Cordillera in the 19th Century', in: Alfred W. McCoy and Ed. C. de Jesus, *Philippine Social History* (1982), 39–56.

Seagrave, Sterling. *The Marcos Dynasty.* New York, Fawcett Columbine 1988.

Sevenhoven, J.J. van. 'Java, ten dienste van hen die over dit eiland wenschen te reizen', *Tijdschrift voor Nederlandsch Indië*, 2, 1 (1839).

Shepherd, Verene A. (ed.). *Slavery Without Sugar: Diversity in Caribbean Economy and Society Since the 17th Century.* Gainesville, University Press of Florida 2002.

Siberry, Malcolm. *The Story of Vulcan Works from 1830 to 2002*, prepared by Malcolm Siberry for MAN B & W Diesel Ltd, Ruston, U.K., posted at http://www.enginemuseum.org/bbv.html.

Sijthoff, P. *Verslag van de Honger en Watersnood in de Residentie Semarang uitgebracht door de Commissie ingesteld bij Gouvernements besluit dd 2 Juli 1902*, No. 8, Batavia, Landsdrukkerij 1902.

Sleeman, Michael. 'The Agri-Business Bourgeoisie of Barbados and Martinique', in: P.I. Gomes (ed.), *Rural Development in the Caribbean*, London and New York, C. Hurst and St. Martin's Press 1985.

Sneevliet, H. to W van Ravesteyn, 10–5–1916, Document 114, in: F. Tichelman, *Socialisme in Indonesië* (1985), 366.

Sneevliet, H. 'De Handel van Semarang', in: M.G. van Heel, *Gedenkboek van de Koloniale Tentoonstelling* (1916), 220–54.

———. Correspondence, 1916 (documents 102, 114) in: F. Tichelman, *Socialisme in Indonesië* (1985), 337 and 366–67.

Sola y Bobadilla, José Sixto de, *Pensando en Cuba*. La Habana, Ed. Cuba Contemporánea 1917.

Stanley, Peter W. *A Nation in the Making: the Philippines and the United States, 1899–1921*. Cambridge, Harvard University Press 1974.

———. *Reappraising an Empire: New Perspectives on Philippine-American History*. Cambridge, Harvard University Press 1984.

Stark, E. *Uit Indië, Egypte en het heilige land. Brieven aan zijne vrienden 1910*. Amersfoort, Veen 1910 [1926].

Stevens, Th. *Vrijmetselarij en samenleving in Nederlands-Indië en Indonesië 1764–1962*. Hilversum, Verloren 1994.

Steward, Julian et al. *The People of Puerto Rico*. Champaign-Urbana, University of Illinois Press 1956.

———. 'Perspectives on Plantation', in: Pan American Union, *Plantation Systems of the New World; Papers and Discussion Summaries*. Washington, Pan American Union 1959, 5–12.

Stoler, Ann. *Capitalism and confrontation in Sumatra's plantation belt, 1870–1979*. New Haven, Yale University Press 1985.

———. 'Foreword', in: Lily E. Clerkx, Wim F. Wertheim, *Living in Deli. Its Society as Imaged in Colonial Fiction*. Amsterdam, CASA series 6, VU University Press 1991.

———. 'Sexual Affronts and Racial Frontiers: European Identities and the Cultural Politics of Exclusion in Colonial Southeast Asia', *Comparative Studies of Society and History*, 34 (1992), 514–51.

Stuurman, S. *Wacht op onze daden. Het liberalisme en de Nederlandse staat*. Amsterdam, Bert Bakker 1992.

Suhartono. *Apanage dan Bekel. Perubahan Sosial di Pedesaan Surakarta, 1830–1920*. Yogyakarta, Tiarawacana 1992.

Suryo, D. 'Social and Economic Life in Rural Semarang under Colonial Rule in the Later Nineteenth Century'. Ph.D. diss., Clayton, Victoria: Monash University 1982.

Taselaar, Arjen. *De Nederlandse koloniale lobby. Ondernemers en de Indische politiek, 1914–1940*. Leiden, Research School CNWS, Publ. 62 / Diss. RU Leiden 1998.

Taylor, Jean Gelman. *The Social World of Batavia. European and Eurasian in Dutch Asia*. Madison, The University of Wisconsin Press 1983.

———. *Smeltkroes Batavia; Europeanen en Euraziaten in de Nederlandse vestigingen in Azië*. Transl. by Emile Henssen, Groningen, Wolters Noordhoff 1988.

Thompson, Alvin. O. (ed.). *In the Shadow of the Plantation: Caribbean History and Legacy*. Kingston Jamaica, Ian Randle Publishers 2002.

Thompson, Edgar Tristam. *The plantation: A Bibliography*. Washington D.C. Social Science Monographs, Pan American Union 1957.

Thompson, Lanny. 'The Imperial Republic: A Comparison of the Insular Territories under U.S. Dominion after 1898,' *Pacific Historical Review*, 74, 1 (2002), 535–74.

————. *Nuestras islas y su gente. La construcción del 'otro' puertorriqueño en Our Islands and Their People.* Río Piedras, Centro de Investigaciones Sociales y Departamento de Historia de la Universidad de Puerto Rico 1995.

Tichelman, F. 'De SDAP en Indonesië', *De Nieuwe Stem,* vol. 22 (1967), 683–723.

————. *Socialisme in Indonesië: De Indische Sociaal Democratische Vereeniging,* 1897–1917. Dordrecht, Foris Publ. 1985.

Tillema, H.F. *Rioliana,* Semarang, 1911.

————. *Van Wonen en Bewonen, van Bouwen, Huis en Erf,* Semarang: Tandji 1913.

————. *'Kromoblanda': over 't vraagstuk van 'het wonen' in Kromo's grote land.*'s-Gravenhage, Uden Masman, 1915–1923 (6 vol.).

Tillema-Weehuizen, H.S. and H.F. Tillema. *Kampongwee.* Groningen, s.n. 1919.

Timmins, G. *Made in Lancashire. A History of Regional Industrialisation.* Manchester, Manchester University Press 1998.

Tomich, Dale W. 'Sugar Technology and Slave Labour in Martinique 1830–1848', *Nieuwe West-Indische Gids,* 63, 1–2 (1989), 118–34.

————. *Slavery in the Circuit of Sugar. Martinique and the World Economy, 1830–1848.* Baltimore, Johns Hopkins Unversity Press 1990.

————. 'Small Islands and Huge Comparisons: Caribbean Plantations, Historical Unevenness, and Capitalist Modernity', *Social Science History,* 18, 3 (1994), 339–358.

————. *Through the Prism of Slavery. Labour, Capital and the World Economy.* Lanham, Rowman & Littlefield Publishers 2003.

Tornero Tinajero, Pablo. *Crecimiento económico y transformaciones sociales: esclavos, hacendados y comerciantes en la Cuba colonial, 1760–1840.* Madrid, Ministerio de Trabajo y Seguridad Social 1996.

U.S. Tariff Commission, *U.S. Philippine Trade.* Report No. 118. Washington, U.S. Government Printing Office 1937.

U.S. War Department, Cuban Census Office, *Informe sobre el Censo de Cuba, 1899.* Washington: Government Printing Office, 1900.

————. Porto Rico Census Office. *Informe sobre el Censo de Puerto Rico, 1899.* Washington: Government Printing Office, 1900.

————. Office of the Director of the Census, *Census of Porto Rico, 1899.* Washington, U.S. Government Printing Office 1900.

Varona, Enrique de José. 'Con motivo de las fiestas de Belén', *Revista de Cuba Contemporánea,* (1914), T IV, 357–60.

Varona, Francisco. *Negros: historia anecdótica de su riqueza y de sus hombres.* Manila, General Printing Press 1938.

Velasco y Pérez, Carlos de. *Aspectos nacionales.* La Habana, J. Montero 1915.

Villoldo, Julio. 'Necesidad de colegios cubanos', *Cuba Contemporánea,* Tomo I (Marzo-Abril 1913), 89–112.

Vivoni Farage, Enrique, and Silvia Álvarez Curbelo (eds). *Hispanofilia: arquitectura y vida en Puerto Rico, 1900–1950 = Hispanophilia: Architecture and Life in Puerto Rico, 1900–1950.* San Juan, Editorial de la Universidad de Puerto Rico 1998.

Volkstelling 1930. Deel VI. *Europeanen in Nederlandsch-Indië* (Census of 1930 in Netherlands India. Volume VI. Europeans in Netherlands India). Departement van Landbouw, Nijverheid en Handel. Batavia, Landsdrukkerij 1933.

Vollenhoven, C. van. *Adatrechtbundels*, Serie D, no XXXIII, 's-Gravenhage, Nijhoff 1924.

Wagner, P. *A Sociology of Modernity: Liberty and Discipline*. Routledge, London 1994.

Walker, Herbert S. *The Sugar Industry in the Island of Negros*. Department of Interior. Bureau of Science. Manila, Bureau of Printing 1910.

Weijnschenk-genealogie, see Lach de Bère.

Wernstedt, Frederick L., and J.E. Spencer. *Philippine Island World: A Physical, Cultural, and Regional Geography*. Berkeley, University of California Press 1967.

Wertheim, W.F. 'Conditions on Sugar Estates in Colonial Java: Comparisons with Deli', *Journal of Southeast Asian Studies*, 24, 2 (1993), 268–84.

Wijbrands, K. *Nieuws van de Dag van Nederlandsch-Indië*, 15.11.1910, quoted in: J. Breman, *Koelies, Planters en Koloniale Politiek*. (1992), 316.

Wolf, Eric R. 'On Peasant Rebellions', *International Social Science Journal*, 2 (1969), 286–93.

Zanetti, Oscar, and Alejandro García. *Caminos para el azúcar*. La Habana, Éditorial de Sciencias Sociales 1987.

INDEX